Additional Praise

In *Spain and Its Achilles' Heels: The Strong Foundations of a Country's Weaknesses*, Koldo Casla offers in a very challenging way the main flaws of modern democratic Spain. His thoughtful arguments about the role played by historical legacies help to illuminate the challenges of the present.

—**Pablo Simón, assistant professor at Universidad Carlos III, Madrid**

Koldo Casla has crafted a sophisticated and well-written account of four major historical vulnerabilities in Spain. This is a must-read for scholars and students interested in the country's contemporary politics.

—**Diego Muro, senior lecturer in international relations, University of St Andrews, co-editor** of *The Oxford Handbook of Spanish Politic*

Koldo Casla provides a deep and convincing analysis of how contemporary Spanish politics has been specially marked by the mismanagement of four weaknesses (or Achilles' heels): nationalism, religion, the Francoist past and an immature welfare state. The book is an essential read for anyone trying to understand Spanish politics today.

—**Lluís Orriols, associate professor at Universidad Carlos III, Madrid**

With an original and bold approach, Koldo Casla reveals not only the Achilles' Heels of Spain, but also its Samson's hair, the light and shadow of the country's social, economic, political and cultural reality of recent decades. The author presents a first-hand testimony combined with academic rigour, and this delicate balance allows him to paint a sharp and well-focused picture. Koldo Casla's meticulous, accessible and personal account will be of great value to newcomers to the study of Spanish politics as well as to those already familiar with this one-of-a-kind country.

—**Mathieu de Taillac, foreign correspondent of Le Figaro and Radio France in Spain**

Spain and Its Achilles' Heels

Spain and Its Achilles' Heels

The Strong Foundations of a Country's Weaknesses

Koldo Casla

ROWMAN & LITTLEFIELD
Lanham • Boulder • New York • London

Published by Rowman & Littlefield
An imprint of The Rowman & Littlefield Publishing Group, Inc.
4501 Forbes Boulevard, Suite 200, Lanham, Maryland 20706
www.rowman.com

86-90 Paul Street, London EC2A 4NE

Copyright © 2022 by Koldo Casla

All rights reserved. No part of this book may be reproduced in any form or by any electronic or mechanical means, including information storage and retrieval systems, without written permission from the publisher, except by a reviewer who may quote passages in a review.

British Library Cataloguing in Publication Information Available

Library of Congress Cataloging-in-Publication Data

Names: Casla, Koldo, author.
Title: Spain and its Achilles' heels : the strong foundations of a country's weaknesses / Koldo Casla.
Description: Lanham : Rowman & Littlefield, [2021] | Includes bibliographical references and index.
Identifiers: LCCN 2021037889 (print) | LCCN 2021037890 (ebook) | ISBN 9781538164587 (cloth) | ISBN 9781538164600 (paperback) | ISBN 9781538164594 (ebook)
Subjects: LCSH: Spain—Politics and government. | Political culture—Spain—History. | Political participation—Spain—History. | Spain—Social conditions. | Spain—Economic conditions. | Spain—Ethnic relations. | Catholic Church—Political activity—Spain.
Classification: LCC DP84 .C35 2021 (print) | LCC DP84 (ebook) | DDC 946—dc23
LC record available at https://lccn.loc.gov/2021037889
LC ebook record available at https://lccn.loc.gov/2021037890

Contents

Acknowledgements ix
Map: Spain, Nationalities and Regions xi

1 Spanish Politics Beyond Franco and Catalonia 1
2 Achilles' Heels: The Strong Foundations of a Country's Weaknesses 9
3 The Territory and the People: How Many Nations? 23
4 Dealing with the Past: Franco's Legacy 67
5 Who Weaves the Social Safety Net? 103
6 'It's the Church We Have Lit Upon, Sancho': Catholicism and Conservative Politics 135
7 Vulnerabilities Need Not Be Weaknesses 163

Time Line 177
Bibliography 179
Index 199
About the Author 205

Acknowledgements

It is not easy to give a snapshot of Spanish politics in 2021. A deputy prime minister resigns from cabinet to stand as a candidate in a regional parliament, and after a poor result, he resigns from politics entirely. His left-leaning party did not even exist eight years ago. The conservative party is torn between appealing to the far-right and drawing a line in between them. A party that claimed to be liberal and centrist goes from high expectations to all but being wiped out in two years. Catalonia has the umpteenth election, with little change in the power distribution, and another secessionist executive is conformed at the eleventh hour. Halfway through the year, the government pardons nine Catalan politicians imprisoned for sedition and other crimes. And, at the time of writing, there are still six months for New Year's Eve.

'Koldo, focus on the future, not the suffering of the past. It's better to forget.' With affection most of the time, but with occasional frustration, this is a message I received from one or two loved ones when this book was no more than an idea on my mind. I learned a great deal from research. I learned about the topics, but I also learned from people's reactions to the topics. I discovered a thing or two about my own family, more or less distant relatives, anecdotes I was insufficiently familiar with, or even aware of in some cases. I had conversations that I might have never had otherwise. Most of these discoveries did not find their way onto the pages you are about to read. I deem them too personal and you would consider them of little or no relevance. But they do matter to me, and I am glad I had the opportunity to find out about some stories beneath the history.

I have many people to thank.

I would like to start by acknowledging friends and colleagues at the University of Essex for contributing to a friendly and supportive environment despite pandemics and lockdowns.

I presented some of the contents of this book at the Center for Basque Studies of the University of Nevada, Reno, and at the Centre for Catalan Studies of Queen Mary University of London, at online events in October and November 2020. I thank organisers and participants for giving me the opportunity to think aloud and to contrast some conclusions and assumptions.

I am grateful to Rebecca Anastasi, editor at Rowman & Littlefield, for her interest and support.

I am also obliged to Pablo S. Quiza, my aunt Jaione Salazar, my sister Mónica Casla and the Arts Department of the Archbishopric of Pamplona for giving me permission to use their photographs.

María Serrano is the first person I run many of my rough ideas by. Some of them see the light of day, many more María skilfully persuades me to change or drop entirely because they make little sense. She also recommends some of the most interesting books. For many other reasons that I will not share with you, I feel lucky to be María's partner in life.

I want to thank my family in the Basque Country, my mum, my sisters Mónica and Arantxa, my brothers-in-law Joseba and Peio, my nieces Izaro and Iratxe, and my nephew Iñigo.

I have lived abroad for most of the last 13 years, during which time I have kept looking back carefully from afar. I could figuratively feel the stretch in my legs, with one foot in Spain – large enough so I could always have at least one toe on the Basque Country – and the other one in the UK, where I live. The Portuguese *saudade* and the Welsh *hiraeth* are rather distinctive words that find no suitable translation in other languages but that nonetheless share a meaning. They can be defined as the longing for a land and a time that is not there anymore and therefore one can no longer return to. I was told that both *hiraeth* and *saudade* imply a sense of regret. That is not what I feel at all. However, I have certainly felt an occasional sense of disorientation from missing some of the references of what is taken as normal in the society of origin and in the one of destination. I am not the first migrant to feel this way. Questioning so-called normality is a healthy exercise, but such disorientation is part of the deal when interpreting politics as an insider outside.

'*Izan zirelako, gara; garelako, izango dira.*' The sentence in Basque has had evolving meanings over the years. It can be translated as 'because they were, we are; because we are, they will be', and it captures a sense of historical trajectory, a forward-looking connection with one's roots. I for one use it with a minimal dose of idealism and with the critical keyboard with which I type this book. But I use it, above all, as a token of remembrance of those close to our hearts who are no longer with us, and to whom one owes at least a portion of one's place in this world.

London, 25 June 2021

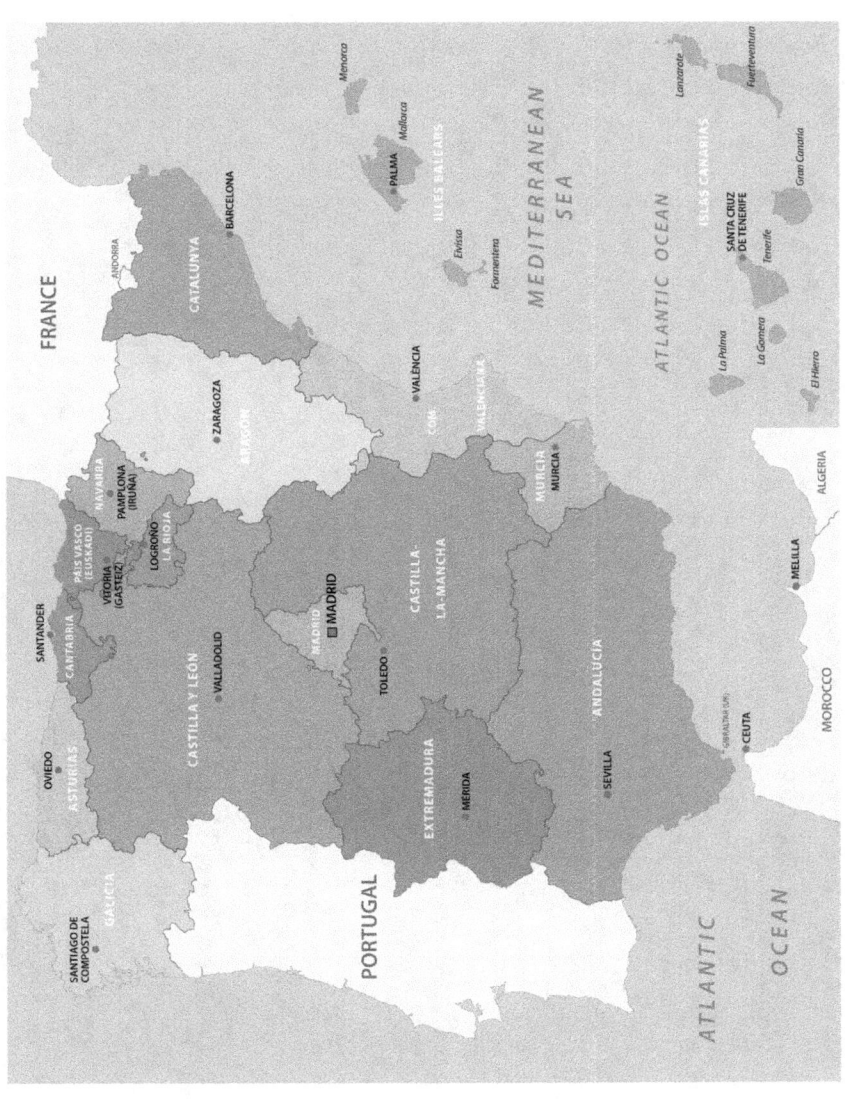

Figure 0.1 Spain, Nationalities and Regions. Source: GettyImages-861148802.

Chapter 1

Spanish Politics Beyond Franco and Catalonia

On 1 October 2017, roughly 2 million people took part in a referendum organised by the Catalan government, a referendum that had been declared illegal by the judiciary. The regional government had promised that, if the majority of votes were positive, they would declare independence unilaterally within two days. 'Yes' they did win overwhelmingly, but the Catalan authorities did not declare independence. Instead, they issued an ambiguous statement acknowledging the referendum's result and reaffirming their determination to become an independent State. After a few days of confusion and tension, the Spanish government invoked a constitutional procedure never used before to replace the Catalan authorities with men and women chosen from Madrid. Regional elections were held in an uneasy calm weeks later, as a result of which the balance of power between pro- and anti-independence forces barely changed. Powers were returned to a new Catalan executive supported by the same parties of the previous one, under a new president who expressed his admiration for his predecessor, now exiled in Belgium, as well as his commitment to follow through with the independentist process. Two years later, Spain's supreme court sentenced nine pro-independence politicians to between nine and 13 years in prison for sedition and other crimes, including misuse of public funds.

Four days before the referendum, the U.S.-based magazine *Foreign Policy* picked this headline for one of its online dispatches: 'Spain is flirting with another civil war.'[1] The author made clear on Twitter that he was not happy with the title, which suggests it was an editorial choice. Fast forward two years. It is October 2019, and Andrew Hussey publishes an article in the

---

[1] James Badcock, "Spain Is Flirting with Another Civil War," *Foreign Policy* (online) (27 September 2017).

British magazine *New Statesman* to explain the relatively sudden rise of the far-right party Vox as a by-product of the country's agitated and contested relationship with the legacy of Islamic Al-Andalus, which ended more than five centuries ago. Hussey told me he did not decide the title, which means someone else thought this was going to be punchy: 'The new Spanish civil wars.'[2] One month later, Vox would win 52 seats in the lower house and 15% of the votes in the general election; 3.6 million people bestowed their trust on them.

These two examples are indicative of a widespread view in international news desks: that Spain's twenty-first-century politics can be interpreted or explained in one way or another by reference to the Civil War (1936–1939) and Francoism (1939–1975). If the analysis or the discussion is long enough, whatever the topic, sooner or later someone will draw the connection. Such connection is not without merit. The war accentuated socio-economic and political divisions, cut short hundreds of thousands of lives, and led to a lengthy dictatorship where democracy and rights were suspended. Many of the economic and political institutions of the twenty-first century are the result of the lessons rightly or wrongly learned from that experience. But the Civil War and Francoism are not the master independent variable beneath everything else in politics. The past, or rather the way the past is dealt with in the present, is indeed one of the strong foundations of Spain's weaknesses. But it is not the only one.

In the last 10 years, new political players have upended the traditional two-party system; the far-right is back in business after four decades of quiet; Euskadi Ta Askatasuna's (ETA) terror is history; one of the wealthiest regions has not been lost, but it was a near thing; and society survived the painful austerity policies of one economic crisis to find themselves in the middle of another one, this one stemming from a pandemic. The 2010s were awkward in many ways. And yet, in spite of everything, Spain still has one of the highest life expectancies, is a world leader in organ donations, harbours a long list of UNESCO heritage sites, has a very high rate of trilingual citizens due to its linguistic diversity, is a safe country with low levels of criminality, and in general is a fun and enjoyable place to be.

Cervantes, Lorca, Picasso, Almodóvar and so on, Spanish culture has wonderful ambassadors, and as is usually the case, most of the best-known ones are men. But interest in Spain far exceeds gastronomy, arts and literature. Spanish history and politics are followed by an international community of journalists, academics and keen observers. Yet, despite the archives and the shelves full of books, it is still shocking to read how easily commentaries can

---

[2] Andrew Hussey, "The New Spanish Civil Wars," *New Statesman* 148, no. 5492 (11 October 2019), 30–3.

fall back on clichés about violence or the purportedly homogenous desire in certain territories to separate from the rest of the country. Those desires do exist. But nothing is homogenous in Spain.

This book is a story of Spanish politics beyond Franco and Catalonia. As could not have been otherwise, the book also talks about Franco and about Catalonia, but it puts them in a wider context, tracking the historical roots of the political tensions that make Spain the captivating yet troubled country that it is today.

Why was Franco exhumed from the Valley of the Fallen in late 2019? How is it that he was there in the first place? Why did Catalonia erupt *all of a sudden* in October 2017? Why do not you hear so much about the Basque Country anymore? How did Podemos gather momentum so quickly in 2014 to 2015, and why did half of that support vanish five years later? Isn't it counter-intuitive that a Catholic-majority country may also have the most LGBT-friendly society in the world,[3] and was one of the first to legalise equal marriage in 2005, or euthanasia in 2021?

Understanding the most significant events in recent Spanish politics requires spelling out the unspoken but enduring foundations of the country's deepest fears and weaknesses, its Achilles' heels. In Greek mythology, an Achilles' heel is a vulnerability that can lead to downfall despite the apparent general strength of the full body. For a country, I use this term to refer to the underlying factors that, while by no means unique, are characteristic of that particular society, delimit what is possible and shape the political debate. They are the primary political frailties without which a country's politics cannot be properly comprehended.

In this book I present four of Spain's Achilles' heels, one for each foot of a dancing couple. While doing my research, I discussed the work behind the book with friends and colleagues, Spanish and not, and I was encouraged by the fact that the argument left no one indifferent. They kept me on my toes, pushing me to elaborate the narrative and justify my choices. Much of their input made me refine some ideas, add new ones and discard others. I hope the coming chapters will persuade you of the good reasons to focus on these four heels. I believe they are most enduring and distinctive foundations. But there could be others.

In one of the earliest conversations in a pub in north London, an Irish friend asked me about the possible influence of colonialism on Spanish politics. After all, Spain used to be an empire on which the sun never set. Three-and-a-half centuries of direct rule changed the metropolis as it transformed the colonies, most visibly in Latin America. Any remaining grandeur was gone with

---

[3] Pew Research, *Global Views on Morality* (April 2014).

the loss of Puerto Rico, Cuba and the Philippines in 1898. Parts of Morocco, Equatorial Guinea and Western Sahara would be under Spanish control for the greatest part of the twentieth century. Morocco became independent in the 1950s, Equatorial Guinea in the 1960s, and the status of Western Sahara remains unsettled after Spain illegally handed over the effective control over the territory to Morocco – initially to be split with Mauritania – in 1975 to 1976. The end of the old empire provoked a political and socio-economic crisis accompanied by a literary revival with the talented writers of the Generation of '98, which included Antonio Machado, Miguel de Unamuno, Pío Baroja and Ramón María del Valle-Inclán. The fin de siècle saw also the advent of regenerationism, a loose intellectual and political current that relied on science as method and on Europe as horizon with the aim of modernising Spain and liberating it from its backwardness. Of diffuse contours, Unamuno, José Ortega y Gasset, Joaquín Costa, Manuel Añaza or Ramiro de Maeztu formed part of the broad church of regenerationism. In a relatively recent book, Colomer argues that, due to injudicious imperial adventures, Spain missed the opportunity to consolidate a modern nation State in the nineteenth century: 'The empire made Spain, and the failure and dissolution of the empire unmade Spain.'[4] Colonialism is part of Spain's history, and it does carry explanatory power, but I would relativise its significance in Spanish politics in the twenty-first century. The role of the decline of the empire in the construction of the Spanish nation is covered in chapter 3.

In a delicious bakery in an east London alley, someone raised the question of feminism and resistance to it within conservative circles. Women's rights have been central at key moments of Spanish political history. One of the most defining debates in Spain's parliamentarism took place in 1931 between Victoria Kent and Clara Campoamor, two of the only three women in the lower chamber at the outset of the brief but intense republic of the 1930s – the third one was Margarita Nelken. Women had been appointed in political and representative assemblies for some time, but they did not yet have the right to vote. It was believed that women were generally more conservative than men and that giving them the right to vote could put the republic at risk. In the name of progressive politics, Kent advocated kicking the can down the road. In her view, and in the view of many other progressive politicians, Spanish women were not yet ready to participate on an equal footing with men. Due to their lower rate of literacy, it was believed that women would vote whichever way their priest or their husband told them to. Campoamor, on the other hand, made a passionate defence of votes for women as a matter of principle. Her position eventually triumphed, and the 1931 constitution of Spain's republic

---

[4] Josep M. Colomer, *The Spanish Frustration: How a Ruinous Empire Thwarted the Nation State* (London: Anthem Press, 2019), 2.

recognised equal voting rights for men and women. Campoamor famously declared that she was a citizen before a woman, and a woman before a defender of the republic. Eight decades later, millions of women marched and went on a feminist strike on 8 March 2018, International Women's Day, and did so again in 2019. This movement inspired other initiatives in Mexico, Chile, Poland or France. Feminism is very present in Spain's political debate. In Verge's opinion, 'State feminism' has been 'highly entrenched in Spain' since the late 1970s,[5] State feminism being defined as public policy on gender or women's rights, with a focus on the work of women's policy agencies and their interaction with women's rights organisations.[6] Speaking against feminism is, in fact, one of the hallmarks of Spain's far-right's scapegoat populism.[7] Despite its prevalence, the extent to which feminist discourse translates into effective policies and transformative cultural attitudes is an entirely different matter. Violence against women is widely acknowledged as a sad reality and authorities' response leaves much to be desired, irrespective of the fact that the situation may be even worse in other European countries.[8] Women continue earning less than men, are overrepresented in low-income households, and suffer the consequences of rising inequalities and insufficient social spending, topics we will return to in chapter 5.

Spain has the second-largest immigrant population in Europe, after Germany.[9] Many Spaniards have a positive view of migration, with a steady improvement between 2015 and 2019, although opinions differ notably depending on political ideology primarily since the rise of Vox.[10] Having said this, Spain still has a long way to go to embrace the diversity stemming from the social phenomenon of immigration. Since the late 1990s and early 2000s, the number of people born abroad has risen significantly, particularly from North Africa, Latin America and Eastern Europe. Stereotypes and hidden stigmatisation are widely and unconsciously accepted, for example, in the form of mockery of foreign accents, or the identification of certain types of businesses with national communities – the corner shop is still popularly

---

[5] Tània Verge, "Gender Policy," in Diego Muro and Ignacio Lago (eds.): *The Oxford Handbook of Spanish Politics* (Oxford: Oxford University Press, 2020), 618.
[6] Amy G. Mazur and Dorothy E. McBride, "State Feminism since the 1980s: From Loose Notion to Operationalized Concept," *Politics & Gender* 3, no. 4 (2007), 502.
[7] Meaghan Beatley, "The Shocking Rape Trial that Galvanised Spain's Feminists—and the Far Right," *The Guardian* (23 April 2019).
[8] In the UK, 1,425 women were killed by men between 2009 and 2018; 562 were killed in Spain in the same period. (Yvonne Roberts, "'If I'm Not in on Friday, I Might be Dead': Chilling Facts about UK Femicide," *The Guardian* (22 November 2020); Delegación del Gobierno contra la violencia de género, "Fichas de víctimas mortales."). The difference is remarkable even considering that UK's population is around 43% bigger than that of Spain.
[9] Eurostat, Immigration by age group, sex and citizenship (data from 2019).
[10] Carmen González-Enríquez and Sebastian Rinken, "Spanish Public Opinion on Immigration and the Effect of Vox," *Real Instituto Elcano* ARI 46/2021 (April 2021).

known as 'el chino'. More importantly, first- and second-generation Spaniards are still underrepresented in the public space, media, politics, police, judiciary and so on. Casual racism and xenophobia are part of the ground that breeds Vox's far-right, a new and yet old political phenomenon we will talk about several times in the coming chapters.

Introspection is a workout only recommendable for brave individuals and societies. One never knows what may lie behind a closed door deep down inside. Weaknesses, even foundational ones, are potentially unlimited in number. In this book I analyse four of Spain's Achilles' heels. I consider them the most distinctive and defining ones, capable of encompassing other vulnerabilities in Spanish politics, including the mentioned issues related to colonialism, misogyny and xenophobia.

The first deep root of Spain's weaknesses is the disagreement about the number of nations within her, or more precisely, the political tension that emerges from such disagreement. Spanish nationalism, as well as nationalisms in Catalonia, the Basque Country and elsewhere in Europe, are a product of the nineteenth century, a time when different nations and notions of nations competed for their share of political legitimacy. Spain had its first experiences with democracy with the second republic in the 1930s, while Europe's already existing but weak democracies were struggling to survive when they were not breaking apart entirely. The republic began a process of decentralisation for Catalonia, the Basque Country and Galicia, but with the eruption of the Civil War in 1936 there was no time left to see it working. In fact, the latter two regions were granted autonomy after the armed conflict had started. After Franco's fierce rule from the centre, the 1978 constitution envisioned a sui generis model of technically voluntary decentralisation, the 'Estado de las autonomías' ('State of self-governing entities'). Within four years, all regions claimed and obtained some degree of self-government. Historical reasons were given to retain a discrete financial settlement for the Basque Country and Navarra so they could levy their own taxes, which sparked in other corners of the country a sense that they were being treated unfairly. At the same time, the fact that all regions obtained some degree of autonomy created a feeling of 'coffee for everyone' ('café para todos'), a perception of least common denominator that did not satisfy the desires for greater autonomy in Catalonia and the Basque Country. Whether these territories, and indeed others, could be nations remains contentious and compulsive in the Spanish politics of the early 2020s. Is Spain a nation of nations, and would that formulation be analytically or politically helpful at all?

The second heel is the way the country deals with its recent past. For about three decades after Franco's death, a policy of amnesia, silence or purposeful forgetting was explicitly or implicitly accepted by political parties and society at large. A movement in support of the recovery of disappeared bodies and the investigation of crimes committed during the Civil War and the dictatorship gained impetus in the first decade of the current century. It was nonetheless resisted by the right-wing Popular Party and by conservative media, as well as by the leadership of the Catholic Church. The future of the Valley of the Fallen, a fascism-reminiscent public mausoleum where Franco was buried between 1975 and 2019, is up in the air, and public symbols and street names honouring Franco's allies are still visible in parts of the country. Meanwhile, Basque society is licking the wounds of its own memory after ETA announced the end of its violent activities in October 2011.

While neighbouring countries nourished their welfare state in the three decades that followed World War II, Spaniards lived under a dictatorship that claimed to be the European beacon of anti-Communism. By the time Spain joined the club of democracies in the late 1970s, the rest of the Western side of the continent was about to embark on a neoliberal journey of lesser social protection, lower taxes for the wealthy and weaker unions. Spain never put in place a serious national package of social housing: Less than 2% of houses have some sort of public protection, compared to 29% in the Netherlands, 24% in Austria, 17% in Sweden or 16% in France. This is a structural limitation for any left-leaning government, whatever their promises. The public healthcare system is well regarded, but in the area of social security, apart from retirement pensions and unemployment benefits, Spain has not had a suitable social assistance programme for those at risk of poverty and social exclusion. Since the 1990s, each region has had its own scheme but, with some exceptions, regional programmes do not meet European minimum standards of adequacy. Structural underdevelopment of social protection is the third strong foundation of Spain's weaknesses. What sort of country will Spain become with the necessary reconstruction of its economy after Covid-19, after the austerity of the 2010s, and after the financial and banking crash of 2008?

Finally, the book looks at the influence of the leadership of the Catholic Church on conservative politics. The formation of the so-called national spirit in the second half of the nineteenth century and the greatest part of the twentieth century relied on the ideological premise of religious unity under Catholicism. Spain was the birthplace of the Jesuit order as well as of the ultra-conservative Opus Dei. Several members of the latter community held cabinet responsibilities and powerful positions in the second half of the twentieth century, with Franco and after Franco. Catholicism is still widely present in public festivities, including many that are not necessarily religious in character. Together with the fascist Falange and with the Army, the Church was one of the pillars of Franco's regime. Four agreements were negotiated during the Transition to adapt the 1953 concordat to the new democracy. This happened before the adoption of the constitution in December 1978.

Secularists question the compatibility between the four agreements and the constitution, particularly considering the financial privileges of the Catholic Church and its central position in the education system. In the past two decades, the Spanish Episcopal Conference (Conference of Bishops) has been very vocal in defending the unity of Spain as an ethical imperative, which antagonises many people in Catalonia, the Basque Country and elsewhere.

Nation and nations, the past, welfare state and religion are the four edges that delimit the narrative of this book. Together the four circumscribe what is desirable, likely and possible in contemporary Spanish politics. This book is based on the combination of policy research and personal anecdotes. In writing it I chose to keep a geographical distance, but not an epistemological one. I was born and lived in the Basque Country for the first 23 years of my life, and then again between ages 26 and 28. My family was not particularly political, but interest in politics and justice grew in me from a very early age. For most of that time, the Basque Country was a deeply divided society where the democratic game was shaped by a reality of politically motivated violence. Society was divided in political terms, but much less so in geographical terms. This meant that interacting with people whose politics were profoundly different was an ordinary experience. Politically conscious people in general could not reasonably expect that all or many of their neighbours, colleagues, friends or acquaintances would agree with them in relation to some of the most basic questions, including the identification of one's nation or even whether violence can be at all justifiable in politics. These questions were not hypothetical or academic, but very real in the Basque Country of the 1990s and 2000s. Growing up in that environment I learned to be alert and suspicious of tribalism, self-righteousness and narrow-mindedness, starting with my own. My upbringing made me treasure freedom, pluralism, pragmatism and critique, especially self-critique. In that spirit I wrote this book, which I hope will be worth your time.

Chapter 2

Achilles' Heels

The Strong Foundations of a Country's Weaknesses

2.1 WEAKNESS AND DISTINCTIVENESS

Walking up High Holborn, in central London, he asked me, 'Why is it that you enjoy so much living in the UK?' The quizzer was a colleague, an Englishman and an academic, and this was early 2017. The question was not trivial and suggested incredulity. Britain had voted in favour of leaving the European Union (EU) a few months before, and most people in cosmopolitan London did not like the idea of Brexit, let alone people in academia. This colleague and I had worked together on social rights issues in the UK, and the fact that the government had implemented strict welfare austerity measures was in the background of our dialogue. How could I possibly like this place? In one way or another, I had faced the question a number of times before, from British and non-British friends alike. I had my spiel ready to use, with references to books and essays by George Orwell, who had influenced me dearly as a teenager, without forgetting British humour, the theatrics of English oral expression, and London's many parks and lively markets. At the time, I was affiliated with Newcastle University, so I would praise the pride of the north of England and Geordie friendliness, and I would explain why the city of Newcastle reminds me of Bilbao. I would feel the need to clarify that I did not like Britain or England because of Brexit, but in spite of Brexit. Finally, the argument would be inevitably accompanied by the well-rehearsed but insincere assertion that I enjoy fish and chips better than Iberian ham – the truth is I do not like it *that* much. More often than not, my answer would be satisfactory enough and we would move on to something else. That day in High Holborn was an exception. Gobsmacked, my companion pushed back. 'C'mon, there *must* be something you don't like!' Well, true, I believe austerity policies had been very harmful for too many people, even if austerity had been the pattern all over the continent, so the UK was not exceptional in that regard. And class, of course, there are still big inequalities in the UK on the grounds of social class, and while class exists elsewhere, it is *particularly* present and visible in this country. 'Yes,' he responded, 'class is the Achilles' heel of England.' From there we dragged on about how English people enjoy talking so much about class inequality but never seem to be agreeing on anything meaningful that could be done about it.

The choice of words stuck with me. A hero of the Trojan War, son of a goddess and a king, Achilles' was the greatest of warriors in ancient Greece. Strong like no other man, he would have been invincible had it not been for his weak spot, the heel, where he was mortally wounded with a poisonous arrow in battle. Or so does mythology say.

The heel and the homonymous tendon are some of the most human traits. Apes do not have them, and this evolutionary gift is one of the reasons why our ancestors gained an extraordinary advantage in terms of nimbleness and speed. The expression Achilles' heel makes most sense when dealing with robust actors. It is a sort of warning call for people with an overdose of self-confidence, erring on the side of presumption. It is a way of telling them that they are not indestructible. If one does not hold a particularly favourable view of oneself, to be reminded of their Achilles' heel seems entirely unnecessary, harsh even. The Achilles' heel is a constant reminder that, whatever illusions we may hold or be told about ourselves, we all have limitations, we are proficient at making mistakes, we are vulnerable. And that is indeed why kindness is so important to humankind, kindness understood the way Phillips and Taylor do, as 'the ability to bear the vulnerability of others, and therefore of oneself', an ability that is gratifying when 'it connects us with others', but terrifying when 'it makes us too immediately aware of our own and other people's vulnerabilities (vulnerabilities that we are prone to call failings when we are at our most frightened)'.[1]

The Achilles' heels significance and function at an individual level is psychoanalytically complex but intuitively recognisable. But what may such expression mean for a collective, for a political community? The analogy between the agency of individuals and that of societies is never perfect. For starters, most humans have two feet and as many heels. Countries do not. This form of anthropomorphism of the polis begs for a stylistic licence, unless one intends to argue that a given society has no more than two weaknesses. This book is based on the assumption that the metaphor is elastic enough to cover a limited number of them, but not necessarily one or two only.

---

[1] Adam Phillips and Barbara Taylor, *On Kindness* (London: Penguin, 2009), 5 and 14.

'States are people too,' wrote Alexander Wendt.[2] States are human constructs capable of forming interests, purposes, desires and beliefs, and expressing and channelling them through their own social institutions. From this perspective, the idea of the Achilles' heel, singular or plural, one or many, is helpfully expressive and has descriptive and analytic value. A society's Achilles' heel is a distinctive but not necessarily unique attribute, an enduring foundation of a country's weaknesses. Achilles' heels are inherent to all human-made communities, including the most resilient ones. Their existence should not make us forget that Achilles' was in fact the strongest man of his generation. Achilles' heels are underlying factors that may go unnoticed to the bystander's eye, but that delimit what is possible in a given context; they influence discourse and shape the contours of future political decisions. They are, in other words, frailties without which our understanding of local and national politics will necessarily be incomplete.

There is value in initiating the analysis from the acknowledgement of one's vulnerability, which in the case of a country is not an individual but a collective trait. This book is a plea for reflection starting from our limitations and our interdependence, our need for each other. As Judith Butler said, 'Loss and vulnerability seem to follow from our being *socially constituted bodies*, attached to others, at risk of losing those attachments, exposed to others, at risk of violence by virtue of that exposure' (emphasis mine).[3] I revolt against the dangerously popular trend of compulsive positive thinking, where happiness and certainty are placed on an altar, and sadness and doubt are punished. I resist arrogant and yet fragile nationalism. This is an appeal to humility, a challenge to know oneself, not to be complacent, but to grow from the recognition of our own identity and the reality that surrounds us. Identifying and embracing our vulnerabilities is the first step on the way to gaining the skills to change what can be changed, and to gaining the confidence to preserve what should be preserved.

I wrote parts of this book from a relatively small town in the north-western part of the Region of Madrid. This is an area where wealthy families from the capital have their second residence. The zone is largely conservative and many of the people, especially among summer residents, are proudly nationalist. Spain's flags are omnipresent in public squares, balconies and flagstaffs installed in fenced gardens. The far-right Vox won the general election in this town in December 2019 with 29% of the vote, and the right-wing Popular Party (PP) came second with 28%. In the regional elections of May 2021, the combined vote for right-wing parties in this town was two-thirds, with PP

---

[2] Alexander Wendt, *Social Theory of International Politics* (Cambridge: Cambridge University Press, 1999), 215.
[3] Judith Butler, *Precarious Life: The Powers of Mourning and Violence* (London: Verso, 2004), 20.

gaining more than half of all ballots. Emboldened by these and similar results elsewhere, the nationalist and extreme right sometimes appears cocky. Yet, one needs to be very strong to see one's vulnerabilities; hubris is a dangerous weakness.

Belonging and feeling part of something bigger than one's immediate circle is a very human need. The urge to look for reasons to be proud of such bigger *thing* is also understandable. We see it everywhere. Team GB had an outstanding performance during the London Olympics of 2012. I remember British friends expressing on social media how *proud* they were *to be British* as the number of golden medals went up. I do not think they were particularly nationalistic, and I doubt very many of them knew the name of most of the sportsmen and women from before, certainly not in the case of minority sports. And yet, London Olympics became a moment of catharsis and jubilation in the UK. The opening ceremony was particularly ironic in this regard. The central theme was the National Health Service (NHS), an institution cherished by British people as a caring mother. Politicians of all colours compete to persuade the public that their parties have done more than their opponents to make the NHS. And yet, while the country was displaying their national treasure in front of the whole world, the NHS's resources were under serious strain after years of underfunding – which would continue at least until the end of the decade – and a legal reform introduced the very year of the Olympics opened the door to further privatisations of the healthcare system. The hallowed institution was ever less *national*, and the *service* was ever more deficient, but the showpiece looked good in the stadium and on television.

There is nothing wrong with the urge to belong, or with the feeling of content and relief stemming from the pride that emerges from such belonging. I have been reminded of photographs and recollections of migrants living in Spain, who painted their cheeks in red and yellow in July 2010 to celebrate Spain's victories in the football world cup, despite the likelihood that many of them suffered discrimination and disadvantage all too often. Belonging and feeling proud are not inherently bad. Rorty wrote that 'national pride is to countries what self-respect is to individuals: a necessary condition for self-improvement'.[4] Problems begin if society draws the wrong conclusions from collective satisfactions, for example, if winning a football competition distracts us excessively from the fact that the country's welfare state is utterly unprepared to respond to the socio-economic crisis that was unfolding in 2010. As joyful as it can be, a sporting triumph is not going to change such fact.

---

[4] Richard M. Rorty, *Achieving Our Country: Leftist Thought in Twentieth-Century America* (Cambridge, MA: Harvard University Press, 1998), 3.

Collective vulnerabilities are structural and systemic features that endure the passing of time to remain very real in the present day. Society's Achilles' heels are not one's fault any more than achievements of sport teams are not one's merit. For most of us, our individual responsibility in preserving Achilles' heels is limited. Vulnerabilities are often taken for granted, accepted as part of society's being. Like a structural element in a house, it can be painted over or hidden behind furniture. But the structure remains there, and without it we would not have a building at all. We might have a different sort of edifice, but not the one we know. The hole in the analogy is that structural elements are meant to be strong, the strongest feature of the house, in fact, and in our case it is the strong foundations of a country's weaknesses what we are interested in.

From time to time, events expose societies to their own vulnerabilities in a very straight manner, cracking myths, bursting bubbles and disrupting what some thought to be harmony. This might have been one of the many consequences of the Brexit vote in 2016, and the subsequent negotiation within the UK and between the UK and the EU. Among other things, Brexit accentuated territorial divisions and unearthed some uncomfortable truths about England's declining role in global affairs. Across the Atlantic, the killing of George Floyd by a white police officer in Minneapolis in May 2020 was transformed into a moment of reckoning about structural racial inequalities in the United States and in other countries. Back in Europe, the intermittent riots in banlieues of Paris are much more than mere disruptions of public safety; they are a reminder of the deep social and racial inequalities and of the sense of exclusion shared by many first- and second-generation Frenchmen and women, citizen or not. The announcement by King Juan Carlos in August 2020 that he had fled the country was shocking. Spain's former head of State appeared to be running away from judicial investigations into his involvement in a corruption and tax avoidance scandal. Beyond that, the news hit many Spaniards hard in an inferiority complex, in the impression that the shameful things that happen in Spain do not happen anywhere else in Europe.

When confronted with these intense events full of deep meaning, some people react with shame, anger and rejection, some fight back and others respond with shock and disbelief. It is a messy conflation of feelings and sometimes contradictory thoughts. Societies can get divided based on old and new social cleavages – urban–rural, centre–periphery, ethnicity, generational divides and so on – about the interpretation of disruptive and cathartic events, and about the most suitable course of action, potentially giving way to a new crisis.

This book aims to contribute to remove the veil over some of these very real conditions without having to wait for the next crisis. This is a reflection about the problematic relation of a collective subject with herself, an attempt to understand and link up symptoms that are observable with underlying structural factors that may be overlooked. Coming to terms with our personal and collective vulnerability is, I believe, a step in the right direction towards healing – or towards learning to coexist with – some of the divisions that unfold when societies are exposed to their fears and weaknesses. An Achilles' heel may at first be a weakness. Daring to face it, however, is a sign of strength. In Gilson's words, 'Vuln*erability* is not just a condition that limits us but one that can *enable* us. As potential, vulnerability is a condition of openness, openness to being affected and affecting in turn' (emphasis in the original).[5] Being audacious to grow into vulnerability, instead of failing to grow out of it, is a liberation from the self-imposed duty to justify yourself, or to defend at any cost the country you happen to come from. At the same time, exposing the Achilles' heels does not mean being conformist, passive or resigned. Rather the opposite, it is a commitment to honesty and to seeking to understand the way things are in reality, not in our conscious imagination. It is a pledge to work on such basis, facing the uncertainty, accepting our limitations, cultivating what is good and special, and learning to do better in the future.

2.2 DISTINCTIVENESS AND POLITICS (IN THEORY)

Comparative politics is a social science that consists in placing *two or more* cases or countries facing each other with certain variables under control, that is, holding certain things constant while focusing on perceptible differences. The word 'comparison' entails a plurality of units, but depending on the level of abstraction, research can compare a large number of countries, a small number of them – often three or four – or a single case study. Landman explains that a single-country study is comparative if it uses or develops concepts that are applicable to other countries, and/or seeks to make inferences beyond the actual case study, bearing in mind that 'inferences made from single-country studies are necessarily less secure than those made from the comparison of several or many countries'.[6] In other words, single case studies are a form of comparative politics when they apply and contribute to mature ideas that can be relevant in other countries through implicit comparisons. Case studies have the analytical advantage of requiring a low level of abstraction in the sense that they do not need generalised variables to have them contrasted across borders. Unlike analyses that look at a large or even a relatively small number of countries, single case studies permit intensive

---

[5] Erinn Gilson, "Vulnerability, Ignorance and Oppression," *Hypatia* 26, no. 2 (2011), 310.
[6] Todd Landman, *Issues and Methods of Comparative Politics* (London: Routledge, 2008, 3rd edition), 28.

examinations as researchers can dive deep into them. Single case studies may not be equipped to test hypotheses in a positivist sense or to falsify theories hypothesised elsewhere. However, case studies allow the researcher to go beyond mere descriptions to contextualise, historicise and interpret path dependencies and the configuration of units in a country's politics. They also supply sufficient analytical and methodological freedom to generate and cultivate new propositions that others might want to use as the basis of future research.

A case study can be considered interpretive when they have an 'interest in the case rather than an interest in the formulation of general theory'.[7] That is precisely the aim of this book: to spell out the influence of certain underlying conditions on the practice of politics in Spain. Those conditions are presented as four structural vulnerabilities without which the analysis of policy would be short-legged. They are (1) the stubbornness in the disagreement about the number of nations in Spain – one or more, how many more? – (2) the way the country comes to terms with its twentieth century, (3) the past and present holes in the welfare safety net, and (4) the extraordinary influence of the Catholic Church on conservative politics. Bravery to confront these vulnerabilities can turn weaknesses into strengths. This book looks for definitions, motives and goals in actors themselves. Observations are presented and used to sharpen intuition and to inform judgement, not to predict, but to make sense of the way political actors interpret and have historically interpreted structures and their surroundings.

This is a subjective exercise. Much of what I describe in the following chapters is part of me, my upbringing and my identity. I will not distance myself. I will not pretend to be above or away from it. Society is not a lab and I am not a neutral observer. In fact, I would dispute the very existence of such theoretical position when dealing with politics. Countries are, first and foremost, their people. My condition as a researcher is connected to the subject of research, Spain's politics and its controversies. As a passport holder and someone who was born and lived there, I influenced the subject minimally, but I am influenced by it considerably. I deem it necessary to be upfront about my epistemic approach, which is that of critical realism,[8] based on the combination of realism of the observable and subjectivism of the observer. There is an observable world that is understandable only through human lenses, perception and social construction. The study is based on a nuanced aetiology: Causal relations do exist in principle, and they can be inferred from

---

[7] Arend Lijphart, "Comparative Politics and the Comparative Method," *The American Political Science Review* 65, no. 3 (1971), 692.
[8] Andrew Collier, *Critical Realism: An Introduction to Roy Bhaskar's Philosophy* (London: Verso, 1994).

observable variables, but not all causes and not all variables are observable, and therefore causal analysis cannot be entirely satisfying. Causality is complex when multiple causes interact dynamically. Hence, interpretation is key, and knowledge is not universally valid, but relative, contextual and socially produced.

Those are the operating instructions that I give myself to study the strong foundations of Spain's weaknesses. Achilles' heels are a search for defining features, not for uniqueness. Achilles' heels do not constitute supposedly inevitable, necessary or immutable conditions. Everything historically and politically relevant is contingent and dependent upon multiple cultural, ideological and socio-economic factors, present and past. History matters. 'Time,' observed North, 'is the dimension in which the learning process of human beings shapes the way institutions evolve. That is, the beliefs that individuals, groups, and societies hold which determine choices are a consequence of learning through time.'[9] Some events are more structural, others simply take place at the right time and that makes them memorable. In either case, timing and the sequence in which events unfold matter for political path dependence, where 'the probability of further steps along the same path increases with each move down that path'.[10] One must not ignore the profound temporal dimensions of social and political processes, and that's why this book adopts a historical approach to social explanation. Outcomes and events are better gripped when placed in time. History with capital letter reminds us that history with lower case did not need to happen the way it did. There was nothing certain about it, nothing entirely unavoidable or 100% foreseeable. Historicising politics enriches our grasping of past and present phenomena, and strengthens the explanatory significance of the Achilles' heels in a way that will become apparent as we accumulate insights and answers. History shows why and how we got here. It enlightens the trail between past events and the political scenario of the present, making the past politically relevant today.

2.3 POLITICS (IN PRACTICE) AND THE PAST

Franco's Information and Tourism minister, Manuel Fraga, led a marketing campaign in the 1960s with a very catchy slogan: *Spain is different*. The campaign contributed to open the country to the world, attracting millions

---

[9] Douglass C. North, "Economic Performance through Time," *The American Economic Review* 84, no. 3 (1994), 359–60.
[10] Paul Pierson, "Increasing Returns, Path Dependence, and the Study of Politics," *The American Political Science Review* 94, no. 2 (2000), 252.

of visitors and their currencies, and bolstering an industry that took root and remains essential for the country's economy six decades later. Spain is today one of the world's top destinations in terms of the number of international tourist arrivals. Incidentally, while this may have changed in recent years, Spanish institutions have generally contributed to portray a stereotypical image of the country by resorting to bullfighting, flamenco dancing, religious processions, sun and sandy beaches. These items are recognisable in parts of the country, primarily the south and the Mediterranean coast, but visitors risk getting disappointed if they look for these attractions in other regions.

Fraga's slogan served its purposes well, but it quickly outlived the advertising campaign to become a handy catchphrase for one of Spaniards' favourite pastimes: self-flagellation. Political parties in opposition, media and popular discourse in general recurrently build on the idea that the sort of negative things one can hear in relation to Spanish politics cannot possibly happen anywhere else. The former *Financial Times* correspondent in Madrid, Tobias Buck, captured this phenomenon neatly:

> Here was a country that, for all its progress and achievements, never seemed quite sure of its place in the world, a country forever in doubt, always measuring itself against the outside world and more often than not finding itself wanting. I know no nation that criticises itself so frequently and so mercilessly. In my time as a correspondent in Spain, I was told over and over again that *this* – this crisis, this scandal, this election result, this whatever – would never happen in other European countries.[11]

Spain is not unique, for better or for worse it is not exceptional. Robert Fishman summarises the country's ordinariness as follows:

> On a wide range of political outcomes, Spain stands out as an intermediate case that is neither one of the greatest success stories of the last hundred years nor a particularly unsuccessful one. The record of the country's political life is a rather mixed one in numerous respects, yielding episodes and arenas both of success and of failure.[12]

Yet, alongside the self-flagellation, Spain's history in the last two centuries is full of examples of nationalist hubris, with decades of more or less strict

---

[11] Tobias Buck, *After the Fall: Crisis, Recovery and the Making of a New Spain* (London: Weidenfeld & Nicolson, 2019), 10.
[12] Robert M. Fishman, "Spain in Comparative Perspective: Contributions of the Spanish Case to Comparative Political Analysis," in Diego Muro and Ignacio Lago (eds.): *The Oxford Handbook of Spanish Politics* (Oxford: Oxford University Press, 2020), 16.

isolation banging on about Spain's supposed moral superiority. If one looks at nineteenth and twentieth centuries, the sense of superiority, sincere or not, is hardly unique to Spain. Many advanced economies have experienced authoritarianism, and even more are and have been guilty of self-absorption, navel-gazing, *ombliguismo* in Spanish. In the case of Spain, boundless nationalism was the driving force behind the longest-lasting and latest-ending dictatorship in Western Europe, a dictatorship that silenced freedom and diversity expressing suspicion and rejection of all forms of foreign influence. Spain managed its way out of that dictatorship with a negotiated rupture in the late 1970s, the so-called Transition to democracy, but fragile nationalism did not disappear.

A cliché of the Spaniard is that of a man or a woman who has no time for insolence. While this can be a virtuous stance, when cool is not kept, it can result in self-conceit, for which there is a fitting expression: a 'bullfighting attitude' (*actitud torera*). People are mercifully diverse, and they were not born to fit in boxes or tags. Like all generalisations, this one is unfair even if there might be an element of truth to it. However, Spain's international image has not benefited from much subtlety in history. Treated as a monolithic group, Spaniards have been disfigured in mean stereotypes. Stanley Payne roughly summarises the typical labels put on Spain by foreigners over the centuries: cruel, bloodthirsty, sadistic and destructive in the sixteenth and seventeenth centuries; militarily weak, ignorant, lazy and unproductive in the second half of the seventeenth century; and in the eighteenth century, culturally picturesque and romantic but of little political relevance in the nineteenth century; and a combination of all of the above in the twentieth century.[13] Álvarez Junco documented many of the prejudices spread by European commentators in the eighteenth and nineteenth centuries: while the rest of Europe was being enlightened, common wisdom was that Spain represented a cultural and political identity incompatible with progress.[14] Montesquieu described Spain as a land of backwardness, degradation, laziness and fanaticism, where people were blinded by religion, rulers and inquisitors were 'incapable of any degree of light or instruction; and a nation must be very unhappy that gives authority to such men'.[15] Speaking of literature, despite the richness of the golden age of sixteenth and seventeenth centuries, Voltaire believed there was 'nothing interesting in Spain except the Don Quixote'.[16]

---

[13] Stanley G. Payne, *Spain: A Unique History* (Madison: University of Wisconsin Press, 2011), 5–6.
[14] José Álvarez Junco, *Spanish Identity in the Age of Nations* (Manchester: Manchester University Press, 2011), 65–84.
[15] Charles de Secondat, Baron de Montesquieu, *The Spirit of Laws: Book XXV. Of Laws in Relation to the Establishment of Religion and its External Polity* (1748, translated by Thomas Nugent, 1752, revised by J. V. Prichard), section 13.
[16] Alfonso de Savio, "Voltaire and Spain," *Hispania* 7, no. 3 (1924), 163.

Perhaps the most infamous description is the country's entry in the revised *Encyclopédie Méthodique* of 1782, written by Nicolas Masson de Morvilliers, which included these not so encyclopaedical remarks:

> But what is owed to Spain? After two, four, ten centuries, what has she done for Europe? It resembles those weak and miserable colonies in constant need of the protective arm of the metropolis: it is necessary to help her with our arts, our discoveries; it looks even like those desperately ill who, unaware of their illness, repel the arm that gives them life. Nevertheless, if a political crisis is needed to leave this shameful lethargy, what is she waiting for? The arts are asleep there, and so are the sciences, and trade! She needs our designers for her manufactures! Scholars are forced to learn hiding our books! She lacks mathematicians, physicists, astronomers, naturalists! Without the support of other nations, she has nothing of what is required for a siege.[17]

These are only some of the illustrative examples of historic prejudices about Spain, prejudices that in some cases have lived on to this day. In May 2020, while European governments were discussing the financial response to Covid-19, the Dutch weekly Elsevier came out against any transfer of money from the Netherlands to indebted EU countries, Italy and Spain in particular: 'Not a penny more to the south of Europe,' read the message on the magazine's cover. A drawing depicted two blond people working hard on top, and at the bottom a moustachioed man drinking wine and a brunette woman in a bikini playing with her smartphone by the swimming pool.

These descriptions are, in any case, caricatures not only of Spanish society but of the country's portrayal in international and European commentaries. Some clichés stand the test of time, but growing interdependence and ever more accessible travelling – when there is no pandemic around – means that, thankfully, opinions are more nuanced, plural and variable. Looking back, nonetheless, is a helpful exercise. Over years and centuries, an international image of Spain has been painted with a broad brush. This is the norm for every country, and Spaniards must have contributed to do the same about

---

[17] Encyclopédie méthodique ou par ordre des matières, Géographie moderne, Vol. I (Paris: 1782), 565: *"Mais que doit-on â l'Espagne? Et depuis deux siècles, depuis quatre, depuis dix, qu'a-t-elle fait pour l'Europe ? Elle ressemble aujourd'hui à ces colonies faibles & malheureuses, qui ont besoin sans cesse du bras protecteur de la métropole : il nous faut l'aider de nos arts, de nos découvertes ; encore ressemble-t-elle à ces malades désespérés qui, se sentant point leur mal, repoussent le bras qui leur apporte la vie ! Cependant, s'il faut une crise politique pour la sortir de cette honteuse léthargie, qu'attend-elle encore ? Les arts sont éteints chez elle ; les sciences, le commerce ! Elle a besoin de nos artistes dans ses manufactures ! Les savants sont obligés de s'instruire en cachette avec nos livres ! Elle manque de mathématiciens, de physiciens, d'astronomes, de naturalistes ! Sans le secours des autres nations elle n'a rien de ce qu'il lui faudrait pour faire un siège."*

other societies. At the same time, perhaps influenced by international representations, Spaniards have formed an opinion of themselves, which has had a defining influence over their national character, or characters, as we will discuss in the next chapter.

In and out, those views and opinions are not immutable. Spanish society has reached the present through a long and bumpy road, with its moments of joy and its many moments of sorrow. The path ahead is not predetermined – even if it partly depends on the trajectory thus far – and the speed, direction and purposes of the whole trip are up for discussion. Weaknesses do not need to be intractable, and vulnerabilities are weaknesses only when they are overlooked. Working out the future is a task for the present, and doing so successfully requires learning lessons from the past. Historicising politics, in this sense, is an interpretation of the past from this moment, a dialogue between the contexts of yesterday and today. In E. H. Carr's words, 'The past is intelligible to us only in the light of the present; and we can fully understand the present only in the light of the past.'[18] Facts of the past are only available through the present time, when both the collection of events and their interpretation take place.

Addressing the strong foundations of a country's weaknesses requires facing and embracing the past, having it very present. Accepting it as it was, good and bad by contemporary standards, is not the same as glorifying the preterite. Facts and events are not capable of change, but our interpretation of them can adapt and evolve. Despite the apparent paradox, the past sometimes needs to change, and societies need to be open to reconsider the conclusions they draw from it. As we will see in chapter 4, studying Francoism matters not so much for what the regime meant in the 1940s, 1950s, 1960s and early 1970s, but for the impression it left on Spain's institutions and politics in the democracy that followed. In other words, Francoism matters for what it says about the present and for what we can learn from it for the future. This applies to Spain as it does to other countries. Writing about the U.S. retrospection into the influence of slavery over contemporary forms of racism, Hannah-Jones encapsulated the idea with dexterity:

> Citizens don't inherit just the glory of their nation, but its wrongs too. A truly great country does not ignore or excuse its sins. It confronts them and then works to make them right. If we are to be redeemed, if we are to live up to the magnificent ideals upon which we were founded, we must do what is just.[19]

---

[18] E. H. Carr, *What is History?* (London: Penguin, 1990, 2nd edition), 55.
[19] Nikole Hannah-Jones, "What is Owed," *New York Times* (30 June 2020).

Remembrance is key to revisit the foundations, weak and strong, that made a country what it is today. Political communities are built, financially, structurally and culturally, on certain premises that might have been a morally irrelevant matter in the past, but that can become less than acceptable in retrospect as humanity evolves and societies mature. It is imperative to question the moral standing of those premises, and to interrogate about who benefited from them politically and economically speaking. The conventional anniversaries and celebrations of the supposed birth of nations, their independence and other memorials are exactly the right time for such critical reflection. Growing into our collective vulnerability means remembering and commemorating differently, resignifying the past with less pride but with greater recognition. After all, the Achilles' heels are the first part of our body to touch the ground when we start a walk.

Chapter 3

The Territory and the People
How Many Nations?

3.1 THE OLDEST NATION IN EUROPE OR A PRODUCT OF THE NINETEENTH CENTURY?

I remember a dinner once, I believe it was summer 2012, when I witnessed a polite dialectic confrontation between two senior representatives of the parliamentary human rights commissioners of Andalusia and Catalonia. It was in the context of a two-day meeting of ombudsman commissioners from different parts of Spain, and I was there representing the Basque one. I do not recall what the discussion was about, and I do not think it mattered either, but it was certainly not about any significant political issue. At some point one of them launched what the other perceived to be a cliché about the people in the part of the county he was from. After a while, calm was awkwardly restored, and we all hunkered down for the night in our hotel rooms. When I went down for breakfast the following morning, the Andalusian gentleman happened to sit at the same table. Between coffee sips he mumbled, '*They* think they've always been so great; one thousand years ago, *we* used to take baths in scented water while *they* were barbarians!' The way he said it, he meant no acrimony and it was humorous in fact.

In 1846, the English travel writer Richard Ford described Spain as 'a bundle of small bodies tied together by a rope of sand'.[1] One century later, the country and/or its appearance to the external observer apparently had not changed much. Another English author, Gerald Brenan, wrote in 1943 that 'Spain is a collection of small, mutually hostile or indifferent republics held together in a loose federation'.[2] Spain was, in his view, the land of the *patria*

---

[1] Richard Ford, *Gatherings from Spain* (London: John Murray, 1846), 4.
[2] Gerald Brenan, *The Spanish Labyrinth* (Cambridge: Cambridge University Press, 1943), xx.

chica, the small motherland, a country where personal allegiance is pledged first and foremost to the place of birth, understood in a minimalist sense. Pride is local, close to one's upbringing, expressed in what's different from the other – not necessarily superior but certainly not inferior. Difference can be historical, gastronomic, musical, linguistic – with different languages, idioms and words – phonetic – in the form of regionally recognisable accents – and political. Ford, Brenan and others painted a picture of Spain as a country full of small motherlands, a picture that was valid in the nineteenth and twentieth centuries, and to *some* extent remains so in the twenty-first century. This chapter deals with the extent to which that portrayal is or is no longer tenable, and with the corresponding tensions that derive from endurance and change of national identities within Spain.

Brenan's book was both a laudatory representation of the people and a furibund diatribe of its rulers, including the then relatively new dictatorship led by Francisco Franco. Franco was the surviving leading figure of the military coup of July 1936, coup that resulted in a bloody civil war that lasted three years and killed more than half a million people. Franco's coup and the subsequent regime were sustained on three pillars: the Fascist Party Falange, the Army and the Catholic Church. Brenan observed that throughout history the Church had been 'the cement that held' together the territories that conformed what was to become Spain.[3] Over the centuries, the Catholic Church had played a unifying role, sometimes by force, sometimes by consent, a role only comparable to that of the monarchy. Both crown and faith would find a shared mission and spread a collective idea and purpose, sowing the seeds of a nation (more on this in chapter 6).

The seeds were not sown evenly, though. In parts of the field, crops were mixed. At the turn of the nineteenth to the twentieth century, influential local actors in the Basque Country and Catalonia, and with more limited resonance in Galicia and Andalusia, began to cultivate their own nations. They did so with a combination of romanticism and economic interests, some bourgeois, some traditional, some progressive. Eventually, these political projects would conflict with the idea of Spain as a single nation, an idea that, as we will see, was not in fact that much more ancient.

The consequences of the contention about the singularity and multiplicity of nations remain vivid today, and by no means are they unique to Spain. Some of these consequences are personal, deeply engrained and hard to rationalize. I read Tobias Buck's *After the Fall* and Jason Webster's *Violencia: A New History of Spain* over Christmas 2019. Both books were published that year and I recommend both, particularly Buck's, to anyone interested

---

[3] Ibid., 61.

in the immediate and longer-term causes of Spain's political challenges. Presumably unaware of each other's choice, different publishers seemed to agree a massive stripy red, yellow and red Spanish flag was the right choice for the covers. Both books look alike on the shelf from a distance. I read them one after the other while visiting family, starting on my way to the airport in London, continuing in Madrid and ending the second one in my home town, San Sebastian, in the Basque Country. While the cover did not bother me much in London, the colours strangely appeared more noticeable in Madrid, especially when leaving home with one of the books under my arm. By the time I got to San Sebastian, I am embarrassed to admit, I considered leaving the dust jacket in the suitcase. I knew most people would not care, but I could not help being oddly self-conscious about it. In the end, I came to the conclusion that I would feel more ridiculous removing the wrapper than leaving it alone, so I chose this second course of action.

As a political construct, the nation is a product of the nineteenth century. This applies to Spain, as does to Catalonia and the Basque Country, and indeed to most other nations in Europe.[4] Of course, this does not mean that there were no political realities before 1800 corresponding to what we came to denominate Portugal, Hungary, Denmark, and so on. Each with their own unique and yet contingent history, European nations emerged and evolved within relatively well defined and yet contested territories. As political realities, the territories and their rulers have shaped the continent's history – in fact, the history of the world – for centuries. As political constructs, however, nations are much more recent phenomena. The territories had been there for a very long time before nations were awakened in the last two centuries.

Spanish conservative politicians and commentators contend that Spain is the oldest nation in Europe. Sometimes they add that it is 500 years old, referring implicitly to the time of the Catholic Monarchs, Fernando of Aragon and Isabel of Castilla, who funded Columbus's adventure and occupied Granada in 1492. Widower Fernando conquered the Kingdom of Navarra in 1512. One could take that period as the surfacing of a new political reality that would later be transformed into a nation. By that token, other political entities could compete in age: England, France, Scotland, Sweden and so on. It is unquestionable that there has been a political structure responding to the name of Spain that has been part of Europe's and the world's history for more than five centuries. If a nation is a self-identified collective bestowed of sovereignty, it is profoundly revisionist to misuse the word 'nation' to speak

---

[4] David Edgerton argues that the British nation is a product of the twentieth century, in particular of the post-War era, when Britain transitioned from an empire to a nation, a process accompanied by its own challenges (Northern Ireland, Scotland, Brexit, diversity and racism, etc.). (*The Rise and Fall of the British Nation: A Twentieth-Century History*, London: Allen Lane, 2018).

about a time when the will of the people was systematically ignored by the rulers, in Spain and everywhere, a time in fact when the consciousness of the people as a collective subject simply did not exist.

It is true, however, that leaving colonialism aside, together with Switzerland and Portugal, Spain is one of the few European states whose borders have not moved since the Napoleonic Wars. That is a historical fact that allows many possible interpretations, but it is undeniable that, geographically speaking, Spain has endured the passing of time better than most. So far Spain has excelled at the test of resilience.

Identifying objective criteria for nationhood – such as common language, ethnicity, history, territory, cultural traits and so on – remains an impossible task. All those supposedly objective criteria are by definition contested, in some cases considered *theirs* by people in multiple territories, and sometimes shared only among an elite who claims to speak on behalf of a far larger group of people, *the* people. As an alternative to the objectification of the nation,[5] the subjective idea of the nation, famously summarised by Renan in 1882 as 'an everyday plebiscite',[6] is no less unsatisfactory. Despite the appeal of implicit consciousness and the theoretical freedom of choice, the reasoning is inevitably circular: a demos must precede the plebiscite, but in this subjective idea of the nation the demos is taken for granted, demos without which we have no nation.

With different emphases, Gellner, Anderson and Hobsbawm spoke of nations as socially constructed categories that emerge in a given historical moment and secure their continuity by creating imagined communities that transcend generations and death.[7] The nation is a very young political concept. Its connection with a political unity is a product of the nineteenth century, and the recognition of the people as the collective holder of sovereignty dates from the later decades of that century. Understood in this way, the idea of a political project of the nation comes first, followed by the institutionalisation of the idea through the State, and finally the people, the mass that reluctantly, enthusiastically, casually or unknowingly sustains the nation and its institutions. In Hobsbawm's words, 'Nationalism comes before nations; nations do not make states and nationalisms but the other way around.'[8] Like

---

[5] Margaret Moore, "On National Self-Determination," *Political Studies* 45, no. 5 (1997), 906.
[6] Ernest Renan, *What Is a Nation? And Other Political Writings* (New York: Columbia University Press, 2018), 261–2.
[7] Ernest Gellner, *Nations and Nationalism* (Oxford: Blackwell, 1983); Benedict Anderson, *Imagined Communities: Reflections on the Origin and Spread of Nationalism* (London: Verso, 1983); E. J. Hobsbawm, *Nations and Nationalism since 1780: Programme, Myth, Reality* (Cambridge: Cambridge University Press, 1992, 2nd edition).
[8] Hobsbawm, *Nations and Nationalism*, 10.

the French, the German or the Italian with their own, the common Spaniard comes last in the construction of his or her nation. For Gellner,

> a mere category of persons (say, occupants of a given territory, or speakers of a given language, for example) becomes a nation if and when the members of the category firmly recognize certain mutual rights and duties to each other in virtue of their shared membership of it. It is their recognition of each other as fellows of this kind which turns them into a nation, and not the other shared attributes, whatever they might be, which separate that category from non-members.[9]

Álvarez Junco and De la Fuente write that Spain's historiography is in part the story of a narrative that constructed a collective identity.[10] The tension between history, memory and national identity is, once again, not unique to Spain. We saw it plainly in France with the publication of the 2021 Stora report about the memorialisation of the Algerian War.[11] In fact, Hayden White would argue, by endowing the past with meaning, wherever they are the historian cannot escape the manufacture of present politics through past history:

> The historian arranges the events in the chronicle into a hierarchy of significance by assigning events different functions as story elements in such a way as to disclose the formal coherence of a whole set of events considered as a comprehensible process with a discernible beginning, middle, and end.[12]

In the case of Spain, the tension between centre and periphery has played a central role in the construction of the nation. The political articulation of Spain in the last 150 years has resulted from a sort of tug of war between centralising forces, increasingly on the right-hand side of the political spectrum, and on the other hand left-leaning and federalist forces, as well as regionalist, nationalist and separatist ones. Understanding Spanish politics requires understanding the dialectics between centre and periphery. The process of liberalisation and democratisation of the State in the nineteenth and twentieth centuries took place while the relationship between centre and periphery was being worked out. The idea of Spain as a nation has been built in opposition to parallel and sometimes incompatible political projects, projects that in

---

[9] Gellner, *Nations and Nationalism*, 7.
[10] José Álvarez Junco and Gregorio De La Fuente, *El relato nacional: Historia de la historia de España* (Madrid: Taurus, 2017), 10.
[11] Benjamin Stora, "Les questions mémorielles portant sur la colonisation et la guerre d'Algérie" (January 2021).
[12] Hayden White, *Metahistory: The Historical Imagination in Nineteenth-Century Europe* (Baltimore: Johns Hopkins University Press, 2014), 6.

some cases intended to federalise the State, but in other instances envisioned its fragmentation into separate confederations when not fully independent countries. To this day, it is not easy for Spaniards to agree on a collective expression they can take as their own. Not surprisingly, Spain is one of the few States that has no official lyrics in its *national* anthem. Two other countries can say the same thing, both afflicted with a very painful recent past: Bosnia-Herzegovina and Kosovo.

The process of institutionalisation of Spain as a nation State was led *from* the geographical centre, Madrid, but not necessarily *by* the centre. Madrid has been the capital city of Spain since Felipe II decided so in the mid-sixteenth century. The court had been itinerant up to that point. Despite the king's whim, villages and cities retained much of their clout and self-governing power until eighteenth and nineteenth centuries. Álvarez Junco writes that

> the Hispanic monarchy (had not been) a united State but a disparate collection of kingdoms and feudal domains, with subjects who spoke a variety of languages, who were characterized by substantial differences as regards laws and taxes, and who even had to pay tolls when they journeyed between the different territories.[13]

The turn in the formation of the State happened in the nineteenth century, with milestones such as the creation of the stock exchange in 1831; the division of Spain in provinces for administrative purposes in 1833; the establishment of Guardia Civil as a quasi-military force with policing duties in 1844; the merger of several financial institutions into a single Bank of Spain in the 1850s; common currency, the *peseta*, in 1868; and the adoption of the criminal code of 1848, and the civil code of 1889 – this one still in force, after numerous amendments. Multiple players took an active role in the articulation of centralising institutions during the alternatingly authoritarian, conservative and liberalising decades of the nineteenth century, as well as during the so-called Bourbon Restoration in 1874 to 1923, and the dictatorships of the twentieth century under Miguel Primo de Rivera in 1923 to 1930 and Francisco Franco in 1939 to 1977. Not all of these actors were Castilian. Plenty came from Galicia, Basque Country, Catalonia, Andalusia and so on and they were as Galician, Basque, Catalan and Andalusian as those who resisted the centralising impetus from those regions. The word 'Madrid' is commonly used in Spain's political parlance to refer to the central administration and implicitly to those who favour centralising politics, as in *Madrid* decides this, or *Madrid* imposes that. However, the city of Madrid does not deserve this unionist characterisation any

---

[13] Álvarez Junco, *Spanish Identity in the Age of Nations*, 49.

more than other smaller cities, and a number of influential individuals from the periphery have contributed decisively to construct an idea of Spain as a nation State that should be ruled from the centre.

The politics around the nation's connotations is reflected in the evolving meaning of the term as defined by the Royal Spanish Academy. The Academy was set up in the early eighteenth century to 'clean, set and give splendour' to the Spanish language, as their motto goes. The Academy was born with the agenda of promoting linguistic unity in the territory, and it is the most authoritative voice about what is supposed to be *proper* in Castilian Spanish. Similar institutions exist in Latin America, the United States and Equatorial Guinea for the different variants in the Spanish-speaking world. Since 1780, the Royal Spanish Academy publishes a dictionary of the Spanish language. The current edition, number 23, dates from 2014, and it is the first one published together between Spain's academy and the academies abroad. The Academy's difficult job is both an expression of the way certain words are used at a given point in time, and a trigger of new interpretations of those words, including politically loaded ones. Until 1869, the term *nación* was defined by the Royal Spanish Academy simply as the 'aggregate of inhabitants in a province, a country or a kingdom, and the very country or kingdom'; in that year's edition, number 11, the meaning was complemented with two new entries to add that a nation was also 'the State or political body that recognises a supreme centre of common *government*', and 'the *territory* and its individual *inhabitants*, considered as a whole' (emphasis added). At some point in the mid-nineteenth century the nation was therefore redefined as an equation that combined government, territory and the people. Fast-forward 64 years, and the Montevideo Convention of 1933 would use those three key elements to establish what is customarily understood as a State, adding a fourth one, namely the capacity to enter into international relations. In the 15th edition of 1925, the word *nación* gained a new entry in the Royal Academy's dictionary to also mean the 'set of people that have the same ethnic origin and, in general, speak the same language and possess a common tradition'. A reference to ethnicity as a defining element of the nation remained in the dictionary until the 22nd edition of 2001.[14] More disturbing is what happened to the word *patria*,

---

[14] All editions of the Royal Academy's dictionary, and other extremely valuable sources as far back as the fifteenth century, are now available online in the *Nuevo Tesoro Lexicográfico de la Lengua Española*. 1852: "*Conjunto de los habitadores en alguna provincia, país o reino, y el mismo país o reino.*" 1869: "*El Estado o cuerpo político que reconoce un centro común supremo de gobierno. Se dice también hablando del territorio que comprende, y aun de sus individuos, tomando colectivamente.*" 1925: "*Conjunto de personas de un mismo origen étnico y que generalmente hablan un mismo idioma y tienen una tradición común.*" 2001: "*Conjunto de personas de un mismo origen y que generalmente hablan un mismo idioma y tienen una tradición común.*"

motherland. Until 1925, *patria* was the 'place, city or country where one is born', but that year the 15th edition took a jingoistic turn, and motherland became, as the first acceptation, 'this nation of ours, including all the material and immaterial things, past, present and future, that enthral patriots' loving support'. A more neutral definition had to wait five reviews of the dictionary until the 20th edition of 1984; since then, *patria* is the 'land of birth or adoption arranged as nation, to which a human being feels attached legally, historically or affectively'.[15]

The word 'nation' did not emerge in the nineteenth century, but that is when the nation acquired a specific political meaning. This applies not only to the Spanish nation, but also to the Basque and the Catalan ones. Álvarez Junco resorts to the Catholic icon of *Mater Dolorosa*, the sorrowful mother, to symbolise Spain's nationalism as a reaction to Basque and Catalan nationalisms, which began to construct their own imagined communities in the nineteenth century.[16] Spanish nationalism found its raison d'être as a counterweight, as the guardian of the State versus those trying to break the union apart. Against that perceived threat, Spanish nationalism, in Álvarez Junco's metaphor, was mournful and hurt, created as a reaction and as a resistance to an outsider within, an apparent other that had to be kept inside by all means necessary.

The resistance to ideas or actors stemming from the outside world has been central to the construction of the Spanish nation. Conservative forces presented and framed liberalism in the second half of the nineteenth century and Socialism and anarchism in the twentieth century as alien to the Spanish identity. Basque nationalism in that era would also reject those ideas as foreign. The construction of a collective identity of the self in opposition to the other also applied in retrospect. It was propagated with mythical references to popular revolts during the Napoleonic occupation, confrontation that would become the *War of Independence*. The day when the people of Madrid rose up against French troops, 2 May 1808, is to this day honoured with a bank holiday in the capital. The narrative is embellished with the story of the mayor of Móstoles, then a small town near Madrid, who dared to declare a war against the almighty France with a municipal edict. The people took up arms against Napoleon's troops, but the irony, as observed by Ronald Fraser, is that the military victory did not give way to a victory for liberalism, let alone democracy: 'At

---

[15] 1914: "*Lugar, ciudad o país en que se ha nacido.*" 1925: "*Nación propia nuestra, con la suma de cosas materiales e inmateriales, pasadas, presentes y futuras que cautivan la amorosa adhesión de los patriotas.*" 1984: "*Tierra natal o adoptiva ordenada como nación, a la que se siente ligado el ser humano por vínculos jurídicos, históricos y afectivos.*"

[16] *Mater dolorosa* is the original name of the 2001 book in Spanish, published 10 years later in English as *Spanish Identity in the Age of Nations*.

an enormous cost of lives and destruction and the almost certain loss of its colonies, patriot Spain had in the end fought to restore an absolutist monarchy.'[17] Fernando VII returned to the throne and reigned with an iron fist for two more decades after the war.

Distant history was revisited from the early stages of the construction of the Spanish nation praising the supposedly extraordinary ability of the natives to resist the outsider. It began with the romanticisation of the Roman siege of Numancia in the second century BC. The defensive spirit of that local population more than two millennia ago is broached when talking about contemporary underdogs, *defensa numantina* being commonplace in sporting commentaries. Numancia was often invoked in Franco's time to praise how Franco supporters sheltered in 1936, during the Civil War, in the Alcázar of Toledo against an overwhelming republican loyalist siege.[18]

Revisiting old history to suit the political nation-building agenda is not exceptional to any country. Nevertheless, the way it was been done in Spain has some significant and dangerous implications for the present time. For example, to this day influential voices on the right-hand side of politics speak about the roughly eight centuries (711–1492) of coexistence of Moorish and Christian kingdoms as a 'reconquest' of the former's lands by the latter. Such coexistence was by no means peaceful, but it was not a unidirectional nationalist Christian crusade either.[19] During the electoral campaigns of 2019 the far-right Vox and the right-wing Popular Party (PP) competed in the use of the word *Reconquista* in their hustings in Asturias, in the north, and Andalusia, in the south, the two territories where the reconquest supposedly began and ended, respectively.[20] The initiation of that magnified campaign of more than seven centuries is credited to one Don Pelayo, king of Asturias in the early 700s. That long period is presented as if an imagined Spanish identity had existed in the eighth century and was only entirely restored when the last Muslim monarch of Granada was kicked out of the Peninsula on 1 January 1492. The real history of religious diversity, unlikely alliances and mercenaries on all side is an inconvenient truth when the political agenda consists in presenting Spain as some sort of historically immutable reality.

---

[17] Ronald Fraser, *Napoleon's Cursed War: Popular Resistance in the Spanish Peninsular War* (London: Verso, 2008), 480.

[18] Jason Webster, *Violencia: A New History of Spain: Past, Present and the Future of the West* (London: Constable, 2019), 56–7.

[19] Mark R. Cohen, *Under Crescent and Cross: The Jews in the Middle Ages* (Princeton: Princeton University Press, 2008); Darío Fernández-Morera, *The Myth of the Andalusian Paradise: Muslims, Christians, and Jews under Islamic Rule in Medieval Spain* (Wilmington: Intercollegiate Studies Institute, 2016).

[20] El Periódico, "Casado apela a la Reconquista después de Vox: primero Andalucía, luego Asturias" (11 January 2019).

In that spirit, in the last two centuries the architects of the imagined national community of Spain have favoured the view of Spain as a Christian nation united against a Muslim outsider. This is so despite the fact that Moors lived in the Peninsula for longer than Romans or Visigoths did before them, and for longer than time has passed since Isabel and Fernando got married in Valladolid in 1469.

Spain's national identity would be inextricably tied to Catholic religion, an axiom that was supported by two handy myths. Firstly, it was opportunely popularised that Saint James the Apostle chose the Peninsula to proselytise the message of Jesus of Nazareth. The mysterious *discovery* of the apostle's remains in the Galician city of Santiago de Compostela in the nineteenth century helped to keep alive the legend of the founder of both religion *and* nation. And secondly, the conversion to Catholicism of Visigoth king Recaredo in the sixth century was presented as a momentous decision that somehow marked the recognition of that religion as official in a unified kingdom.[21]

It would be wrong to talk about conservatism, Catholicism and Spanish nationalism as if they had been perfectly and continuously aligned in Spanish politics. Influenced by the French Revolution and by European liberalism, the nation-building project of the first half of the nineteenth century had a centralising drive, but it was largely liberal and secular. Actually, in early-nineteenth-century Spain's liberals set an example that would be followed all over the world in using the banner of liberalism as a political platform. Nation-building was formulated in the first half of the century as an alternative to the absolutism and fanaticism of King Fernando VII. Payne wrote that Spain was the first power 'to break down over the issue of unsuccessful colonial war and repression', when the military rose against the monarch in 1820 and reinstated the 1812 liberal constitution.[22] That liberal interim lasted only three years, until 1823, and it was followed by the restoration of the absolutist rule. The captain-general who led the liberal uprising, Rafael del Riego, was tortured, hanged and beheaded. A song composed in his honour would become Spain's anthem during the second republic in the 1930s. Spain's political liberalism of the early 1800s inspired the decolonisation of Latin America, and legitimised it from an Iberian perspective. Spain's liberals supported Panhispanism, a project that originated in the newly separated countries of Latin America to build cultural, social and political bridges with the former metropolis. Panhispanism would not reach very far. A conservative version would emerge in Spain in

---

[21] Álvarez Junco, *Spanish Identity in the Age of Nations*, 266–8.
[22] Stanley G. Payne, "Spanish Conservatism 1834–1923," *Journal of Contemporary History* 13 (1978), 766.

the early twentieth century, this one focused on celebrating the old empire under a different name: *Hispanidad*.[23]

Nation-building was a liberal project in the first half of the century, but around the 1850s Spanish nationalism found common ground with conservatism. In the later decades of the century, the country began to flavour capitalism in small doses. It did so in profoundly uneven ways, with an incipient railway system, mining and heavy industry in Asturias and the Basque Country in the north, and in Catalonia in the east. An economic elite in these regions came together to favour policies to bolster their comparative advantage. At the same time, a new social class was born, the working class, which quickly learned to preach Socialism and anarchism, ideas that were gaining traction in other European countries. While capitalism started to take root in parts of the periphery, Spain's new Catholic nationalism favoured costly imperial battles in the name of God and Motherland in Morocco, starting in late 1850s all the way to the 1920s.[24] The nineteenth century was a time in history when European powers invested in sustaining and expanding their colonies; Spain, however, lost its territories overseas – Puerto Rico, the Philippines and Cuba to the United States in 1898 – and it was also largely unsuccessful in its imperialist undertakings in Africa.[25] The expensive and disastrous colonial adventures raised public debt uncontrollably and did also provoke profound social divisions and anxieties in an impoverished population that had more mundane priorities, such as getting by on very little.[26] And yet, pride and nostalgia for the *grandeur perdue* would be essential to sustain the idea of the Christian nation, especially when the Army was the only truly functioning authority of the central government in the nineteenth century. Since 1910, every 12 October has been a *national* bank holiday, a day to honour with military parades both the supposed apparition of the Lady of the Pillar to Saint James the Apostle, and the arrival of Columbus's fleet in the Americas, two birds with one stone (figure 3.1).

As said earlier, Spain is one of the few European countries to survive the last two centuries with its borders unchanged. Spain kept its distance from moments of transformation: the 1848 revolutions had little or no repercussion in the country, at least not in the short-term. Spain also stayed away from major international conflicts. The Austro-Hungarian and the Ottoman empires paid the heaviest price for doing the opposite. At the same time, and partly as a result of the semi-voluntary confinement, Spain progressively

---

[23] Álvarez Junco, *Spanish Identity in the Age of Nations*, 316–7.
[24] Ibid., 302–3.
[25] Juan J. Linz, "Los nacionalismos en España: Una perspectiva comparada," *Historia, antropología y fuentes orales* 7 (1992), 130.
[26] Paul Preston, *A People Betrayed: A History of Corruption, Political Incompetence and Social Division in Modern Spain 1874–2018* (London: William Collins, 2020), 27–78.

Very little left but honor. *Philadelphia Inquirer.*

Figure 3.1 Spain in 1898, as represented in the *Philadelphia Inquirer*. Source: José Álvarez Junco

moved to the sidelines of Europe. Spain managed to move stealthily for decades, until the 1936 to 1939 Civil War became a test bed for the World War that would follow. Up to that point, the country had avoided international military confrontation directly, but it had however experienced a significant amount of armed violence. Apart from tons of coups and uprisings, some successful and some not, Spaniards fought each in open battle three times in just over a century, the two *Carlista* wars in 1833 to 1840 and 1872 to 1876 – not to forget the smaller confrontation of 1846 to 1849, territorially confined to Catalonia, known as the war of the *matiners*, the 'early risers' – and the most famous and brutal one in 1936 to 1939. All these conflicts had certain drivers in common. The place of Catholicism in society was one of them (see chapter 6). The tension between centre and periphery, later to be centralism versus federalism, or mononationalism versus plurinationalism, was another one. The wars are fortunately now in the history books, but the knot of the underlying tension between centre and periphery has not been untangled yet.

3.2 IN PURSUIT OF A 'CONSTITUTIONAL FITTING'

The mononational view of Spain triumphed in 1939 and it became the official and only acceptable position in the regime. Until mid-1970s, General Franco led a political system for 'one, great and free' nation, *una, grande y libre* being one of the mottos of the dictatorship. Francoism saw itself as the force that had ensured Spain did not succumb to Communism and did not disintegrate. Spain would be neither *roja* ('red') nor *rota* ('broken'). The dictatorship sustained an ideology of cultural homogeneity, single national identity and centralised decision-making. Unlike the initial nation-building project of early nineteenth century, this nationalism had no liberal agenda.

Francoism repressed the national question but did not settle it. The debate re-emerged strongly during the Transition to democracy, the milestone between Franco's death in November 1975 and the adoption of the constitution in December 1978. In those three years, parties and leaders that had been ostracised and persecuted sought a compromise with politicians that had been in power during the regime but were prepared to accept the rules of democracy. Together, but opposing each other forcefully, they looked for a 'constitutional fitting' (*encaje constitutional*) to the nation/s and the regions, a solution to a conundrum that had shaped Spain politically for more than a century. Centrifugal and centripetal actors needed some sort of consensus about the polity in a new democracy, an arrangement about the future distribution of power between the regions and the central government in Madrid. The problem, they would soon learn, was that someone's roof was somebody else's ceiling: what some took as the absolute maximum of decentralisation tolerable was actually the bare minimum for others.

In the late 1970s, Spanish parties on the left, the Socialist or social-democratic PSOE and the Communist PCE, used to make references to the right to self-determination in their manifestos. However, these statements were more programmatic than substantive. Conceived as political reactions to the centralism of the dictatorship, progressive parties did not intend to recognise the right of any region to separate from the rest of the country unilaterally.[27] The Spanish left was trying to appeal to voters in Catalonia and the Basque Country, where decentralisation was a hegemonic demand. The malleable language with which Communists and Socialists treated self-determination suggested an empty signifier of self-government, but not a path to independence. The constitutionalisation of the right to self-determination was in fact debated in the drafting process. The representative of the pro-independence Basque left party Euskadiko Ezkerra ('The Left of the Basque Country'),

---

[27] Andrés de Blas Guerrero, "El problema nacional-regional español en los programas del PSOE y PCE," *Revista de Estudios Políticos* 4 (1978), 155.

Francisco Letamendia, tabled an amendment to that effect. The amendment was rejected with 5 votes in favour, 268 votes against and 11 abstentions. Communists, Socialists and even Catalan nationalists made clear that they were in favour of decentralisation or federalism, but that the possibility of independence was not on the agenda.[28] Even though they used the words in hustings and manifestos, they did not see a place for self-determination in the constitution.

Article 2 set a compromise, whose cryptic formulation evinces the tricky political juggling:

> The Constitution is based on the indissoluble unity of the Spanish Nation, the common and indivisible homeland of all Spaniards; it recognises and guarantees the right to self-government of the *nationalities* and *regions* of which it is composed and the solidarity among them all.[29] (Emphasis added)

Just like in English, the word *nacionalidad* ('nationality') means belonging or citizenship of a certain country. With the 1978 constitution, the word acquired one additional meaning in Spanish constitutional law, as it now also refers to those Spanish regions that are deemed to have a defined historic or cultural identity, as difficult and controversial as it may be to identify them. Despite their novel character, *nacionalidades* were not new in political discourse. In 1876, the statesman Francesc Pi i Margall compiled some of his political speeches and articles in a volume under that title.[30] Born in Barcelona and president of Spain during the brief republic of 1873 to 1874, Pi i Margall was one of the tallest figures of the republican and federalist movement of the late nineteenth century.

The 1978 constitution distinguishes between 'nationalities' and 'regions', but nowhere does it say which ones are which. In fact, the constitution does not mention the territories by name, with the exception of references to the *foral* system of Navarra and the Basque Country (about *foralismo*, see section 3.4), the special fiscal regime of the Canary Islands, and the autonomy of the North African enclaves, Ceuta and Melilla. The distinction between nationalities and regions appears to be left deliberately open. Territories chose different ways of defining themselves in the law when the process of decentralisation began between 1979 and 1983, and a number of them have changed the label

---

[28] Session's Record of Congress (*"Diario de Sesiones del Congreso de los Diputados"*), 21 July 1978, no. 116, 4563–72.

[29] *"La Constitución se fundamenta en la indisoluble unidad de la Nación española, patria común e indivisible de todos los españoles, y reconoce y garantiza el derecho a la autonomía de las nacionalidades y regiones que la integran y la solidaridad entre todas ellas."*

[30] Francesc Pi i Margall, *Las Nacionalidades* (Madrid: Imprenta de Eduardo Martínez, 1877, 2nd edition).

in more recent reforms; the Basque Country, Galicia, Andalusia, Valencia, Aragon, Canary Islands and Balearic Islands see themselves as 'nationalities' or 'historical nationalities'; Asturias, Cantabria and Castilla and León are 'historical communities'; Extremadura and Murcia are 'regions' or 'historical regions'; and Madrid, La Rioja and Navarra have avoided the reflective question entirely.[31] As a result, there are few simple *regions* left among Spanish regions.[32] Incidentally, for the first time uniqueness was a prominent feature in Madrid's regional elections in May 2021, when the successful candidate of PP, Isabel Díaz Ayuso, argued that there is a special *Madrileño*-style way of life that would make the region different.[33]

Title VIII of the constitution gave to the unspecified territories the ability to constitute themselves in *self-governing communities*, regions – and nationalities – with constitutionally recognised powers. *Self-governing community* is another peculiar expression used in Spain's constitutional system, and nowhere else as far as I know. Drafters consciously evaded the word 'federal', a word that was politically loaded, associated with the left for a hundred years and with the republican regime that Franco's troops rose up against in 1936. The federal second republic provided the democratic space for the political articulation of regionalism and nationalism in the Basque Country, Catalonia, Galicia and Andalusia, inspired in the latter two cases by Alfonso R. Castelao and Blas Infante respectively. The 1931 constitution envisioned that territories could conform themselves in self-governing regions, but only three of them had time to take meaningful steps. Catalonia gained autonomy in 1932. Despite popular attempts in 1931 and 1932 to develop a single model for Navarra and the Basque Country together, disagreements between Socialists, Basque nationalists and Navarrese traditionalists meant that Navarra was not included in the Basque self-governing statute, which was only adopted in October 1936. By then, most of the territory had already fallen under the control of Franco's troops. Galicia held a confirmatory plebiscite in June 1936, but the Civil War broke out only one month later, and the process was irremediably called off. The 1978 constitution established a quicker and easier procedure to gain autonomy for those territories that had approved draft statutes of autonomy 'in the past' (Second Transitional Provision), a euphemistic way of referring to the republic, the only past that could matter for these purposes. This applied to the Basque Country, Catalonia and Galicia. Andalusia also managed to follow the quick

---

[31] Antonio Bar, "A Nation of Nations? A Reply to Joseph H.H. Weiler," *International Journal of Constitutional Law* 17, no. 4 (2019), 1313.
[32] Santos Juliá, "Apenas quedan ya regiones en España," *El País* (6 November 2017).
[33] Javier Casqueiro, "¿Hay una forma de vivir a la madrileña como dice Ayuso? Los candidatos opinan," *El País* (29 April 2021).

procedure set out in Article 151 of the 1978 constitution, the alternative to the lengthier general procedure of Article 143.

Article 1 of the 1931 constitution said Spain was a 'comprehensive State' (*Estado integral*) with self-governing municipalities and regions. The 1978 constitution, however, did not define the type of State in terms of its territorial arrangement. Commentators call it 'the State of self-governing entities', *Estado de las autonomías*. Whatever it did, the constitution did not set up a federation. In 1978, it was clear that it was only a matter of time before the Basque Country, Catalonia, Galicia and Andalusia sought and gained autonomy. But it was not settled that any of the others would follow suit, and in fact it was far from certain how many other regions there were, or even where their territorial limits lied. The general principle was established in Article 137: 'The State is organised territorially into municipalities, provinces and the self-governing communities *that may be constituted*. All these bodies shall enjoy self-government for the management of their respective interests' (emphasis added).[34] Therefore, in accordance with that phrasing, self-governing communities were not mandatory; they could have not been constituted. By 1983, however, 17 regions had self-governing executives and legislatures covering the whole of Spain, with a legally established division of powers between them and the central government in Madrid. Ceuta and Melilla would gain relative autonomy in 1995. A process that started with the political demands in a few territories ended up in what a government minister famously called 'coffee for everyone' (*café para todos*).

If one day stands out in the process of decentralisation, that is 23 February 1981, when a small group of armed officers kidnapped the whole chamber of deputies for 24 hours, possibly the only coup ever broadcast live on television. While no political party backed the failed coup explicitly, especially not when it became clear it would fail, the intellectual and material leaders of the coup were particularly critical of the decentralisation process. An increasing number of loud voices sounded the alarm against what they saw as the dismemberment of the nation. The centre-right UCD and the centre-left PSOE agreed on a roadmap to stop this from happening with new legislation to 'harmonise' and close the decentralisation process with the view to levelling out the powers between regions.[35] While the first step of harmonisation was partly stopped by the constitutional court in 1983 in the LOAPA case,[36] the ideological tide had shifted drastically towards the containment of the

---

[34] "*El Estado se organiza territorialmente en municipios, en provincias y en las Comunidades Autónomas que se constituyan. Todas estas entidades gozan de autonomía para la gestión de sus respectivos intereses.*"

[35] Pere Ysàs, "Democracia y autonomía en la transición española," *Ayer* 15 (1994), 106.

[36] Constitutional Court, Judgment 76/1983 (5 August).

transfer of powers to the regions. The two main Spanish parties agreed to do this, without reservations in the case of PP, which replaced UCD as the new reference on the right-hand side of the chamber after 1982. Regionalist and nationalist parties would always retain a relatively strong representation in the lower chamber, with 30 to 35 deputies out of 350, who would strive to preserve the power of the regions vis-à-vis the centre.

Has the constitutional fitting of the territories been a success story? On the one hand, considering where Spain was in 1978 and how it has evolved in the last four decades, one could draw positive conclusions focusing on the 'balance of power between governments through the vertical and horizontal division of powers, (which permitted) different parties and groups to participate in regional executives and to influence public policy, acting as a check on other governments'.[37] On the other hand, the way the constitution distinguished between areas of power that were reserved to central government and those that could be transferred to the regions (in Articles 148 and 149) 'opened the gate for broad competition for further transfers of powers on non-regulated issues'.[38] As we will see later, the tension between the central government and Catalonia was particularly intense in the 2010s, while recentralisation gained support in other parts of Spain. The two phenomena reinforced each other and, combined, they paved the way for the emergence of Vox in 2018 to 2019.

As said earlier, apart from the common use as citizenship, in Spain a *nationality* can also be a region with a special historic or cultural identity. It is recognised as such in the Royal Spanish Academy's dictionary we have already spoken about. Drawing a line between territories that deserve such special consideration and those that do not can be an impossible task. Having said that, it should be uncontroversial that some territories, currently self-governing regions, were created from scratch in the early 1980s, and they had no prior collective subjectivity. It is the case of the Region of Madrid, one of the wealthiest and most populous parts of the country, which was disjointed from other provinces of Castilla, the region Madrid had historically belonged to. Other relatively controversial decisions were taken in the process, as was the fusion of northern Castilla with León, a political decision rejected by some and accepted reluctantly by many in the latter. While not the noisiest of debates, the issue remains alive: In December 2019, the City Council of León

---

[37] César Colino, "Decentralization in Spain: Federal Evolution and Performance of the Estado Autonómico," in Diego Muro and Ignacio Lago (eds.): *The Oxford Handbook of Spanish Politics* (Oxford: Oxford University Press, 2020), 77–8.

[38] Josep M. Colomer, "Political Institutions in a Comparative Perspective," in Diego Muro and Ignacio Lago (eds.): *The Oxford Handbook of Spanish Politics* (Oxford: Oxford University Press, 2020), 163–4.

passed a motion urging the reconsideration of the merging into what they saw as a 'fictitious region'.[39]

Irrespective of the historical longevity of the region or nationality, the distribution of power between central and regional authorities is regulated in 'statutes of self-government' (*estatutos de autonomía*). The statutes are adopted by an act of the Spanish parliament by an overall majority, and in some cases, they need to be confirmed via referendum by the people living in the region. Importantly, the process is based on the starting point that all the powers were originally concentrated by the central government in Madrid. Once the statutes are passed, neither the Spanish parliament nor the central government should interfere with the powers under regions' remit. Yet, Spanish authorities retain significant powers in important policy areas, as well as the basic regulation of policies that have been transferred to the regions for further development, including health and education. Whenever centre or periphery believes their counterpart has exceeded the limits of its powers, the constitutional court is supposed to arbitrate the disagreements, of which there are plenty. Some of them have been heated in recent years, not only but particularly in relation to Catalonia.

3.3 THE CATALAN QUESTION

Much changed in the relationship between Catalonia and the rest of Spain after the reform of the Catalan statute in 2006, and after the constitutional court declared the statute partly invalid in 2010. That the fire heightened in the context of a global financial meltdown and a profound socio-economic crisis was not coincidental and only made things worse. Spain and Catalonia got to an epitome of fracture on 1 October 2017. That day Catalan authorities held an *illegal* referendum on independence, and the world saw Spanish police using excessive force against people gathered in and near polling stations. That the referendum was contrary to Spanish and Catalan law could hardly be disputed. Whether democracy should matter more than legality on that occasion was a different matter. Whether any democratic wish about independence ought to involve the whole of the Spanish population, or only the Catalan people, was, again, a different matter.

After the result, the Catalan government was equivocal about whether the result – largely supportive, 90%, but with a low turnout of 43% – legitimised a unilateral declaration of independence. Critics doubted the reliability and overall validity of the result because the referendum had not followed

---

[39] James Badcock, "Spanish Province Passes Historic Motion to Split from 'Fictitious Region'," *The Telegraph* (29 December 2019).

a legally established procedure with the corresponding guarantees of fairness. Apologists responded that a legally established procedure is what they wanted, but the Spanish State did not let them have it. In any case, in response to the Catalan government's ambiguity about what they intended to do next, on 27 October, the Spanish senate resorted to a mechanism, constitutionally envisioned in Article 155 but never used before, that would allow the central government to replace Catalan authorities and to issue instructions directly to Catalan civil servants. Catalan elections were held in December in an atmosphere of confrontation. The distribution of seats between those in favour and against independence barely changed, and the independentist coalition *remained* in power, or technically *returned* to power when the Article 155 mechanism expired in June 2018. Pro-independence politicians who had adopted a leading role in the preparation of the referendum were detained. Some escaped and left the country. Judicial proceedings ended in a supreme court ruling and prison sentences for sedition for nine pro-independence politicians in October 2019.

Orwell wrote that 'every nationalist is haunted by the belief that the past can be altered'.[40] The relationship between Catalonia and the rest of Spain is the story of a clash of legitimacies between two constructed national identities. The past should not be altered at whim, Orwell warned us. Let us then take a look at the rear mirror and see how those identities evolved and interacted over time before 2006 and 2010. Spoiler alert: There was nothing inevitable about 1 October 2017, and the relationship between Catalonia and the rest of Spain has not always been of rage.

Many people abroad know about the Balearic Islands (Majorca, Menorca, Ibiza and Formentera), Canary Islands, much of Andalusia and other touristic destinations, but Catalonia has been for some time the region one hears the most about outside Spain. Spaniards living in other regions understandably complain about the disproportionate attention that Catalonia gets in media and politics. They and their land have their own problems, but they do not seem to be covered as widely. While this is a fair point, I will nonetheless spend some time on Catalonia, not only because it has been the hottest point of contention in the last decade, but also because I think Brenan was right when he wrote in 1943 that 'the Catalan question is . . . one rather special instance of the general problem of Spanish regionalism'.[41] I still believe what I said some pages ago, Spanish politics are much more than Franco and Catalonia, but we can learn a lot about the country's national vulnerabilities by spending some time talking about this land.

---

[40] George Orwell, "Notes on Nationalism" (1945).
[41] Brenan, *The Spanish Labyrinth*, 38.

Like Spain's and other European nationalist projects, Catalan nationalism is a product of the nineteenth century. Uneven capitalist development and cultural modernisation since the 1850s gave birth to a new elite in and near Barcelona whose economic interests did not coincide with those of the landowners in Castilla and the south. The fiasco of the federalist attempt of the first republic of 1873 to 1874, and the centralising impetus from Madrid at the end of the third Carlista war in 1876, pushed the Catalan bourgeoisie to support a new political project, Catalanism, to favour their special interests. The loss of Cuba in 1898 increased the sense of resentment among Catalan manufacturers and traders, who had significant investments on the island. The ruling class in Madrid was held responsible for such loss because they failed to factor in the U.S. determination to exert their influence in the Caribbean. In all, the loss of Cuba had severe consequences for Spain's economic position and international recognition as a colonial power.[42]

Despite their frustration with the Spanish establishment, in the early decades of the twentieth century the Catalan bourgeoisie played two political games at once. On the one hand, they supported politically and economically a growing regionalist movement that demanded self-government. That was Catalanism. On the other hand, when the political situation allowed it, they did not hide their resolve to remain as involved as possible in the management of power in Madrid. In fact, regionalisms in Catalonia and elsewhere in the late nineteenth century and early twentieth century were attempts to reshape the idea of Spain, trying to influence the fate of the whole in one direction or another, rather than dismembering it. About this time, Núñez Seixas writes:

> Catalan mainstream nationalists never gave up the hope of incorporating the Spanish regionalist movements into a common political project aimed at reshaping the entire structure of the Spanish state, within which Catalonia would then exercise a sort of 'modernizing hegemony'. Intellectual and cultural dynamics of regional affirmation throughout Spain did not imply the promotion of distinct 'minority nationalisms', but rather a vehicle for regional and local affirmation of the concept of a Spanish nation.[43]

With dramatic switches, the double game would remain a feature of Spanish politics at different moments of the twentieth century, and remains so on and off in the twenty-first century. For example, the most influential man in the Catalanist movement in the first three decades of last century, Francesc Cambó, became a minister of the king's government in 1918 and 1921. No

---

[42] Preston, *A People Betrayed*, 53.
[43] Xosé-Manoel Núñez, "The Region as Essence of the Fatherland: Regionalist Variants of Spanish Nationalism (1840–1936)," *European History Quarterly* 31, no. 4 (2001), 494.

one captured the ambivalence of the Catalanist juggling better than Niceto Alcalá-Zamora, who reprimanded Cambó for attempting to play the roles of Bolivar in Catalonia and Bismarck in Spain at the same time.[44] Alcalá-Zamora would later turn to republicanism and became the longest-serving president of the second republic, between December 1931 and April 1936.

The relationship between Catalonia and the rest of Spain has been a succession of periods of more or less sincere collaboration and more or less open hostility. In October 2017, Catalan president Carles Puigdemont declared Catalonia would be an independent State, but immediately asked the Catalan parliament to suspend the effects of such declaration. The statement was profoundly confusing and to this day it is still debated if he did or did not announce that Catalonia would be open for international recognition and UN and European Union membership. That would be in fact the third time in history that a Catalan State would be declared, fourth if one considers the revolt of 1641, when local oligarchs proclaimed a new republic under the protection of the king of France. The lyrics of *Els Segadors*, the Catalan anthem, are inspired by that revolt. The other two declarations took place in 1931 and in 1934. The first one was pronounced by Francesc Macià as soon as the Catalan Republican Left ('Esquerra Republicana de Catalunya') obtained the largest number of votes in Catalonia in the local elections of 12 April 1931, from which the Spanish republic would emerge. As soon as the results began to be known, Macià promised that Catalonia would be a republic within an Iberian federation. The *Generalitat* or Catalan government was set up in 1932. In 1934, the new Catalan president, Lluís Companys, declared the Catalan State within a federal republic. Companys and other Catalan leaders were imprisoned and the right-wing government in Madrid suspended Catalonia's self-government. Franco would have Companys executed in Barcelona after the Civil War, in 1940.

During the debate about the Catalan statute of self-government in 1932, the philosopher and then member of parliament, José Ortega y Gasset argued that, while the Catalan problem is not exceptional or unique, it cannot be resolved and be done with; it is part of Spain's history and politics, it is a 'problem for life' that can only be dealt with or 'brought along' (*conllevar*).[45]

---

[44] Session's Record of the Courts ("*Diario de las Sesiones de Cortes*"), 10 December 1918, no. 105, 3468: "*Yo quiero advertirle una cosa: no se puede ser a la vez Bolívar en Cataluña y Bismarck en España.*"

[45] Session's Record of the Constitutional Assembly ("*Diario de Sesiones de las Cortes Constituyentes*"), 13 May 1932, no. 165, 5575: "*Yo sostengo que el problema catalán, como todos los parejos a él, que han existido y existen en otras naciones, es un problema que no se puede resolver, que sólo se puede conllevar, y al decir esto, conste que significo con ello, no sólo que los demás españoles tenemos que conllevarnos con los catalanes, sino que los catalanes también tienen que conllevarse con todos los demás españoles.*" In Spanish, *conllevar* can mean to suffer or to put up with the consequences of something, but also to get along with someone.

Ortega used that speech to oppose the statute of self-government on the table, which he thought would risk Spain's unity. History has shown that Spain's unity can endure not one but 17 statutes of self-government at once. Having said that, and leaving the superficial political question aside, Ortega's fundamental point about society's need to embrace and bring its own problems along in the future still holds true today, nine decades after he pronounced those words in parliament.

Franco's dictatorship imposed cultural homogeneity, prohibited political parties and centralised all powers in Madrid. Catalan bourgeoisie had to adapt to the new circumstances, and building the Catalan nation was put on hold. Fraser put it this way in 1976:

> Without denying the specificity of the Catalan nation and its culture, *politically* bourgeois Catalanism defined itself by its progressiveness in contradistinction to reactionary centralism – until faced with losing power or being swept away by proletarian uprisings. This gave the Catalan bourgeois and petty-bourgeois parties a more advanced, progressive appearance, which was not always belied, particularly in its petty-bourgeois variant – but did not prevent them putting class above 'nation' when the former was threatened.[46] (Emphasis in the original)

A Catalan elite did in fact benefit from the extraordinary economic growth of Spain in the 1950s, 1960s and 1970s. At the same time, however, social and cultural expressions of opposition to the regime were not uncommon, despite being illegal and persecuted. In 1963, the French newspaper Le Monde opened with an interview with the abbot of the renowned monastery of Montserrat, Aureli Escarré, where the monk denounced the repression of Catalan language, and expressed the view that Catalonia was indeed a nation and that the Spanish regime did not deserve to be called Christian.[47] The interview exasperated Franco and Escarré was forced to leave Spain and move to Italy.

Self-government of the regions became one of the shared demands of both Spain's left and nationalist and regionalist forces in Catalonia, and beyond, when democracy began to return to Spain in the late 1970s. Despite the differences between them, particularly with the attempts to stop the decentralisation process in the 1980s, the Catalan social-democratic PSC – associated with Spain's PSOE – the green and post-Communist coalition, and the pro-independence Catalanist left (ERC) agreed to run together as part of a single list in the elections to the Spanish senate every four years until 2008 in the

---

[46] Ronald Fraser, "Spain on the Brink," *New Left Review* I–96 (1976), 6.

[47] Le Monde, "Le régime espagnol se dit chrétien mais n'obéit pas aux principes de base du christianisme," (14 November 1963).

so-called Entesa (Agreement). The right-wing nationalist coalition that ruled Catalonia between 1979 and 2003, Convergència I Unió (CIU), sustained the minority governments of both Felipe González (PSOE) in 1993 to 1996 and José María Aznar (PP) in 1996 to 2000. Cambó's strategy of pushing for self-government in Barcelona while remaining critically influential in Madrid appeared to be as valid 75 years later. Back to the left, in another expression of collaboration beyond disagreements about the nation, pro- and anti-independence parties of the Entesa coalition got into power in Catalonia for the first and, so far, only time in 2003, and they stayed together not without difficulties until 2010.

One-third of the statutes of self-government of different regions were renewed in the 2000s; Catalonia's was one of them. In a campaign rally in November 2003, Spanish social-democratic contender José Luis Rodríguez Zapatero vowed to sign off any new statute passed by the Catalan parliament. Three years later, as prime minister he learned that he would not be able to meet that promise. The text drafted in Barcelona was endorsed by 120 of the 135 deputies of the Catalan parliament – all except the unionist and conservative PP. However, when the text reached Madrid, certain provisions were modified because Spain's deputies casted doubt on their constitutionality. The most emblematic modification was this: The draft originally said in the first article that Catalonia was a 'nation', but the Spanish parliament moved that word to the politically symbolic but legally immaterial preamble of the statute. The right-wing nationalist CIU accepted the change, but the left-leaning ERC did not, despite sharing government with Spain's social-democrats in the Catalan government. ERC deputies in the Spanish parliament abstained and asked the Catalan people not to go to the polling station when asked to express their view in referendum. Three in four Catalans who voted did vote in favour of the new statute in 2006, but less than half of the population exercised their prerogative.

TPP voted against the new statute in Barcelona and in Madrid, and they brought it to the constitutional court because in their view the 2006 statute, despite the changes introduced in Madrid, was still incompatible with the 1978 constitution. PP appealed against certain provisions of the Catalan statute that were literally the same as those of other statutes. This double standard antagonised many in Catalonia. The party's campaign did not end with the legal action. PP organised rallies around Spain to frame the Catalan statute and PSOE's government as threats to the unity of the Spanish nation. Conservative leaders preached Catalanophobia and called for the boycott of Catalan products, symbolically represented in the local bubbly, cava. The strategy was not going to be fruitful in Catalonia, but that did not matter. PP intended to gain votes in the rest of Spain by fuelling hostility towards Catalans and their desire for greater self-government, a desire shared by pro-independentists, nationalists and federalists. At the same time, an apparently increasing number of messages emerged from Catalonia with unfair stereotypes about other parts of Spain, represented as more prone to partying than working. With about 15% of the population, Catalonia concentrated 20% of Spain's GDP, and the tension was ripe for malicious politicians to make the case that Spain was a drag on Catalonia's finances. The motto '*Espanya ens roba*' ('Spain is stealing from us') became popular in certain political environments.

In June 2010, the constitutional court's ruling gave the green light to most of the 2006 statute, but not all of it.[48] The decision was 500-page long and dealt mostly with technical questions about the binding or advisory nature of certain statutory reports, or about the extent to which the powers of Catalan authorities were exclusive or shared with the central government in Madrid. It is fair to say that the vast majority of Catalans – or Spaniards, for that matter – did not read the ruling, neither would they appreciate the legal nuances. Politically, however, the court's decision was received in Catalonia as yet another diminution of their self-government. What's more, this time the emendation did not even emerge from a legislative authority, but from 12 unelected legal experts selected and appointed by political parties in the Spanish parliament. The ruling of a court sitting in Madrid was received with a large demonstration in Barcelona led by the top brass of Catalan politics carrying a banner that said '*Som una nació, nosaltres decidim*' ('We are a nation, we decide').

Participation at rallies on the national day of Catalonia, or *Diada*, on 11 September grew in size every of the following eight years. At the same time, the celebration became an ever more divisive issue. Unlike most national festivities, which tend to rejoice at victories, Diada commemorates the fall of Barcelona in Spain's war of succession in 1714, after which regional powers were taken away by the Spanish king, Felipe V, the first one of the French House of Bourbon, the same royal family that sits on the throne today, represented by Felipe VI. The year 1714 is the reason why large crowds started to chant for independence on the 14th second of the 17th minute during Barça matches in the stands of Camp Nou stadium. Diada used to be celebrated by all political parties, nationalist or not, each framing the day to their advantage. In the 2010s, non-nationalist and anti-independence parties chose not to participate in the public gatherings, which became large, festive, peaceful and explicit demonstrations for an independent Catalan republic. According to some accounts, the invigorated movement for independence encompassed

---

[48] Constitutional Court, Judgment 31/2010 (28 June).

different sectors of the population, including the working class.[49] According to other accounts, however, support for greater self-government, a referendum and ultimately independence has always been and remains higher among those with higher incomes and with university degrees.[50]

The post-statute controversy also saw the emergence of a new political party, Ciudadanos ('Citizens'), sturdily opposed to independence and in favour of stopping when not reversing Spain's decentralisation. Ciudadanos was born as *Ciutadans* in Catalonia in 2006, where it became a significant force in 2012 and obtained the largest number of votes in 2017, when right-wing and left-wing pro-independence forces concurred separately. The party quickly expanded to other regions and reached the third position in Spain's general election of April 2019. However, it lost five out of every six seats when the election was held again seven months later, after the left's inability to find a working arrangement between them. With a booming far-right Vox and a steady right-wing PP, Ciudadanos struggled to find its place. As observed by Gray, 'from the outset, voters perceived Ciudadanos to be further to the right than the party's own perceptions of itself, and it started to attract far more disillusioned PP voters than PSOE voters'.[51] In the Catalan elections of February 2021, Ciudadanos fell from top position and 25% of the vote to just over 5%, and in the Madrid elections of May 2021, Ciudadanos collapsed and disappeared from the regional parliament. The results showed that a liberal centrist ticket is in desperate need for a radical change of strategy if it aims to have a voice in Spanish politics.

The pro-independence surge in Catalonia in the 2010s cannot be explained without two key factors: the economic crisis and a fundamental change in the strategy of the conservative Catalan nationalist front. Led by Artur Mas, the right-wing CIU returned to power in 2010, and quickly began implementing deeply unpopular policies aimed at tightening public spending. In a context of rising evictions and unemployment, anti-austerity *indignados* ('outraged') groups mushroomed all over Spain, also in Catalonia, similar to the so-called Occupy movement of other countries (see section 5.2).[52] At the same time, CIU and several of its leading figures, including Jordi Pujol, president of Catalonia between 1980 and 2003, had been immersed in shameful corruption scandals. President Mas was hoping to persuade the new Spanish prime minister Mariano Rajoy (PP) to change the financial allocation mechanism

---

[49] Donatella della Porta and Martín Portos, "A Burgeois Story? The Class Basis of Catalan Independentism," *Territory, Politics, Governance* 9, no. 3 (2021), 391.
[50] Thomas Piketty, *Capital and Ideology* (Cambridge, MA: Harvard University Press, 2020), 920–1.
[51] Caroline Gray, *Territorial Politics and the Party System in Spain: Continuity and Change since the Financial Crisis* (Abingdon: Routledge, 2020), 141.
[52] Raphael Minder, *The Struggle for Catalonia: Rebel Politics in Spain* (London: Hurst & Co, 2017), 6–11.

so Catalonia could retain a greater share of the tax levied in the territory. However, Mas had little leverage over a Spanish PM who enjoyed an overwhelming majority in the Spanish parliament, and who was not keen to renounce to an important source of revenue in the middle of a deep recession. Empty handed, Mas announced snap regional elections for September 2012. 'Faced with a clear opportunity to blame central government for Catalonia's economic situation', it was at that point that Mas and right-wing nationalists prioritised the agenda of Catalonia's self-determination.[53] Haunted by corruption and the unpopularity of austerity, CIU lost a large number of votes, and while they remained the first party, governing alone was no longer an option. Reluctantly CIU formed a coalition with the rising left-leaning and independentist ERC. As part of the deal, Mas agreed to hold an informal consultation on Catalan independence. Such consultation took place in November 2014, when 80% of the people voted in favour of independence, even if the result was tainted by a low turnout of around 40%. Austerity policies continued both in Catalonia and in the rest of Spain, but Catalan politics were now constantly presented as a choice between remaining part of Spain or going separate. Right-wing nationalism endorsed that binary narrative, even though, unlike ERC, CIU had never supported independence before. In the opinion of Barrio and Rodríguez-Teruel, the two nationalist parties entered into an 'outbidding competition', each one trying to ensure that they were not overtaken by the other party as the most ardent defenders of independence in the public eye.[54]

Mas reinvented himself from an austerity-prone politician into a street protester. Rotted by corruption and internal divisions, that was the end of CIU, but right-wing nationalism went on through a collection of political parties that were successful in successive elections. Catalans were called to the polling station again in 2015. The overall representation of pro- and anti-independence parties did not change significantly, and a coalition of right-wing and left-wing pro-independence parties emerged victorious. Mas was replaced by a little known independentist mayor of the medium-sized city of Girona, one Carles Puigdemont.

The new Catalan government supported by the same left-wing and right-wing nationalists announced their determination to organise an independence referendum. They assured the population that this new plebiscite would somehow be endowed with greater legal and political significance than the one of 2014. The Catalan parliament passed legislation with a roadmap of

---

[53] Richard Gillespie, "The Contrasting Fortunes of Pro-sovereignty Currents in Basque and Catalan Nationalist Parties: PNV and CDC Compared," *Territory, Politics, Governance* 5, no. 4 (2017), 418.

[54] Astrid Barrio and Juan Rodríguez-Teruel, "Reducing the Gap between Leaders and Voters? Elite Polarization, Outbidding Competition, and the Rise of Secessionism in Catalonia," *Ethnic and Racial Studies* 40, no. 10 (2017), 1776.

what was supposed to happen between the referendum and the unilateral declaration of independence – assuming as everyone did that the result was going to be positive – as well as after such declaration. The two fundamental laws were rushed through the Catalan parliament over 48 hours in early September 2017. These laws were appealed by the Spanish government to the constitutional court, which swiftly declared them unconstitutional. The referendum was ruled illegal by the courts, but the Catalan government went ahead anyway on 1 October. Independence yes or no had been a mantra for five years if no more, constantly debated on the media and in the streets. However, there was no official campaign in the weeks prior to the referendum, and to the extent that there was an unofficial one, only those who supported independence took part in it. The others refused to participate in what they saw as an unconstitutional sham. This meant that no one made the case for *better together*. Reasons were given not to engage, but reasons were not given to vote against independence. Catalan police refused to use force in polling stations, but the Spanish government sent police forces from other parts of the country to stop the ballot. Shocking violent incidents took place in the morning, with allegations of excessive use of force.[55] Appalling videos and photographs circulated on social media, and international media covered the news widely. That's when many outside the country realised suddenly that something big was going on in Spain. While unofficially counted, about two million people representing over 90% of voters inserted a pro-independence ballot; 43% of electors was said to have taken part in the referendum.

The division within Catalonia and between Catalonia and the rest of Spain had never been deeper in living memory. Scenes of police violence upset many not only in Catalonia, but elsewhere in Spain, and the international image of the government and the country got seriously damaged as a result. Two days after the referendum, King Felipe VI addressed a shocked, confused and divided country. The king of Spain accused the government of Catalonia of having 'repeatedly, consciously and deliberately' violated the constitution and the statute of self-government. He said that they had 'infringed the democratic principles of any State under the rule of law (and) undermined the harmony and peaceful coexistence of Catalan society itself', adding that they had shown 'unacceptable disloyalty towards the powers of the Spanish State'.[56] Media and opinion polls reported that the king's hard-hitting statement did provide solace to many Spaniards, possibly also to a number of Catalans. At the same time, however, the message frustrated most people in Catalonia, some of whom perhaps secretly hoped that the monarch would hold out an olive branch. The speech exasperated Catalan authorities,

---

[55] Human Rights Watch, "Spain: Police Used Excessive Force in Catalonia," (12 October 2017).
[56] Message from His Majesty the King (3 October 2017).

who recalled how one of Felipe VI's direct Bourbon ancestors had centralised powers taking them away from Catalonia in 1714.

As said earlier, the jury is still out about whether president Puigdemont did or did not declare that Catalonia had become an independent State in October 2017. Be that as it may, the Spanish senate resorted to a constitutional provision never used before, Article 155, to implement direct rule in Catalonia in accordance with the legal framework, including the statute of autonomy, which, despite commentaries,[57] was not and could not be suspended within the law.

Direct rule was in place for a few months until a new Catalan government was formed sometime after the snap regional election of December 2017. The intensely anti-independence Ciudadanos received the largest share of votes because the two main pro-independence parties, on the left and right, ran separately. However, the distribution of seats between those in favour and those against independence remained approximately the same. A lot had happened, but not much had changed. Voices in other parts of Spain demanded the continuation of direct rule in Catalonia, but powers were restored in June 2018.

Puigdemont and several Catalan government ministers fled Spain and moved to Belgium, Scotland, Germany and Switzerland soon before direct rule was imposed. Had they not done so, they would have probably faced the same fate of the ministers, other politicians, and two civil society leaders, who were detained and prosecuted for rebellion, sedition, misuse of public funds and contempt of court – refusal to comply with judicial rulings. The trial was livestreamed on Youtube, with initially high but soon waning popular interest. The supreme court issued its judgement in October 2019, acquitting all the defendants of rebellion but condemning nine of them to between nine and 13 years in prison for sedition, including controversially the two civil society leaders Jordi Sànchez and Jordi Cuixart.[58] The decision was criticised by large and peaceful demonstrations in Catalonia, and smaller ones in other parts of Spain, as well as some violent disturbances in the streets of Barcelona. In April 2021, the constitutional court dismissed the first claim by one of the Catalan politicians, Jordi Turull, for alleged violation of his fundamental rights.[59] Two of the nine members of the court, however, issued dissenting opinions because the sentences were excessive given the relatively ambiguous wording of the crime of sedition; they also argued that the sentences should have been better adjusted to each convict's individual responsibility. Similar rulings were issued, or are expected to be

---

[57] Bonnie N. Field, "Legislative Politics in Spain," in Diego Muro and Ignacio Lago (eds.): *The Oxford Handbook of Spanish Politics* (Oxford: Oxford University Press, 2020), 211.
[58] Supreme Court, Judgment 459/2019 (14 October).
[59] Constitutional Court, Judgment 91/2021 (22 April).

issued, in relation to the other Catalan politicians in prison. Legal counsels announced they intended to appeal to the European Court of Human Rights in Strasbourg. Meanwhile, the Spanish government received requests for executive pardons. In May 2021, Prime Minister Sánchez implied that his government would be ready to grant pardons because, he said, the constitution is based on dialogue, not revenge: 'There is a time for punishment and there is a time for concord.'[60] The government made the pardons official in June, justifying the measure as a matter of 'public interest', and making it conditional upon the recipients not committing a serious crime over a period of between three and six years.[61] The pardons were supported by religious leaders in Catalonia, as well as employer representatives and trade unions in Spain, but were strongly criticised by right-wing parties. At the time of this writing, in mid-2021, the government is also pondering a reform of the criminal code, which could reduce the sentence for the crime of sedition the Catalan politicians were initially punished for.

3.4 THE BASQUE COUNTRY, *FORALISMO* AND A NATIONAL QUESTION SHAPED BY VIOLENCE

The Basques have always aroused the curiosity of foreigners. In 1787, John Adams, later to be the second president of the United States, praised the Basques this way: 'While their neighbors have long since resigned all their pretensions into the hands of kings and priests, this extraordinary people have preserved their ancient language, genius, laws, government, and manners, without innovation, longer than any other nation of Europe.'[62] In 1955, Orson Welles devoted to the Basque Country one of his BBC documentaries, set in a bucolic town in the mountains of the French Basque Country, not far from the border with Spain, a border, says Welles in the introduction, that 'has always been more a theory than a fact . . . People who live here are neither French nor Spanish. They are Basque. The rise and fall of other republics and kingdoms have never made them forget that they are Basque.'[63] Basque language is radically different from Spanish and French, or indeed any other language alive, incomprehensible for anyone except for its one million or so speakers. In the family tree of languages, Basque has no mother or siblings. Its origins

---

[60] Session's Record of Congress, Plenary ("*Diario de Sesiones del Congreso de los Diputados, Pleno y Diputación Permanente*"), 26 May 2021, no. 106, 6: "*La Constitución española recoge en su espíritu tanto el castigo como la concordia. Hay un tiempo para el castigo y hay un tiempo para la concordia.*"
[61] Royal Decrees 456/2021 to 464/2021, of 22 June.
[62] John Adams, *A Defence of the Constitutions of the United States* (London: C. Dilly, 1787), 16.
[63] Orson Welles, "The Land of the Basques" (1955).

and survival have been a riddle for linguists for a very long time. You may not know this, but Adam and Eve communicated in Basque, or so I say when the exceptionality of the Basques comes up in casual conversations, not caring much if my interlocutors realise that I am only half joking.

Incidentally, '(being) Basque' is translated into Basque language as *euskalduna (izatea)*, meaning that who speaks, literally that who *has*, the Basque language. This definition must be taken with a pinch of salt, because at least half of the population living in the Basque Country would not be Basque otherwise, since they do not speak the language. The number of speakers has been growing thanks to younger generations, and significant efforts are being made privately and publicly – less so in *Iparralde*, 'The North', the French Basque Country – to promote the knowledge and use of the language. Having said that, the relationship between Basque and Spanish – or French – is still of complex diglossia: One language – Spanish or French – is understood and could be potentially used by everyone, while the other – Basque – is not, and the two languages – Spanish and Basque, French and Basque – coexist in a single territory and community, but their use is stratified depending on the sphere and topic of conversation.

Between 2009 and 2011, I lived in Denver, where I was a postgraduate student of International Relations. My second year I taught Basque language as a volunteer in the *Euskal Etxea* ('Basque House') of Colorado. My students were the descendants of some of the thousands of Basque shepherds from the French and the Spanish Basque Country and Navarra who migrated to the United States – Idaho, Nevada, Utah, and other states in the area – in the late nineteenth and early twentieth centuries. My pupils' ages ranged from 30s to 70s and their knowledge of the language was basic. For months we went over and over the same sentences and songs, which probably says more about my limited pedagogic skills than about their learning capabilities. But they were keen, and they proudly preserved other cultural expressions that I had grown up with in the Basque Country, especially gastronomy and Christmas festivities. The Basque heritage was recognisable in their first or last names, sometimes both. Their names and in some cases their physical appearance suggested they were Basque. With the Rocky Mountains in the background, most other things did not. All of this I found fascinating and I never got entirely used to it. They were American citizens, and many of them enjoyed visiting the Basque Country every year or two. Some still had cousins or distant cousins there. Despite all that, it was my impression that some in the group had developed an idealised version of the Basque Country in their heads as a beautiful, green, rural and mountainous land unaltered by globalisation and resolute to break away from Spain and France. I remember feeling torn between the urge to burst a bubble and the second thought, which was no other than why bother. That was one of their core beliefs, which I had to respect, particularly when one way or another, their beliefs made little difference, just like my own beliefs make little difference. Furthermore, the group was extremely kind to me; they were the most welcoming and generous hosts.

Basque politics are slightly different from Spanish politics. However, being Basque nowadays does not mean that you will necessarily agree with Welles that you are neither French nor Spanish. To be honest, that was not the case when Welles said so in 1955 either. For example, the current leader of Spain's ultranationalist and far-right-wing party Vox, Santiago Abascal, was born and grew up in the Basque Country. In January 2020, Abascal denounced to the delight of his 51 colleagues in the Spanish parliament that, by granting their support to the investiture of PSOE's Pedro Sánchez as prime minister,

> the separatists, the caciques of the Basque Nationalist Party are doing what they always do in this traditional and mean-spirited game of profiteering from each of Spain's weaknesses, either by picking the fruits of (ETA's) terrorism or the fruits of the (independentist) coup d'état in Catalonia.[64]

Abascal was denouncing as a sign of profiteering and weakness what had been a relatively stable feature in Spain's institutional politics for at least three decades. Since Prime Minister Felipe González lost his absolute majority in 1993, the Basque Nationalist Party (PNV, *Partido Nacionalista Vasco*) has played a significant role in Spanish politics with both left-wing and right-wing governments in Madrid. Its small representation (five to seven seats out of 350) has sometimes made all the difference in tight races. The appearance of respectability of their spokespersons and their pragmatism allowed them to position themselves in the ideological centre of Spanish politics. In exchange for their support for both PSOE and PP governments, PNV managed to pass legislation and budgets in the Basque parliament with the backing or the acquiescence of regional deputies of those parties. PNV currently shares power with PSOE in the Basque executive since 2016, as did between 1986 and 1998. Apart from the Basque parliament, one must bear in mind multi-level governance, with quasi-parliamentary institutions of the three Basque provinces, Gipuzkoa, Bizkaia and Araba. Directly elected by the people, these provincial assemblies regulate taxes and appoint the executives that will levy them. While their representation decreased considerably in the 2010s, in

---

[64] Session's Record of Congress, Plenary (*"Diario de Sesiones del Congreso de los Diputados, Pleno y Diputación Permanente"*), 4 January 2020, no. 2, 45: *"Los separatistas, los caciques del Partido Nacionalista Vasco a lo suyo en este juego ya tradicional y miserable de sacar tajada de cada debilidad de España, bien sea recogiendo las nueces del terrorismo o las nueces del golpismo en Cataluña."*

the 1980s, 1990s and 2000s, PP and PSOE were relatively strong in Araba, which was an additional incentive for all parties to reach a mutually beneficial consensus: You let me govern here, and I will let you govern there.

Between 2015 and 2018, conservative prime minister Mariano Rajoy ruled Spain with a minority executive. Two new political stars had risen in Spanish politics, Podemos on the left and the economically liberal Ciudadanos somewhere around the centre. The two would eat seats away from the traditional gatekeepers, social-democratic PSOE and conservative PP. Rajoy lost his majority after a series of corruption scandals and years of disliked austerity policies. But he held on to power negotiating every vote in the chamber. In that parliament, Rajoy had two main partners in Madrid: 32 deputies from Ciudadanos and five from PNV. Together with his 134, they were just enough most of the time – the lower chamber has 350 members – unless pretty much everybody else voted against him. However, while Ciudadanos was reasonably comfortable with PP's economic policies and Jacobinism, ideology did not explain PNV's support.

That unlikely alliance has ancient roots and is called *foralismo*.

PNV was honouring its party name, not the Spanish acronym PNV, but the name in Basque, EAJ. The reader may find surprising that EAJ and PNV do not mean the same thing. EAJ stands for 'Euzko Alderdi Jeltzalea', meaning 'Basque Party fond of God and the old laws' (J for 'Jel-tzale', 'jaungoikoa eta lege zaharren zalea'). The so-called old laws are more commonly known as *fueros*. The reference to God is due to the devout Catholicism of the PNV founder Sabino Arana, and indeed the widespread religiosity primarily in the non-urban population of the Basque Country of 1895, when the party was born. Leaving God aside, PNV-EAJ's politics during Rajoy's second government are understandable in light of Basque history, going back centuries in time.

The fueros, hence *foralismo*, are the unique foundation of the first Basque nationalism, and of much of the contemporary one. Throughout history, fueros were the collection of laws and conventions that regulated private and public life in the territories that are now known as the Basque Country and Navarra. Swearing to respect and protect them was one of the things that Spanish monarchs were expected to do upon coronation. A variety of fueros existed in other parts of Spain, but they were all taken away in a process of centralisation that began in the early eighteenth century. Catalonia lost them in 1714 after the local nobles supported the losing side in the succession war that took the French Bourbon family to the Spanish throne. Seeking an origin for the resistance, Catalonia idealised 1714 just like many Basques idealised 1512, the year when the Kingdom of Navarra was absorbed by Castilla and Aragon. In 2011, a left-leaning pro-independence coalition was formed to run for the Spanish congress and senate in the Basque Country and Navarra. The name of the coalition was Amaiur, in reference to the last Navarrese fortress standing against the troops of King Fernando the Catholic. The symbol of the 'arrano beltza' ('black eagle'), seen in marches of the pro-independence left, is borrowed from the heraldry of Navarrese monarchs of the twelfth and thirteenth centuries.

Unlike their Catalan counterparts, Basque aristocracy sided with the winning side in the succession war of the early 1700s. However, they picked the losing side in the succession or Carlista wars the following century. The Carlista side was profoundly antiliberal, as they were keen to preserve local traditions, of which the fueros were a typical expression. At the end of the last Carlista war, in 1876, the Basque fueros were taken away. However, only two years later, in 1878, a new scheme was set in place that gave the three Basque provinces the authority to levy taxes. A negotiated percentage of the collected amount would be wired to the Spanish treasury. The 'economic concert' ('concierto económico') was born. In Navarra a similar model, the 'economic covenant' ('convenio económico'), had been in place since 1841. The system remains in force to this day, suspended by Franco only for Gipuzkoa and Bizkaia between 1937 and 1980 as a punishment for having resisted his coup of July 1936. Araba and Navarra, where the coup succeeded from the beginning, conserved their fiscal prerogatives.

PNV was born to preserve the economic concert and to restore the fueros to the maximum extent. Compared with the 'outburst of literary creativity' in the Catalonia of late nineteenth century, wrote Payne in 1964, Basque nationalism surfaced in a much more 'narrow, provincial and gray' setting.[65] Less sophisticated in its origins perhaps, but Basque nationalism would prove to be no less effective in the democratic arena. Resorting to history and tradition, PNV filled a new political space to advocate for autonomy and co-sovereignty shared with the crown.[66] With the passing of time, the defence of fueros would be reframed as self-government. In fact, the 1978 constitution recognises the unique character of Basque and Navarrese self-government in this particular way in the First Additional Provision: 'The Constitution protects and respects the historic rights of the territories with fueros. The general updating of such regime shall be carried out, where appropriate, within the framework of the Constitution and of the Statutes of Self-government.'[67] A democratically elected Basque government was set

---

[65] Stanley G. Payne, "Spanish Nationalism in the Twentieth Century," *Review of Politics* 26, no. 3 (1964), 410–1.
[66] Joseba Agirreazkuenaga, "Las oportunidades de construcción del Estado liberal español: La 'España Foral'," *Ayer* 35 (1999), 145.
[67] "*La Constitución ampara y respeta los derechos históricos de los territorios forales. La actualización general de dicho régimen foral se llevará a cabo, en su caso, en el marco de la Constitución y de los Estatutos de Autonomía.*"

up in 1980, and in early February 1981, King Juan Carlos visited the iconic town of Gernika, in a move that was interpreted as the crown's recognition of Basque self-government. In his speech, the king referred to the fueros as an expression of 'Basque unique features' and as an 'essential part of the project that facilitated and encouraged the inclusion of the Basque Country in the very definition of Spain'.[68] Leaders of Herri Batasuna (Popular Unity) stood up, chanted for independence and disrupted the event. Two-and-a-half weeks later, a group of military officers hijacked the Spanish congress in an attempted coup d'état (see sections 3.1 and 4.2) (figure 3.2, figure 3.3).

Within the current constitutional framework, apart from the Basque Country and Navarra, no other region or nationality can claim to enjoy historic rights like theirs. Handling their own taxes gives Basque and Navarrese institutions a level of fiscal and financial autonomy far greater than that enjoyed by Catalan authorities or indeed any other regional government. From the perspective of foralismo, the 1979 Basque statute of self-government is the twentieth century scaffolding of the bilateral relationship with Spain the PNV has always been eager to look after. Driven by pragmatism, PNV's negotiations with PP and PSOE in Madrid are framed as efforts to maximise the potential of the current framework, while seeking ways to replace it with

Figure 3.2 King Fernando the Catholic swears to respect the *fueros* of Biscay in Gernika in 1476. Source: Wikimedia Commons: https://commons.wikimedia.org/wiki/File:Fernando_El_Catolico_Guernica.png

---

[68] El País, "El Rey defiende en Guernica la democracia y las instituciones tradicionales vascas," (4 February 1981): "*Hecho diferencial vascongado*" and "*parte esencial del proyecto que posibilitó y estimuló la incorporación vascongada a la propia definición de España.*"

Figure 3.3 King Juan Carlos in 1981 in the moment when pro-independence politicians attempted to disrupt the event. Source: EFE

another one that could expand self-government to new policy areas. PNV's historical strategies have oscillated in a 'pendulum' between pragmatism and claims for sovereignty.[69] Some party members occasionally speak about it, particularly the youth branch, but breaking away from Spain entirely remains at odds with the core principles of foralismo. The farthest PNV went in this regard was the proposal articulated by Basque premier Juan José Ibarretxe in 2003 to 2005 for a new political statute in the form of a free association between the Basque Country and Spain. While it enjoyed enough support in the Basque parliament, even from within the pro-independence left, it was amply rejected in the Spanish parliament, and remains buried ever since.

PNV's strategy in the 2010s was substantially different from Catalonia's right-wing nationalism. Historically, conservative nationalists in the Basque Country and Catalonia have both been broad churches, and the two forces have combined ambitious narratives of nationhood with cooperative approaches towards the authorities in Madrid.[70] However, there are disparities between them in relation to how they dealt with generational renewal,

---

[69] Ludger Mees, "Nationalist Politics at the Crossroads: The Basque Nationalist Party and the Challenge of Sovereignty (1998–2014)," *Nationalism and Ethnic Politics* 21, no. 1 (2015), 45.

[70] Bonnie N. Field, "The Evolution of Substate Nationalist Parties as Statewide Parliamentary Actors: CiU and PNV in Spain," *Nationalism and Ethnic Politics* 21, no. 1 (2015), 136.

leadership succession and loss of power in 2003 to 2010 for CIU in Catalonia and 2009 to 2012 for PNV in the Basque Country.[71] These contextual differences, alongside the existence of an economic concert in the Basque Country, and the failure of Catalan nationalists to secure one in 2010 to 2012, would explain their different strategies between Catalan contestation, including claims of secession, and Basque accommodation.[72] PNV favoured territorial accommodation, which Muro defines as 'the capacity of states to contain conflict within the mechanisms and procedures embedded in existing institutional arrangements'.[73]

PNV's influence is far greater than what its historic vote share of 30% to 35% in the Basque Country may suggest. The party's first political symbol is now the official flag of the Basque Country, *ikurriña*, which resembles the Union Jack, but with a white cross over a green saltire on a red background. With more or less enthusiasm, the principle of foralismo, at least in relation to taxation, is endorsed by all other political parties in the Basque Country. Even the pro-independence left, representing 20% to 25% of the vote, accepts the financial arrangement of the economic concert as a minimum floor of self-government, although they would probably add that foralismo is a perilous distraction from the ultimate goal of independence. Most parties are comfortable with an institutional arrangement where power and resources are internally distributed between the Basque government and each one of the three provincial authorities, which is where power used to lie in distant epochs of foralismo. As indicated previously, each provincial authority has its own directly elected parliament – 'Juntas Generales' in Spanish, 'Batzar Nagusiak' in Basque – and their executives are in charge of tax collection and distribution. The pro-independence left tends to see this structure as an anachronism, but pragmatically they accept to work within those parameters.

The neoforalismo of the economic concert explains why tax revenue transfers from and to Madrid are not such a visceral point of contention in the Basque Country, unlike Catalonia. The concert is negotiated bilaterally between Basque institutions and the Spanish government, and the Spanish parliament either approves the outcome or rejects it in its entirety, with no room for amendments. Tax revenue remains in the Basque Country, from which a negotiated quota is transferred to Spain's central treasury. The specific quota does not depend on the amount of Basque collection, but on Spain's budget for policy areas that have not been devolved or assigned to

---

[71] Gillespie, "The Contrasting Fortunes of Pro-Sovereignty Currents in Basque and Catalan Nationalist Parties," 406.

[72] Richard Gillespie, "Between Accommodation and Contestation: The Political Evolution of Basque and Catalan Nationalism," *Nationalism and Ethnic Politics* 21, no. 1 (2015).

[73] Diego Muro, "Territorial Accommodation, Party Politics and Statute Reform in Spain," *Southern European Society and Politics* 14, no. 4 (2009), 453.

the Basque Country. As observed by Gray, this arrangement 'encourages efficiency since the Basque region loses out if its own tax collection increases more slowly (or decreases more quickly) than that of the Spanish state'.[74] In this regard, the concert serves two purposes at once: 'While the Basque nationalists seek increasing fiscal autonomy verging on sovereignty within Europe, Spanish governments see it as a form of fiscal decentralization within Spain remaining subordinate to Spanish legislation.'[75]

If one combines the electoral backing of PNV and the pro-independence left coalition EH Bildu ('Unite Basque Country'), Basque nationalism has never been stronger than in the present time. And yet, you have not heard so much about Basque independence recently while Catalonia sometimes seems tied to Spain by a cat's whisker. The fueros are one of the main reasons why.

Violence is the other key factor, or to be more precise, lack of violence. If foralismo has been part of the unique character of Basque politics for a very long time, nearly the same could be said about violence. As we will see later (section 4.4), the Basque Country has much work to do to lick its wounds after 40 years of Francoism and 30 more of Euskadi Ta Askatasuna's (ETA) violence. Only in the last decade has the Basque society been given the chance to build bridges where there was animosity.

ETA tainted the international image of the Basque Country. A comparative study shows that, for decades, ETA's violence was essentially the only issue about the Basque Country that was covered in leading media from France, the UK and the United States. For example, 95% of news about the Basque Country in The New York Times between 1959 and 2018 were about ETA.[76]

ETA ('Euskadi Ta Askatasuna', 'Basque Country And Freedom') was a supposedly left-leaning revolutionary movement for Basque independence. Formed in 1959, ETA's motto 'Bietan Jarrai' ('Keep on both') referred to the idea that the goal was to be achieved by combining politics and armed violence. ETA claimed its first victim in 1968, but most of its killings took place in the late 1970s and in the 1980s. In the early years, under the dictatorship, ETA mostly carried out low-intensity actions, distributing political propaganda, graffitiing walls and setting off small explosive devices in urban areas. ETA became better known internationally when they killed Franco's prime minister, Luis Carrero Blanco, with a car bomb in December 1973. Understood by many in the Basque Country as a reaction to the dictatorship, a poll in February 1976 showed that 23% of Basques believed terrorism would

---

[74] Caroline Gray, "A Fiscal Path to Sovereignty? The Basque Economic Agreement and Nationalist Politics," *Nationalism and Ethnic Politics* 21, no. 1 (2015), 69.
[75] Ibid, 63.
[76] Isabel C. Martínez, *ETA en la prensa internacional: Una aproximación al tratamiento del terrorismo en los diarios franceses, británicos y estadounidenses de referencia* (Vitoria-Gasteiz: Centro Memorial de las Víctimas del Terrorismo, 2019), 114.

contribute to the democratisation of Spain, and 22% thought terrorism would continue after the adoption of a statute of self-government.[77] In the late 1970s, according to Tusell, about 13% to 16% of Basques saw ETA members as patriots and 29% to 35% believed they were idealists.[78] Progressively ETA lost support, but it took time. ETA went through a number of ideological splits in the 1970s. The most significant one took place in the so-called sixth assembly of 1973 to 1975 between ETA-pm ('polimili'), which advocated a single leadership for political and armed operations superimposing the former to the latter, and ETA-m ('mili'), which favoured a governance model of coordinated but organically autonomous structures for political and military strategies. The largest of the two, ETA-pm, was dissolved in the mid-1980s, and its members joined existing democratic parties or left politics altogether. ETA-m, however, went on with their murders, kidnapping and extorsion for 25 more years. They claimed their last victim in 2010, and announced the definitive cessation of their actions on 20 October 2011. The complete dissolution had to wait until May 2018. Overall, ETA was responsible for 850 deaths, but this figure underestimates the pervasive sense of fear they generated. In the last 15 years of their existence, ETA targeted specifically politicians, academics, police officers, journalists and civil servants who disagreed with their totalitarian agenda. Approximately 3,300 men and women were forced to live with police escort.[79] In a territory of slightly more than two million inhabitants, it was hard not to know someone who paid a high price for being who they were, sometimes the highest of all prices, their life. In my case, this includes a primary schoolmate, whose father – a police officer – was killed by ETA, a teacher in the same primary school, whose husband – a journalist – was also murdered by ETA, a sport teammate's father, who reluctantly moved to Madrid after receiving serious threats, at least one of my professors at university, and my former boss, the Basque parliament's high commissioner for human rights between 2004 and 2014, Iñigo Lamarca, whose name appeared on one of ETA's hit lists.

ETA was created during the dictatorship by disgruntled young activists who were disappointed with PNV. Non-religious and officially Marxist since the fifth internal assembly of 1966 to 1968, ETA perceived an excess of complacency in PNV leaders in exile. ETA's narrative presented violence as the consequence of a long-lasting historical problem. Initially, at a time of national liberation movements all over the world, and in accordance with

---

[77] Fraser, "Spain on the Brink," 15.
[78] Javier Tusell, *Spain: From Dictatorship to Democracy: 1939 to the Present* (Malden: Blackwell Publishing, 2007), 300.
[79] Antonio Santos, "El Gobierno vasco estima que 3.300 personas vivieron a diario con escolta entre 1990 y 2011," *El Correo* (8 April 2016).

Marxist historical materialism, the problem was capitalism at least as much as Spain's military occupation. Over time, however, and through multiple transformations and fragmentations in the 1970s and 1980s, ETA exclusively focused on its nationalist agenda for the independence of the Basque Country. Until its disappearance in recent years, for those remaining in ETA, violence was still not *the* problem, but a symptom of a deeper problem: That the Basque nation was being oppressed by a dictatorial Spain and that only self-determination could break the chains.[80]

Wieviorka's interviews and focus groups with grassroots PNV members in 1987 show that many saw themselves as the political parents of supporters of Herri Batasuna (HB), ETA's political arm at the time. Many were biological parents as well as political. HB voters were seen as immature, but these PNV core voters in the late 1980s believed that Basque nationalism benefited from the pressure exercised by ETA on the State, while also thought that ETA on its own could achieve nothing. They interpreted ETA's Marxism and revolutionary language as alien to the Basque identity. For traditional PNV voters, the social clout of ETA and HB among the youth was overwhelming.[81] PNV leaders would later admit that it took the party and Basque institutions way too long to recognise the harm suffered by ETA's victims, and to clearly distance themselves from ETA and HB not only in terms of the means, but also in terms of the goals.[82]

Up until very recently, violence was normalised in Basque society to an extent that now seems hard to believe. On 20 August 2001, a car explosion at Aldamar Street in San Sebastian killed a woman and seriously injured her toddler grandson. No one claimed responsibility, and police hit a dead end and never charged anyone. My sister was a DYA volunteer at that time, a charity that provided emergency medical response. Her crew was called in. The day after, newspapers in Spain and all over the world showed a photograph of my sister consoling the toddler's aunt, who was also in the car at the time of the explosion. Years later, my sister allowed me to read that day's entry in her diary, which began like this: 'Today I have attended my *first* bomb attack.' She was 21 years old, and only a few hours after facing such tragedy, she was expecting that more were likely to come (figure 3.4).

The Basque Country leads a totally different life now, a life where no political idea is persecuted. As put bluntly but effectively by the former *Financial Times* correspondent in Madrid, Tobias Buck, 'Basques today are counting

---

[80] Diego Muro, "Nationalism and Nostalgia: The Case of Radical Basque Nationalism," *Nations and Nationalism* 11, no. 4 (2005); Gaizka Fernández-Soldevilla, "Mitos que matan: La narrativa del 'conflicto vasco'," *Ayer* 98 (2015).

[81] Michel Wieviorka, "Militantes del PNV analizan la lucha armada," *Ayer* 13 (1994).

[82] Público, "Urkullu admite que el Gobierno vasco debió haber actuado 'antes y mejor'," (5 June 2015).

Figure 3.4 The author's sister, Arantxa Casla, in the middle, and one other DYA volunteer attend to the victim of the explosion on 20 August 2001. Source: Pablo S. Quiza

Michelin stars, not bodies.'[83] Desirable or not, advocating for independence should be a perfectly legitimate political option in a democracy. Political groupings might form new alliances in the future and voice a more explicit demand for independence. Depending on the circumstances, such demand could gather at least as much support in the Basque Country as it did recently in Catalonia. But for now, peace is an exciting new experience in the Basque Country. It feels too fragile and it is too precious. Public support for independence is relatively low, 27% in June 2019, being the preferred option for three in four voters of the pro-independence left EH Bildu and one in four of PNV voters.[84] This is so in spite of some of the strongest electoral performances of both PNV and EH Bildu, the former with 39% of the votes and the latter with 28% in the Basque elections of July 2020. This is only a hypothesis, but it is not unreasonable to speculate that both PNV and EH Bildu obtained such good results partly because independence is not currently on the agenda; if it was, one might expect that some would choose an anti-independentist ticket instead. Much more work remains to be done to strengthen the social bonds in a society that up to very recently remained profoundly divided in political

---

[83] Buck, *After the Fall*, 167.
[84] Euskal Herriko Unibertsitatea—Universidad del País Vasco, *Eusko Barometro: Estudio periódico de la opinión pública vasca* (June 2019), 46.

terms. Luckily, such division was ideological, not entirely geographical and certainly not genealogical, which gives reason to be cautiously optimistic about the likelihood of rehabilitation of trust in the Basque society in the years to come.

3.5 NATIONALISMS, BUBBLES AND AMBIGUITIES

What we talk about when we talk about nations is a good question. What we are *not* talking about while we do is a better one.

Spaniards disagree about how many nations there are in Spain. Identity questions are captivating but tend to be reductionist. After all, no one holds one single identity. In a free society, one's national identification does not tell us much about one's religion, sexual orientation, ethnicity, political views or anything else. Spain's national questions have not been settled in the last two centuries, and nothing suggests they will be settled anytime soon. Such questions are reflective, fascinating and inevitable. With a specific focus on Catalonia, the national question was very much alive in the 2010s, but this has not been a historically constant feature in Spanish politics. The debate about the nation or nations has come and gone depending on the political situation, the interests at play, and the concurrence of other urgencies. The question will not disappear, neither does it have to, but it does not need to be harmfully divisive if handled appropriately.

If the discussion is to be had between people living in what we know as Spain, interlocutors would do well to think about what other political issues may not be receiving sufficient attention while they talk about their nation and nations. What miseries does a party hide, and what policies can a ruling party quietly push forward, while the public debate in Catalonia and in the rest of Spain is framed in the simplistic terms of free Catalonia versus united Spain? Whatever one thinks about Catalan independence, that the question erupted in the middle of a profound economic crisis polemically handled with austerity-driven policies should not escape anybody's attention. Socio-economic anger can take many forms, nationalism being one of them, centrifugal or centripetal.

The Catalan question of the last decade is a reminder of the danger of bubbles in politics. Echo chambers are unfortunately a universal phenomenon, magnified by social media. Political groupings do a lip service to the communities they intend to serve when they ignore each other, giving their followers the false impression that they are stronger than they actually are. Muddling through the national question will require overcoming essentialisms and blasting the bubbles that Spaniards and Catalans have let grow over the years. We shall see how the relationship evolves, with a progressive coalition in Madrid, and a new pro-independence government in Catalonia since May 2021, with the left-leaning ERC for the first time on top.

A fundamental difference between Catalan and Basque nationalisms is that while the former got increasingly frustrated when they failed to exercise decisive influence over the State, the latter chose to live with it *ignoring* the State as much as possible. During the last independentist decade, Catalan authorities pursued the direct and constant confrontation with the State. The strategy achieved little political success at a very high social cost in the form of rising polarisation in Catalan society. On the other hand, while the Catalan strategy of the 2010s has its supporters in the Basque Country, hegemonic Basque nationalism favours a particular form of 'banal nationalism',[85] understood as the everyday and nearly casual representation of belonging to a community presented as national, even if lacking State-type institutions. Spanish remains more widely spoken than Basque in most of the Basque Country, unquestionably so in urban areas. However, other cultural expressions, as well as Basque flags and maps, are prevalent throughout. Spain is usually talked about in Basque politics as a very influential actor that lives next door. Even non-nationalist politicians avoid using the word 'national' when referring to Spain, and they consciously or unconsciously often speak of Spain as a third-party plural ('they'), while Basque institutions would be 'us' or 'ours'. From a sovereigntist perspective, a critic might argue that banal nationalism is a distraction from the end goal, no other than achieving full independence. Others might respond that, with a relatively high degree of self-government, particularly on tax and financial matters, the realistic approach is a combination of banal nationalism accompanied with the right amount of pressure and influence in Madrid.

Politically speaking, the Spanish nation was born in the nineteenth century. Apart from the military, in that century Spain's central government had few institutions that were firmly established and adequately endowed. Historians disagree about whether the State failed to penetrate society because it was too oppressive or because it was not strong enough.[86] The ambiguities about the national question since the 1970s are a consequence of that historical reality. In the spirit of the Achilles' heels, ambiguities are vulnerabilities, but they do not need to be weaknesses; they are only so when they are ignored, when they are not embraced. A sign of one of those ambiguities is the lyrics-free Spanish anthem. Not at all dissonant with the republicanism and federalism of the nineteenth century, much of the Spanish left tends to hoist regional flags – by region, for these purposes, I mean nationalities as well – with greater comfort than the Spanish flag. Right-wing forces are often unchallenged in

---

[85] Michael Billig, *Banal Nationalism* (London: Sage, 1995).
[86] Álvarez Junco, *Spanish Identity in the Age of Nations*, 321.

the so-called defence of the symbols of the Spanish nation, and Spain's left is caught wrong-footed in times of crisis of the nation and the nations. The ultimate circle to be squared is in Article 2 of the constitution, which says that Spain is 'indissolubly united' and an 'indivisible nation', but also 'recognises' that an indeterminate list of 'nationalities and regions' have a 'right' to govern themselves and a duty to be supportive of each other. Weiler has tried to fix the problem with a very Solomonic solution where Catalonia, and presumably other territories as well, would be recognised as 'nations', but this recognition would not entail the right to unilateral secession. In his view, Spain's constitution should start by saying that 'Spain is a Parliamentary Monarchy, an Indivisible State, Member of the European Union Composed of a Nation of Nations'.[87] The effort is commendable. Whether it will go anywhere is another matter. Being uncertain about the nation is a characteristically Spanish feature, and there is no indication this will change in the foreseeable future.

---

[87] Joseph H.H. Weiler, "A Nation of Nations?," *International Journal of Constitutional Law* 17, no. 4 (2019), 1306.

Chapter 4

Dealing with the Past
Franco's Legacy

4.1 IN THE VALLEY

I visited the Valle de los Caídos (Valley of the Fallen) for the first and, so far, only time in July 2018. The reader would find the valley 50 kilometres north of the city of Madrid, in the Guadarrama Mountains. It is located within the limits of the municipality of San Lorenzo de El Escorial, 'escorial', literally the 'slag heap' chosen by Felipe II in the mid-sixteenth century for the construction of his palace and spiritual retreat.

The Valley of the Fallen is the location of a gigantic mausoleum of Fascist flair built over 20 years by the men who lost the Civil War between July 1936 and April 1939. As a sort of expiation through suffering, many of the men were forced to redeem their sins in very hard conditions as a penance for siding with the losing side.

General Francisco Franco inaugurated the site on 1 April 1959, on the 20th anniversary of the end of the war from which he emerged as the supreme ruler. Franco chose that particular setting, and his eagerness was such that he even designed the initial sketches and insisted on being consulted on architectural changes and details.[1] The venue includes an underground crypt – named basilica by John XXIII when he visited in 1960 embedded into the rock – a Benedictine abbey, and a 150-metre-high Christian cross, the tallest of its kind in the world, noticeable miles away. It is one of the most prominent features of the mountain range that greets travellers landing at Madrid from the north.

---

[1] Paloma Aguilar, *Memory and Amnesia: The Role of the Spanish Civil War in the Transition to Democracy* (New York and Oxford: Berghahn Books, 2002), 74.

That summer of 2018, two names were visible to the visitor of the crypt: José Antonio Primo de Rivera, founder of the Spanish Fascist Party Falange and executed during the war in 1936, and Francisco Franco himself, who died in bed on 20 November 1975. Only José Antonio remains there at the time of this writing, in mid-2021. The two tombs flanked the altar, a position normally reserved to towering religious figures in Catholicism. In caskets, urns and boxes, more than 30,000 people are buried in a mass grave on both sides of the crypt, a safe distance away from the altar. The personal details of most of those who defended the Spanish republic against Franco are not recorded. Those who fought for Franco and 'fell for God and for Spain', on the other hand, have their names remembered. One of them in this second group is Ricardo Salazar Fernández, my great-grandfather, killed in action in Castellón, on the Mediterranean coast, in spring 1938. While the war would go on for 12 more painful months, that crucial battle struck a nearly definitive blow to the loyalist side by reducing and splitting in two the territory under their control.

The supposed purpose of the Valley, as formulated by Franco's regime, was to serve as a 'national expression of atonement and reconciliation'. More than six decades have passed since the inauguration, and if there has been any atonement and reconciliation in Spanish society, this place has had very little to do with it. But for now, let me tell you a bit more about my first and only visit to the Valley of the Fallen.

Since the return of democracy, and up until a few years ago, a visit to the Valley was a sort of nostalgic pilgrimage. Only those on the hard right did it, some of whom chose and choose it for their weddings and the first communions of their offspring. A relatively sudden turn of events in the summer of 2018 prompted me, and other curious observers, to visit the mausoleum for the first time. Led by Pedro Sánchez, the social-democratic party PSOE unexpectedly returned to power as a result of a motion of non-confidence in the conservative prime minister, Mariano Rajoy. Never before had a motion of this kind succeeded. Triggered by a criminal court ruling that condemned Rajoy's Popular Party (PP) in a corruption scandal, nearly all the opposition parties voted against him, among them the pro-independence Basque and Catalan deputies represented in the Spanish lower chamber. One of the very first promises by Pedro Sánchez's new government was this: Franco's remains were going to be exhumed. More than four decades after Franco's death, the monument was back on the news, and I felt the urge to see the place with my own eyes.

It was five o'clock of a hot, sunny and summery evening in Madrid's mountains. Our car was the third in line to enter the gates of the vast complex, with the Valley and the hill on top of which we would find the famous monument. To our right, a television presenter was practicing with her crew. Franco was once again on the news.

The ticket was 9 euro per person, 18 in total since there were two of us in the car. It was our turn and my sceptical partner asked, 'Where is this money going?' Clearly not the first time the question had been posed to the person at the counter. 'This is a national park. National heritage. It belongs to the State.' So we paid.

Driving carefully up a steep road, after a few turns right and left we arrived at a parking lot. I counted 20 cars there, with many more empty spots. We walked by the ticket hall of a funicular train that would take the visitor to the foot of the imposing cross, but the train was not on service.

We went up the stairs and walked to a point facing the monument, gigantic and overwhelming, just as I had imagined it. On both the left- and the right-hand sides of the façade one finds Spain's coat of arms, not the contemporary one, but the one used in the dictatorship, including the eagle that Franco borrowed from Fernando and Isabel. The Catholic Monarchs of the fifteenth century were glorified by Franco, and they would remain ubiquitous in right-wing memorabilia after his death. Thought to have brought the kingdoms of Castilla and Aragon together under one single ruling couple, Isabel and Fernando defeated the last Moorish kingdom of Granada and ordered the expulsion of Jews from the peninsula in January 1492 (section 3.1). This is the very same year when Columbus arrived in the Americas in their name, unleashing what would become one of history's hegemonic empires. This past grandeur engendered pride in sentimental nationalists of the twentieth century. Pride and nostalgia for a conveniently reimagined past were condensed in the black eagle in Franco's coat of arms. But the Valley 'belongs to the State', or so had said the civil servant upon our arrival. How could one justify two enormous pre-constitutional dictatorial symbols in a national park in the twenty-first century (figure 4.1, figure 4.2, figure 4.3)?

Intoxicated by the imposing size of the building and the cross in front of me, I started wondering about other visitors' motivations. Were they devotees perhaps, or just curious? When I got into the building, right before the metal detector, I discovered I was not allowed to take pictures. I did not ask why. A long dark corridor led to the crypt. The corridor had large historical motifs hanging on the walls. Big golden letters informed the visitor that the monument had been inaugurated by Franco and Pope John XXIII, in this precise order, in 1959 and 1960.

I walked down the aisle in silence to the point where José Antonio Primo de Rivera was buried. Behind the altar, I supposed, Franco. The tomb read simply 'José Antonio', assuming the visitor would be well aware of what specific José Antonio we are referring to. There was no explanation of who he was. There would be nothing in writing about Franco either, or indeed

Figure 4.1 Valley of the Fallen. Source: Wikimedia Commons: https://commons.wikimedia.org/wiki/File:Valle_de_los_caidos_by_forcy-cruz_y_basilica.jpg

Figure 4.2 Spain's coat of arms before 1981. Source: Wikimedia Commons

Figure 4.3 Spain's coat of arms after 1981. Source: Spain's Official Gazette "BOE" https://www.boe.es/buscar/doc.php?id=BOE-A-1981-29376

about anyone or anything else, nothing about the history of the building or the 30,000 men buried metres away. Facing José Antonio, right behind me, a young teenager quietly asked a question in English to a Spanish woman who appeared to be the mother of a friend of the teenager's: 'Who was this?' The lady, possibly in her 40s, replied that José Antonio had been a prime minister in Franco's time. That information was incorrect. José Antonio Primo de Rivera was executed in November 1936, at the early stages of the Civil War. He could not have been in any of Franco's governments. A short text would have enlightened that curious English-speaking girl and her Spanish friend's mother. But there was no key anywhere. I completed the semicircle and found Franco's tomb on the other side of the altar, decorated with two bouquets of fresh flowers. After a while I walked away. I looked back and I noticed two men and two women approached the grave after me. They were old enough to have lived under the dictatorship. One of the men made the sign of the cross. The Valley of the Fallen 'belongs to the State', but nowhere does it say who Franco and José Antonio were.

Before my visit, I had the suspicion that my great-grandfather might be buried in the Valley. His son, my grandfather, had mentioned the possibility to me years ago in what I took as a precious moment of complicity. No one in the family had been able to confirm it, neither were they keen to discuss the matter. 'How could I find out if a relative of mine is buried here?' I asked one of the attendants working in the monument, who wore a badge that said 'National Heritage'. 'That you should discuss with the Benedictine monks in the abbey.'

I walked up to the abbey, no more than 10 minutes away from the basilica. I knocked on the door, which was half open. I came in and I immediately found a monk in his 80s sweeping the hallway. The friar told me they believed the government's estimations of 30,000 or so bodies fell short of reality. But the congregation did not know for sure how many souls they were guarding. I had the name, the place of birth, and the battle where he died, and therefore the approximate date when it happened. 'That should be enough, but bear in mind we don't have the records of all the deceased.' That was a gentle way of saying that if the man in question did not fall for God and for Spain his name was much less likely to be in the system. Thankfully for these purposes, my great-grandfather did die for God and for Spain. 'Send us a letter, please.' Can I send an email instead? 'You could try that.'

We left at seven. The television crew was still by the gate. The following day, I checked the abbey's website and I wrote an email to the address I found there, which seemed official and professional enough. I received no response, so I followed up a week later via telephone. Someone at the other end of the landline told me that the official address was not used for those enquiries. I was supposed to email directly the friar in charge of the archive, and the person on the phone gave me the details, a personal account, which I suspect was not in full compliance with data protection law, but that's for another book. I received the response from a mysterious Mr A. Álvarez two days later, on 4 August 2018. The body of Ricardo Salazar Fernández had been transferred from Castellón to the Valley of the Fallen on 24 March 1959, one week before Franco's pompous inauguration. I later matched and confirmed this information with the Ministry of Justice's online map of graves from the Civil War.[2]

If we were to believe the Francoist propaganda, the Valley of the Fallen was supposed to heal wounds and reconcile losers and winners from the war. But as pointed out by Aguilar,

> No reconciliatory texts exist at the Valley. If reconciliation had really been its intention, we might have expected the victors to have included a lavish range of symbolic and conciliatory statements. It is a monument infested with religious symbols, but lacking any evident political message.[3]

---

[2] Ministry of Justice, Map of graves online.
[3] Aguilar, *Memory and Amnesia*, 83–4.

Dealing with the Past

Figure 4.4 Army hat used by my great-grandfather Ricardo Salazar Fernández; kept in a safe box by my grandfather José Luis alongside other memories until the day of his death in March 2019. Source: Jaione Salazar

With no narrative, one can only assume the monument itself was the message. But, in that case, its meaning has to be open to reinterpretation by successive generations. And the younger ones have been asking questions lately (figure 4.4).

4.2 THE PACT OF SILENCE

The British historian Paul Preston calls it 'the Spanish Holocaust': On top of 300,000 dead soldiers, 200,000 men and women were executed extrajudicially far from the battlefield between July 1936 and April 1939, three quarters of them in areas controlled by Franco and his allies; at least 20,000 supporters of the republican side were killed in the war's aftermath well into the 1940s.[4] These figures do not even start to account for the pain and suffering of those who were imprisoned, lost their job, were otherwise punished, fell into poverty, fled their country or died in concentrations camps in Europe during World War II. Franco's dictatorship went on for more than three decades. In different ways, repression persisted with no political rights, censorship and lack of press freedoms, regular declarations of state of emergency particularly in the Basque Country, torturing of political dissidents,

---

[4] Paul Preston, *The Spanish Holocaust: Inquisition and Extermination in Twentieth-Century Spain* (London: Harper Collins, 2012).

homophobic discrimination, and subjugation of any expression of cultural diversity, which was seen by the regime as a threat to the homogeneity of the 'one, big and free' nation, in the vocabulary of the time.

Franco died peacefully on 20 November 1975. Six years earlier, he had appointed Juan Carlos, the grandson of the last king, Alfonso XIII, dethroned in April 1931, as his successor. Juan Carlos swore to give continuity to the regime, but it soon became clear to Franco loyalists that it was not going to be easy to keep Francoism alive without Franco. The king's prominence in the return of democracy is one of the big points of contention in contemporary history. For some, Juan Carlos had a clear agenda to take Spain into the club of European democracies, and that is why he put relatively liberal figures in key political positions, starting with the prime minister Adolfo Suárez in July 1976. Those who have a favourable view of Juan Carlos's reign commend the way he defended democracy in a televised address when a group of army men attempted a coup d'état on 23 February 1981. Others, however, express the view that the king's actions were not a sincere expression of his democratic convictions. He would have no choice but to support a controlled transition away from the dictatorship, as that was the only way to preserve the monarchy's institutional position in front of growing internal and external pressures to democratise the country. The monarchy's position was not at all secured during the Transition. Suárez admitted in an interview in 1995, which was only aired in November 2016, that he made sure the monarchy would be shielded in the Political Reform Act,[5] one of the two landmark legal instruments of the Transition, together with the 1978 constitution. The monarchy was shoehorned into the Political Reform Act so that the government could say that the people supported the king, because 94% of them endorsed the act in a referendum in December 1976.[6] The most critical even fuel the idea that the king was in fact behind the 1981 coup, an accusation that has never been sufficiently proven. The actual involvement of the king is something that there will be speculation about at least until the confidentiality of the case summary is lifted, which will only happen in the 2030s, unless the law on official secrets is modified before. Be that as it may, the king's position was strengthened significantly when, with parliament hijacked, he went on television to call on the army men to cease on their illegal action, something that, Cercas says, 'no-one else could have done'.[7] That day, 23 February 1981, became in the collective memory an unforgettable instant that would define much of contemporary Spanish history, a day after which the king's

---

[5] Political Reform Act 1/1977, of 4 January.
[6] Eldiario.es, "Adolfo Suárez no sometió a referéndum la monarquía porque las encuestas le dijeron que perdería" (18 November 2016).
[7] Javier Cercas, *Anatomía de un instante* (Madrid: Random House Mondadori, 2009).

favourability rate rose sharply and remained high for three decades if no more.

Let us rewind a few years. Spain's Transition from Francoism to democracy lasted approximately three years, beginning with Franco's death in November 1975, and finishing with the adoption of the constitution in December 1978. I believe it is important for millennials and future generations to admit that the previous two generations did the best they could in the most difficult of circumstances, with rising unemployment, fear of a right-wing military uprising and political violence in the streets. More than 180 people were killed by armed groups on the left and right, and by the police, in 1976 to 1978.[8] The Transition was a time of compromises and pacts between sworn enemies, between some who had ruled the previous regime and some who had experienced their repression first-hand, including torture and exile. The generation that decided the 1970s found themselves in an impossible scenario to bequeath their children a democracy, as imperfect as it may be, and I have absolutely no reason to believe that those children would have done it any better.

The Transition is seen as a founding moment in Spain's democratisation. Yet, imperfect it was. As pointed out by Sánchez-Cuenca, 'the most important characteristic of the transition was not "consensual politics", but rather control of the institutional reforms by the Francoist elites up to the holding of the first democratic elections.'[9] The Transition was, in fact, a managed transition, which was the path designed by post-Francoist elites, who defended as a matter of principle that the Transition had to take Spain 'from the law to the law' ('de la ley a la ley'), allowing the regime's ruling class to retain 'full control of the political situation: the reforms ultimately depended on their approval'.[10] The establishment very consciously wanted to avoid the Portuguese path to democracy represented by the Carnation Revolution of April 1974.[11] Opposition parties on the left, outlawed and persecuted for decades, went along quite possibly because they saw no other choice.

One of the crucial decisions made during the Transition was the pact of silence, which players saw as an essential step to ensure democracy's sustainability. The political pact of silence was articulated in the law through the

---

[8] Omar Encarnación, *Democracy without Justice in Spain: The Politics of Forgetting* (Philadelphia: University of Pennsylvania Press, 2014), 65.
[9] Ignacio Sánchez-Cuenca, "Spanish Democratization: Transition, Consolidation, and Its Meaning in Contemporary Spain," in Diego Muro and Ignacio Lago (eds.): *The Oxford Handbook of Spanish Politics* (Oxford: Oxford University Press, 2020), 34.
[10] Ibid., 38.
[11] Josep M. Valles, "The 1978 Spanish Constitutional Design: Assessing Its Outcome," in Diego Muro and Ignacio Lago (eds.): *The Oxford Handbook of Spanish Politics* (Oxford: Oxford University Press, 2020), 172; Robert M. Fishman, *Democratic Practice: Origins of the Iberian Divide in Political Inclusion* (Oxford: Oxford University Press, 2019).

Amnesty Act 1977.[12] Adopted in October that year, the Amnesty Act followed two partial amnesty decrees of July 1976 and March 1977, and the Political Reform Act 1977, sanctioned and published in January. The very first provision of the Amnesty Act 1977 pardoned all politically motivated crimes, regardless of whether they resulted in death, committed before 15 December 1976, the day the Political Reform Act was endorsed in referendum by more than 94% of the population. For violent crimes whose political motive was 'the reestablishment of public liberties or the vindication of self-government for the peoples of Spain',[13] the deadline was extended six more months, until 15 June 1977, when the first free elections took place, elections that had been made possible by the Political Reform Act 1977. Historiography speaks of this act as a sort of hara-kiri of Franco's legislature barely one year after Franco's death. It was indeed an essential step in order to hold general elections, so a legislative chamber could be formed with the assignment of drafting a new constitution. But the immolation of the Francoist assembly would come at a price: As observed by Encarnación, it allowed 'the old regime to dictate the terms of the transition and accrue considerable power to shape the politics and institutions of the emerging democracy'.[14]

The terms and conditions of the Transition included the extension of amnesty not only to those who did use violence and committed crimes against the dictatorship, but also to those who were violent and committed crimes in support or on behalf of the dictatorship. This includes Antonio González-Pachecho, known as Billy the Kid, an infamous torturer in Madrid in the 1970s. During the Transition, and in the early 1980s, the Spanish government bestowed on him police decorations because of which he received a bonus on his state pension until he died with Covid-19 in May 2020.[15]

The Amnesty Act 1977 remains in force. In recent years, Spain has faced questions and criticism from international human rights bodies because victims of Francoism have not seen justice as a result of the Amnesty Act. Successive governments have defended the act arguing that it 'promoted reconciliation among the Spanish people', it was a key part of a transitional process to democracy that is 'so widely acclaimed within the country and internationally', and it was agreed upon by different political parties in a freely elected parliament.[16]

---

[12] Amnesty Act 46/1977, of 15 October.
[13] *"Móvil de restablecimiento de las libertades públicas o de reivindicación de autonomías de los pueblos de España"* (Article 1(I)(b)).
[14] Encarnación, *Democracy without Justice in Spain*, 54.
[15] Jim Yardley, "Facing His Torturer as Spain Confronts Its Past," *New York Times* (6 April 2014); Pedro Águeda, "Muere por coronavirus el expolicía acusado de torturas 'Billy el Niño,'" *eldiario.es* (7 May 2020).
[16] Government of Spain, *Sixth Periodic Report to the UN Human Rights Committee submitted under Article 40 ICCPR*, UN doc: CCPR/C/ESP/6 (10 May 2013), para. 192, 193 and 196.

Amnesty was indeed one of the three core demands of the democratic opposition in the late stages of the dictatorship and during the Transition. The other two were freedom and 'statutes of self-government', that is, devolution of power to the regions. Amnesty was therefore advocated by the opposition. People responsible for crimes committed against but also on behalf of the dictatorship benefited from the general amnesty. However, not everyone had had the same experience with Francoism. Those fighting it had paid a high price for their political activism as they suffered torture and terror. Those defending the dictatorship had acted with impunity, which the Amnesty Act 1977 simply formalised and extended in the democratic era.

When it reached the plenary of the lower chamber, the Amnesty Bill passed with 296 votes in favour, two against and 18 abstentions.[17] Many of those affirmative votes corresponded to Socialist and Communist deputies, as well as Catalan and Basque nationalists. One of the abstentions came from Francisco Letamendia, the only representative of the pro-independence Basque left party Euskadiko Ezkerra ('The Left of the Basque Country'). For him to vote in favour, he said, the bill should have 'recognised the right of a people to use all the means at its disposal to defend itself against the dictatorship's aggression'; in his opinion, neither the Political Reform Act 1977 nor the June general election – 'a mere formality with no democratic content' – embodied the beginning of a new democracy.[18] Letamendia's intervention is an eloquent expression of the scepticism with which the Basque pro-independence left would interpret the Transition and, until relatively recently, the flexibility with which they would legitimise the use of violence against the State.

But that was not the sentiment of most members of parliament. The union leader and Communist deputy Marcelino Camacho spoke passionately in favour of the Amnesty Bill, despite 'injuries', 'suffering', 'deaths' and 'rancour': 'How could we find reconciliation between us, who have been killing each other, if we do not erase this past for good?'[19] And Xabier Arzalluz, who would later become the long-lasting leader of the Basque Nationalist Party, defended the bill 'simply as forgetting, . . . as an amnesty from all to all . . . Let's forget everything', he said, speaking of the need to infuse into the whole society the idea of forgetting, because 'that's the only way we will be able

---

[17] Session's Record of Congress (*"Diario de Sesiones del Congreso"*), 14 October 1977, no. 24, 974.

[18] Ibid., 970: *"Reconocimiento del derecho de un pueblo a haber utilizado todos los medios que tenía a su alcance para defenderse de la agresión de le dictadura"*; *"fecha puramente formal, no revestida de contenido democrático."*

[19] Ibid., 960: *"¿Cómo podríamos reconciliarnos los que nos habíamos estado matando los unos a los otros, si no borrábamos ese pasado de una vez para siempre?"*

to shake hands without resentment'. It is documented in the session's record that Arzalluz's intervention won a round of applause across the chamber.[20]

The Amnesty Act 1977 is still in force today, and no more amnesties have been approved ever since, despite campaigns calling for it in different contexts in Catalonia – for pro-independentist politicians – and the Basque Country – for Euskadi Ta Askatasuna (ETA) members. In fact, while individual pardons are the executive's prerogative, it is disputable whether another amnesty act would be at all compatible with the constitution, which declares that the law 'may not authorise general pardons'.[21] Leaving the legal debate aside, the existing Amnesty Act has denied victims of serious human rights violations access to justice for crimes committed before 1977.

People who lived through it often remind those who did not that the Spanish Transition was a very difficult and voluble time. People prioritised looking to the future, for which compromises had to be made. Suppressing resentment over the past seemed acceptable when peace and a bright future were the promised prizes. No one got exactly what they wanted, and that would prove that political leaders got the surgical balance about right. Above all, it worked: Spain became a democracy, with its virtues and its flaws, just like any other. Many would say that, from a consequentialist perspective, the outcome was so positive that the process must be deemed worthwhile.

This argument is a powerful one, and the position is strongly held in Spain, at least among Spaniards who remember the 1970s. However, even if one were to accept that the Transition, including the pact of silence, might have been the best option given the circumstances, that would not mean it had no impact on the robustness of Spain's democracy.[22] The effects of the pact of silence went far beyond criminal law. It shaped Spanish politics in much more fundamental ways. One of the consequences was that the right-wing PP, which ruled Spain between 1996 and 2004, and between 2011 and 2018, never felt compelled to renounce Francoism entirely. Their political project emerged from Alianza Popular, an alliance led by former Franco ministers who accepted the democratic turn but did not endorse the Amnesty Act, the constitution or the political process of decentralisation. PP became hegemonic within the right in the early 1980s as a broad church from centre-right liberals to Franco nostalgists. The party evolved and consolidated its place in Spanish democracy without feeling the urge or sufficient pressure to come to terms with its undemocratic origins.

---

[20] Ibid., 968–70: "*Es simplemente un olvido, . . . una amnistía de todos para todos, . . . Olvidemos, pues, todo*"; "*es la única manera de que podamos darnos la mano sin rencor.*"

[21] Constitution 1978, Article 62(i): "*La ley . . . no podrá autorizar indultos generales.*"

[22] Juan Font, "The Quality of Democracy," in Diego Muro and Ignacio Lago (eds.): *The Oxford Handbook of Spanish Politics* (Oxford: Oxford University Press, 2020).

The pact of silence also had an impact on the judiciary. Compared with the dictatorships in Argentina and Chile, Aguilar finds that the 'judicial complicity' with Francoism ran deeper in Spain.[23] Judges were appointed and promoted based on their allegiance to Franco, and the regime relied on them to implement their laws and to put a lid on any attempt of accountability. During the dictatorship, civilian judges were co-opted into the military jurisdiction and court martials. They were reluctant to commence proceedings, let alone to take punitive measures, against the police or the military. Judges and prosecutors actively collaborated with the political-social brigade, conducting no investigation of allegations of torture, and while Franco was alive the supreme court hardly ever questioned the verdicts of the politicised courts of public order. The Amnesty Act 1977 was partly the legislature's response to a very restrictive judicial interpretation of the scope of the two amnesty decrees adopted months before. The negotiated character of the Transition allowed Francoism to remain residually legitimate in influential spheres after the reestablishment of democracy, including the judicial system, which heels over the right-hand side of politics to this day.

Spain's choice to remain silent about the Civil War and Francoism had its consequences in the domain of education as well. As a policy, education underwent a process of decentralisation in the 1980s and 1990s. Leaving aside the possible differences between regions, only in the 1990s did textbooks start to address the persecution during the regime, and well into the democracy, the written material that accompanied history lessons failed to provide a democratic interpretation of the Civil War. Hence, a Francoist narrative prevailed according to which the war had been a regrettable but inevitable event in Spanish history.[24] In an official survey in 2008, only slightly more than 21% of respondents remembered having received a lot or enough information about the Civil War in school, while nearly 70% thought the issue had received little attention or no attention at all. The figures were only slightly better when the question referred to Francoism, with 28% recalling it being covered a lot or enough, for 62% who deemed coverage had been sparse or inexistent.[25]

One important issue that remained largely in the dark for a long time is that of the favours returned by Franco and Francoism to the wealthy families and investors who supported him during the war and continued sustaining his

---

[23] Paloma Aguilar, "Judiciary Involvement in Authoritarian Repression and Transitional Justice: The Spanish Case in Comparative Perspective," *International Journal of Transitional Justice* 7, no. 2 (2013).

[24] Rafael Valls-Montés, *Historia y memoria escolar: Segunda República, Guerra Civil y dictadura franquista en las aulas (1938–2008)* (Valencia: Publicacions de la Universitat de València, 2009).

[25] Centro de Investigaciones Sociológicas, *Memorias de las Guerra Civil y el Franquismo, Estudio 2760* (Madrid: CIS, 2008), 23.

regime later on. With capitalist development, agrarian landownership lost its relative importance under Franco, and it was replaced by financial interests behind a new industrial sector.[26] To this day, Francoist cronyism remains at the origins of some of the most important companies in the country, including more than a handful in the Spanish benchmark stock market index Ibex-35.[27] From the beginning, Francoism showed its determination and effectiveness in changing the history of Spain's big business. The regime contributed to set up some of the largest companies, cutting some enterprises short and lifting others up instead.[28] This was part of a master plan. As far back as 1942, Franco boasted that his 'crusade is the only fight where the rich who went to war returned even richer'.[29]

The effects of the pact of silence were multifaceted and long-lasting. Because of the relative comfort provided by the passing of time, it is hard to imagine the *fear* many Spaniards must have felt in the 1970s. With that word I do not mean only the concern that another military coup could derail the whole process and spoil all democratic wishes. I mean also the anxiety of losing what Spaniards had achieved particularly on the economic front. Spain had been in a behind position in the process of capitalist development for a long time, but the economy boomed in the second half of the dictatorship. It would be debatable whether the economic prosperity of the 1960s was because of, despite of or irrespective of the regime. It can be argued that it was simply Spain's turn to progress economically. Spain's inward-looking post-war coincided in time with World War II, after which the country remained largely isolated in global politics. Spain only recuperated its 1936 levels of per capita income in 1953.[30] The country's economic development trailed that of several Latin American countries in the 1950s; however, by 1975, Spain was among the 10 or 12 most developed economies in the world.[31] Average per capita income more than tripled between 1960 and 1974, and GDP grew at more than 7% annually; only Japan had more impressive numbers.[32] Regardless of what one thinks about the structural factors that may explain Spain's development (an issue we will return to in section 5.1), one can understand why few people would want to put any of it at risk.

---

[26] Ricard Soler, "The New Spain," *New Left Review* I–58 (1969), 10.

[27] Antonio Maestre, *Franquismo S.A.* (Madrid: Akal, 2019).

[28] Albert Carreras and Xavier Tafunel, "National Enterprise. Spanish Big Manufacturing Firms (1917–1990), between State and Market," *Economics Working Paper 93* (Barcelona: Universitat Pompeu Fabra, 1994).

[29] ABC, no. 11385, 22 August 1942, 6: "*Nuestra Cruzada es la única lucha en que los ricos que fueron a la guerra salieron más ricos.*"

[30] Soler, "The New Spain," 4.

[31] Tusell, *Spain: From Dictatorship to Democracy*, 271.

[32] Omar Encarnación, "Spain after Franco: Lessons in Democratization," *World Policy Journal* 18, no. 4 (2001/02), 37; Encarnación, *Democracy without Justice in Spain*, 117.

Migration was an essential ingredient of this economic miracle. People sought jobs and opportunities where they could find them, and the government facilitated emigration, which helped boost the country's productivity and keep unemployment low. It is estimated that one million workers left Spain between 1960 and 1973, more than 90% of whom headed to other European countries.[33] Internal migration was another by-product of the rapid economic growth, with the displacement of people from rural and poorer regions in the south and west towards more affluent and urban areas in the centre – Madrid – the north – Basque Country – and the east – Catalonia. One million people migrated internally between 1950 and 1960, and one million more between 1961 and 1964.[34] In 2007, more than 40% of the population above 50 years of age in the Basque Country and Catalonia were born in another region.[35]

The Spanish philosopher José Ortega y Gasset famously prophesised in 1910 that 'Spain is the problem and Europe the solution'.[36] By the 1970s, Europe was finally in the horizon, but it had become clear that a dictatorial Spain would not be allowed to join NATO, and less so the European Communities. Economic elites understood they did not need Franco or Francoism anymore, and society at large saw in political liberalism a natural next step after the economic liberalisation of the 1950s and 1960s. It became gradually accepted among the economically and politically powerful that only a managed transition could open up the country's institutions to democracy without risking the economy or making ardently nationalist generals nervous.

Deterministic accounts assume that individuals are absolutely rational and perfectly well-informed, capable of evaluating the pros and cons of the political options in front of them. However, political choices are sometimes contradictory, often messy, and never based on all the necessary information. Perceptions of fear and vulnerability, and hegemonic interpretations of history, carry a heavy weight. To understand the choices of the late 1970s, made by political leaders but supported by most people in society, one needs to acknowledge the power of the psychology of silence cunningly instilled by Francoism.

Relatives were lost, families divided, and futures spoiled during the Civil War. Feelings of sadness, hatred and shame ran deep. Over the decades after the war, Spaniards became accustomed to silence. In some cases, it was imposed by force, but over time silence was socialised out of fear of a social

---

[33] Tusell, *Spain: From Dictatorship to Democracy*, 190.
[34] Manuel Martínez, "Algunos aspectos de la coyuntura económica española," *Ruedo Ibérico* 1 (1965), 19.
[35] Unai Martín et al., "Migraciones internas en España durante el siglo XX: un nuevo eje para el estudio de las desigualdades sociales en salud," *Gaceta Sanitaria* 26, no. 1 (2012), 10.
[36] José Ortega y Gasset, *Obras Completas*. Vol. I (Madrid: Occidente, 1946), 513.

breakdown at a community-level, with no need for repressive orders from the authorities. Keeping mum to preserve the social fabric, particularly when a brighter future is promised, is not at all an irrational behaviour. Silence can be 'a therapeutic response to pain and trauma', and 'a practical response or an understanding of the limits of truth-telling'.[37]

Between the 1940s and the 1970s, the regime shifted the official narrative regarding the Civil War from a 'national uprising' ('alzamiento nacional') and a crusade, to the exaltation of peace and reconciliation under Franco as a supposedly unifying figure.[38] As said at the beginning of this chapter, bringing people together was supposedly the reason why the Valley of the Fallen was built and inaugurated on the 20th anniversary of the end of the war. In order to develop a new political discourse, over time the regime gave more prominence to the celebration of 1 April, the day when the war finished in 1939, as opposed to 18 July, when the coup was staged in 1936. For example, the year 1964 came to be known as '25 Years of Peace' ('25 Años de Paz').

Francoism managed to spread the view that the confrontation had been a fratricidal war that had to be dealt with the way families deal with internal conflicts: discreetly. The general discourse was that the big Spanish family had grown apart not only during the republic in the 1930s, but also before with the advent of foreign, liberal, anticlerical and socialistic ideas. The coup had been a saddening but inevitable historical event necessary to reunite previously irreconcilable siblings. Franco and his acolytes could not be held accountable, because they actually sacrificed themselves for the greatest good: saving Spain from atheism, bolshevism and its own rupture. The Civil War had been a mad enterprise, which only had victims, not winners or losers.

As per the Francoist narrative, Spaniards ought to avoid the risk of another confrontation, and in order to do that they had to let the wounds heal by themselves, wounds that were too sensitive and could easily reopen if the pain of the armed conflict was brought to the fore. The narrative was nourished with selective memory, instrumentalist revisionism and widespread falsehoods. This is exemplified by the idea of 'one million deaths' of the Civil War, popularised by the title of a famous novel published in the 1960s. The figure had no empirical basis at all, and we now know it nearly doubles the true number of people who died on the fronts and the rearguard. But the exaggeration contributed to spread the belief that the fratricidal conflict had devastated the whole of society like a mysterious deadly virus would. The reinterpretation of the Civil War as a collective tragedy and the result of Spain's structural backwardness emerged as a topical controversy of the

---

[37] Paloma Aguilar and Leigh A. Payne, *Revealing New Truths about Spain's Violent Past: Perpetrators' Confessions and Victim Exhumations* (Oxford: Palgrave Macmillan, 2016), 78.
[38] Aguilar, *Memory and Amnesia*, 45–50.

historiography of the fourth quarter of the twentieth century.[39] The 1936 to 1939 war had been, after all, the last one of a long succession of uprisings, coups and burning internal confrontations after the so-called Independence War against the Napoleonic troops in 1808 to 1814, including the Carlista wars in the 1830s, 1940s and 1970s, which moulded and divided the country. The great poet Antonio Machado had famously warned a baby Spaniard at the beginning of the twentieth century: 'May God bless you, for one of the two Spains will freeze your heart.'[40] The possibility of another military confrontation was always hanging over everyone's head, not like an imaginary sword of Damocles, but like a cudgel, which seemingly all Spaniards had been holding since Goya's legendary painting. The narrative wanted Spaniards to believe that the Civil War of the 1930s had been the bloodiest of all conflicts, and everyone had been equally responsible for it, equally and collectively culpable. Seeding this idea on Spaniards' minds was Francoism's ideological triumph. The majority was persuaded that during the war both sides had committed the most heinous crimes approximately in equal measure. The goal of reconciliation, which Franco himself had set, made seeking consensus a priority. It was time to move on. The only hope was to draw the new democratic future on a blank slate, leaving behind the past, where there was nothing to learn. In 2008, a survey by the official Centre for Sociological Research showed that while 30% of the people believed Franco had killed more, 36% still thought both sides had provoked the same number of deaths; only 4% attributed more killings to the republicans, while 3 in 10 did not know or did not answer (figure 4.5).[41]

Francoism was resisted internally and questioned externally, but it never collapsed. It was reformed and transformed inside out through a political process that involved Francoist officials as well as democratic leaders that had been outlaws during the regime, many of whom came back from exile for this. All other Western European countries had consolidated their democracies and Spain was, yet again, a historical anomaly.

Eventually, Spaniards managed to break the curse they thought they were under. Their country became a democracy, and in the 1980s it was accepted in NATO and in the European Communities. They had made it possible avoiding confrontation through politics based on consensus, with a great

---

[39] Enrique Moradiellos, "Ni gesta heroica ni locura trágica: nuevas perspectivas históricas sobre la guerra civil," *Ayer* 50 (2003), 29–34; Carolyn P. Boyd, "The Politics of History and Memory in Democratic Spain," *The ANNALS of the American Academy of Political and Social Science* 617, no. 1 (2008), 136.

[40] "*Ya hay un español que quiere / vivir y a vivir empieza, / entre una España que muere / y otra España que bosteza. / Españolito que vienes / al mundo te guarde Dios. / Una de las dos Españas / ha de helarte el corazón*" (Antonio Machado, *Campos de Castilla*, 1912).

[41] CIS, *Memorias de las Guerra Civil y el Franquismo*, 13.

Figure 4.5 Francisco Goya's *Death with Cudgels*, 1820–23. Source: Wikimedia Commons https://commons.wikimedia.org/wiki/File:Francisco_de_Goya_y_Lucientes_-_Duel_with_Cudgels_-_WGA10102.jpg

dose of the compromising that lacked in the 1930s, and with a conscientious effort to forget, to remain silent. With the adoption of the constitution in December 1978, the Transition reached its highest point to become, as Aguilar says, 'the basic founding myth of democracy'.[42] Both the Transition and the constitution were indeed recollected as political resources of the greatest importance for decades, and they remain so for very many people to this day. But for an increasing number the myth began to crumble in the late 2000s and in the 2010s, with the reignition of the Catalan question (section 3.3), and with the socio-economic crisis (section 5.2). Three decades after the adoption of the Constitution, in 2008, 74% of the people expressed the view that the Transition was something to be 'proud of as Spaniards', and the two main reasons given were that it had been generally peaceful and it had put an end to the dictatorship.[43] The proportion of people who felt 'proud' dropped to a still very respectable 67% ten years later.[44] In exchange for democracy there was no *Vergangenheitsbewältigung* for Spain, no coming to terms with the past. In Germany it took 20 to 30 years for the process to kick off, when one generation felt the weight of the baggage that the previous generation had put on them. The German process began with awkward questions. Mutatis mutandis, something similar happened in Spain at the turn of the century.

---

[42] Aguilar, *Memory and Amnesia*, 269–70.
[43] CIS, *Memorias de las Guerra Civil y el Franquismo*, 24–5.
[44] CIS, *Barómetro de septiembre 2018, Estudio 3223* (Madrid: CIS, 2018), 8.

4.3 POLITICS OF HISTORICAL MEMORY SINCE THE 2000s

The expressions *pact of silence* and *pact of forgetting* are generally used interchangeably when referring to the decades after Franco's death. However, Spain's was a pact of silence, not of forgetting. Nobody truly forgot; it was a very deliberate arrangement to avoid confrontation. Because they remembered, Spaniards chose to keep quiet, they chose silence. However, there is a fine line between silencing a memory and forgetting about it. An issue may remain indelible in individual memories, but if talking about it is resolutely avoided, the subsequent generations are left with no choice. The silence of one generation may be the oblivion of the next. The pact of silence of the past becomes the inevitable disremembering of the future. Be it of silence or of forgetting, Spain's pact was not only a political agreement. Families tacitly subscribed to it as well. In 2008, 73% of adults said that when they were children the Civil War was mentioned at home only a bit or nothing at all, and 70% said the same thing in relation to Franco's dictatorship.[45]

But things had begun to change by then: A new generation of political leaders and a new generation of Spaniards were ready and willing to look back, to ask questions and speak up. Thousands of republican sympathisers from the time of the Civil War and the post-war remained 'lying in the ditches' ('tirados en las cunetas') and buried in improvised mass graves with no signposts to remember them. The people that might still know where to find them had only a few years left to live.

The decade of the 2000s saw the emergence of a new movement to 'recover historical memory' ('recuperar la memoria histórica'). This expression, historical memory, used by supporters and opponents alike, tellingly symbolises that, until then, the opportunity to construct a narrative of the past had been missing. A new generation craved memories that could only be partial, selective and socially reconstructed from the present, but memories that needed to be rescued, recovered from under the carpet where they had been swept. They sought an account of the past that could help frame the politics of the present. They sought an explanation of the events during and after the Civil War. They needed to understand the fragile conditions in which the consensus of the Transition was forged. The new generation of the 2000s had heard from their parents that the Transition was the best possible outcome, that certain compromises had to be made to secure an agreement. Now that the Spanish democracy was consolidated, the new generation wanted to review and update the conditions of that agreement. The turn of the century opened the

---

[45] CIS, *Memorias de las Guerra Civil y el Franquismo*, 10–11.

door to a new 'public memory', which Neiman so helpfully defines as 'what every half-educated member of a culture knows in her sinews'.[46]

There was a small attempt in 1979 to recover bodies of republican victims of reprisals in rural Extremadura, near the Portuguese border, but with that one exception, exhumations only started in 2000, when the Association for the Recovery of the Historical Memory was founded.[47] Relatively soon, some of the initiatives to search, exhume and rebury with dignity the victims of the Civil War were funded by regional governments. The first lower chamber motion remembering Franco's victims was passed in the year 2000, tabled by the United Left, a coalition led by the Communist Party. A year later saw the airing of *Cuéntame Cómo Pasó* ('Tell Me How It Happened'), one of the most popular drama series in the history of Spain's television. *Cuéntame* tells the story of a supposedly regular family in a working-class neighbourhood of Madrid that somehow manages to get involved in all of the country's political events from the mid-1960s, through the 1970s and well into the 1980s, approximately one year per season. On the verge of on-demand stream, *Cuéntame* was perhaps one of the last shows to gather whole families in front of the television set one evening per week, and prompted conversations between generations, including plenty between this author and his parents.

In the 1980s and 1990s, the social-democratic party PSOE adopted a low profile in relation to Francoism and its victims. Led by Felipe González, PSOE won the general election in 1982 and remained in power until 1996. It would be unfair to suggest they did nothing to repair the damage caused by Franco's regime, but whatever they did, they did it quietly. Among other measures, González's government returned confiscated assets to trade unions, compensated republican army veterans, and granted Spanish citizenship to members of the International Brigades who were still alive.[48] The International Brigades were Communist volunteers from all over the world – approximately 35,000, including well-known figures like Willy Brandt, Robert Capa, Ernest Hemingway, or Oliver Law, the first black American officer to command a troop of white American soldiers. They travelled to Spain to fight fascism in the Civil War, 'for your freedom and ours', said their motto. Other non-Communist but left-leaning activists also took arms against Franco and his Nazi and Fascist allies, George Orwell among them.[49]

In the 1980s, Felipe González was keen to reintroduce Spain to the world as a modern and future-looking country, an agenda in which 1992 played a

---

[46] Susan Neiman, *Learning from the Germans: Confronting Race and the Memory of Evil* (London: Allen Lane, 2019), 27.
[47] Encarnación, *Democracy without Justice in Spain*, 110.
[48] Ibid., 82.
[49] Giles Tremlett, *The International Brigades: Fascism, Freedom and the Spanish Civil War* (London: Bloomsbury, 2020).

central role: the 500th anniversary of Columbus's arrival in the Americas was also the year of Barcelona's Olympic Games and Sevilla's World Expo. Symbolic measures of memorialisation of the Civil War were not among the priorities of González's cabinets. For instance, to commemorate the 50th anniversary of the beginning of the war, instead of erecting a new statue, the government repurposed a monument in Plaza de la Lealtad (Loyalty Square) in Madrid. The original monument dated from mid-nineteenth century and was set up to praise the popular rebellion against the Napoleonic troops on 2 May 1808, a day remembered with a bank holiday in the capital city. Alongside the inscription as tribute to the victims of the so-called War of Independence against France, the new message, unveiled by King Juan Carlos, read with the upmost equidistance: 'Honour to all those who gave their lives for Spain.' The gesture was brought forward a few months, so the honouring did not take place in 1986, but in 1985, on the tenth anniversary of the king's enthroning.[50] In a press statement on the 50th anniversary of the commencement of the war, 18 July 1986, the Spanish government declared that 'the Civil War is not an event worthy of commemoration' as it 'no longer has – neither should it have – a living presence in the reality of a country whose moral conscience is ultimately based on the principles of freedom and tolerance'.[51]

After eight years in opposition, PSOE regained power in March 2004. Three days before, an al-Qaeda attack had killed 192 and injured hundreds more in Madrid. A year earlier, under Aznar's premiership, Spain had joined the United States and the United Kingdom in their illegal war on Iraq. Despite being abundantly clear that Spain had been victim of jihadist terror, Aznar insisted that ETA was responsible for the Madrid attacks. He even persuaded the UN Security Council to say so in a resolution adopted that very day.[52] The lies became untenable and Aznar's party lost the executive because of them.[53] PSOE was led by José Luis Rodríguez Zapatero, who had just turned 18 when the constitution was voted in referendum in December 1978. Removing Spanish troops from Iraqi soil was one of the first decisions of the new prime minister. Late Francoism and the Transition influenced him and other politicians of his age in a less straightforward way than for the previous political generation. At the same time, however, Rodríguez Zapatero's

---

[50] Aguilar, *Memory and Amnesia*, 208.
[51] El País, "'Una guerra civil no es un acontecimiento conmemorable,' afirma el Gobierno," (19 July 1986): *"No tiene ya – ni debe tenerla – presencia viva en la realidad de un país cuya conciencia moral última se basa en los principios de la libertad y de la tolerancia."*
[52] UN Security Council Resolution 1530 (2004), of 11 March.
[53] Cristina Flesher Fominaya, "The Madrid Bombings and Popular Protest: Misinformation, Counter-Information, Mobilisation and Elections after '11-M,'" *Contemporary Social Science* 6, no. 3 (2011).

grandfather had fought in the republican army and had been executed during the Civil War. On numerous occasions did the prime minister speak about the influence of his grandfather's memory on his politics.

PSOE's government set up an interdepartmental commission to study the situation of victims of the Civil War and Francoism in 2004. The lower chamber declared 2006 the Year of Historical Memory, and after a long process parliament finally passed the Historical Memory Act 2007.[54] The act passed with the opposition of the conservative party PP and the Catalan pro-independence leftist party ERC, the former because they considered it a rupture with the consensus of the Transition, the latter because they thought the act was insufficiently progressive.

The preamble of the Historical Memory Act declares the intention to 'contribute to heal wounds that remain open, (and to) provide satisfaction to citizens who suffered, themselves directly or their relatives, the consequences of the tragedy of the Civil War or the repression of the Dictatorship'. It goes on saying that by 'deepening in the spirit of reunion and concord of the Transition, those citizens are not the only ones being recognised and honoured, the Spanish Democracy as a whole is as well'.[55] Among other measures, the act creates a scheme of State aid for the tracing, identification and recovery of bodies of victims of the war and of Francoist repression who were still missing and buried in mass graves. According to the official Centre for Sociological Research, when the act was adopted, more than half of the population believed that victims' bodies ought to be found and reburied with dignity, and every five in six among them thought it should be the State's responsibility to do so.[56] The Historical Memory Act also ordered the removal of Francoist symbols from public display, with the exception of buildings that could have special artistic, religious or architectural significance; it prohibited political events in the Valley of the Fallen; it extended the right to claim Spanish nationality to surviving volunteers of the International Brigades with no need to renounce their nationality of origin; and it granted a two-to-three-year window to claim the Spanish nationality of origin to the children and grandchildren of those who had fled Spain as a result of the Civil War and the subsequent repression.

---

[54] Act 57/2007, that recognises and broadens the rights and establishes measures in favour of those who suffered persecution or violence during the Civil War and the dictatorship, of 26 December.

[55] "*La presente Ley quiere contribuir a cerrar heridas todavía abiertas en los españoles y a dar satisfacción a los ciudadanos que sufrieron, directamente o en la persona de sus familiares, las consecuencias de la tragedia de la Guerra Civil o de la represión de la Dictadura*"; "*. . . profundizando de este modo en el espíritu del reencuentro y de la concordia de la Transición, no son sólo esos ciudadanos los que resultan reconocidos y honrados sino también la Democracia española en su conjunto.*"

[56] CIS, *Memorias de las Guerra Civil y el Franquismo*, 14–15.

As important as what it included is what it did not. Four issues need to be mentioned. Firstly, the act declared Francoist criminal rulings generally 'unjust' and the judicial bodies 'illegitimate', but it did not annul the sentences; PSOE's government argued that doing so would have put legal certainty at risk. Secondly, the act set up a system so victims could get a declaration of the damage caused, but this declaration excluded any economic compensation from the State. Thirdly, the act did not set up an independent truth commission to investigate the human rights violations committed by the regime. And fourthly, the act left the Valley of the Fallen untouched, with Franco in it. More than a decade would be needed to fix that, with the exhumation of Franco in October 2019. Rodríguez Zapatero ordered the closure of the Valley in 2009, and he set up a working group to look into different options to resignify the Valley in a democratic society. When the conservative PP returned to power in December 2011, they reopened the mausoleum and shelved the recommendations of the working group. The conservative prime minister Mariano Rajoy (2011–2018) also cut funding for the implementation of the Historical Memory Act.

Besides the generational change, one other factor influenced decisively on Spain's early attempts to come to terms with its past. In 1998, former Chilean dictator Augusto Pinochet was arrested in London, where he had gone to receive medical treatment confident of his diplomatic immunity. However, the Spanish judge Baltasar Garzón issued an international arrest warrant against him on account of nearly 100 cases of torture and killings of Spanish nationals living in Chile in the 1970s and 1980s. The House of Lords appellate committee granted the extradition request to Spain ruling that international crimes such as torture could not be covered by the immunity generally recognised in international law to former heads of State. Pinochet was placed under house arrest in London for nearly one-and-a-half years. Both the Spanish government, then led by the conservative José María Aznar, and Tony Blair's UK government opposed Garzón's attempts to prosecute the Chilean dictator. It was unchartered legal and diplomatic territory. Eventually the British secretary of Justice decided that Pinochet should not be extradited to Spain due to health concerns. Pinochet returned to Chile in 2000, and he died there on 10 December 2006, ironically the anniversary of the adoption of the Universal Declaration of Human Rights in 1948.

International human rights law had evolved significantly since the time of Pinochet's coup and Franco's death, in 1973 and 1975 respectively. Emerging from the Inter-American regional human rights system in the late 1980s, it was being increasingly and globally accepted that victims of human rights violations should be entitled to the right to truth, justice and reparation, and that amnesties for most serious crimes are generally incompatible with victims' access to reparation and with States' duty to prevent those crimes.[57] Evolving international law expected countries to embark on an introspection to examine their own history openly and impartially. Advancing on this path, Pinochet's case contributed to the evolution of international criminal law and opened the door to the exploration of universal jurisdiction in other countries. Beyond international law, Pinochet's case had a significant impact in Spain. Spanish society was reminded of its unresolved issues with its own past. Pinochet brought to light the hypocrisy of one country's judicial institutions – Spain – attempting to prosecute crimes committed in a second country – Chile – while those same crimes had been officially forgotten and pardoned in the first one. That the second country was a former colony of the first only made things worse. The hypocrisy was not overlooked by the PR advisers working with Pinochet's legal team. As a master's student at the University of Essex in 2008, I remember listening to one of Pinochet's British lawyers in a panel talking about how 'embarrassed' he felt by Spain's internal contradictions. Sincere or not, the argument carried weight.

Yet, the ascertainment of the contradictions that Pinochet helped bring to the fore did not make the contradictions go away. To this day, the Amnesty Act 1977 remains in force and it is the standing case-law of Spain's supreme court that international human rights obligations do not oblige the State to repeal the act.[58] All those obligations were voluntarily assumed after 1977, and in the court's view the principle of legality allows victims to rely on international treaties *only* after the treaties are binding for Spain, in other words, after 1977; therefore, the Amnesty Act would be safe. The principle also applies to the continuous crime of enforced disappearances. The effects of this crime technically unfold for as long as the disappearance is not investigated, namely, in this case since 1936 or whenever the crime took place until the present day. However, Spain's judges consider that only disappearances that began to occur after the adoption of the relevant domestic or international legislation can be investigated in court, which effectively means that international crimes committed before 1977 remain unpunished. As a result, victims of Francoism have made little progress with Spain's judiciary. That's why they are pursing more uncertain routes bringing their case to Argentina in application of the principle of universal jurisdiction.[59] Victims of human rights violations are being forced to go full circle to get some justice. More than 20 years ago, Chilean victims holding a Spanish passport were given

---

[57] Inter-American Court of Human Rights, *Velásquez Rodríguez v. Honduras* (Judgment of 29 July 1988), para. 181; UN Human Rights Committee, *General Comment no. 20: Prohibition of Torture*, UN doc: HRI/GEN/1/Rev.7 (1992), para. 15.
[58] Supreme Court of Spain, Judgment 101/2012 ("Garzón case") (27 February 2012), 18.
[59] Yardley, "Facing His Torturer as Spain Confronts Its Past," *New York Times*.

hope by the Spanish judge Baltasar Garzón 11,000 kilometres away from their homes. Today, victims of crimes committed in Spain take their long shot in another country of the Southern Cone.

4.4 WHEN THE PAST IS VERY PRESENT: HISTORICAL MEMORY OF THE BASQUE COUNTRY

The coup of 18 July 1936 triumphed in Navarra and the Basque province of Araba. The province of Gipuzkoa fell into the hands of the insurgent army in September, and thereby the connection between France and the republican side was cut off on the northern coast. The remaining Basque territory, Bizkaia, was conquered by Franco's troops in June 1937. Two months before, on 26 April 1937, Nazi bombers assisted Franco by brutally destroying the market town of Gernika, famously immortalised by Pablo Picasso – spelled *Guernica* in Spanish. The bombing had huge symbolism: Gernika was the heart of Basque identity as it is the seat of an ancient assembly of the people of Bizkaia. After his definitive victory, Franco imposed a policy of cultural homogeneity, forbidding the use of the Basque language in public. With an ever more visible and vocal movement calling for democracy and freedom, repression in the Basque Country turned particularly brutal in the final years of the dictatorship. The region was placed under nearly permanent state of emergency and exception between 1968 and 1975.

There were therefore peculiarities that made the experience of dictatorship different from that of other parts of Spain. But the war and authoritarianism absorbed Spain as a whole, and each corner has its own stories of injustice to tell. That is why the prepositions, *in* and *of*, matter. On the one hand, the Basque Country shared the pact of silence with the rest of Spain, and took steps to recover some of the memory in the first two decades of this century. That would be historical memory *in* the Basque Country. But there is another historical memory that is more recent, just as painful, and even more divisive than the other one. It is a memory that is specific *of* the Basques, a memory about which discourses in the Basque Country and in other parts of Spain are worlds apart. I am talking about the memory of ETA's ('Euskadi Ta Askatasuna', Basque Country and Freedom) terror between the 1970s and the late 2000s, the far-right groups' unpunished killings and harassment in the 1970s, the State-supported paramilitary murders with GAL ('Grupos Antiterroristas de Liberación', Antiterrorist Liberation Groups) in the 1980s, and the memory of the torture and ill-treatment of terrorist suspects by the Spanish police.

In Basque politics, the historical memory *of* the Basque Country is more contentious than the historical memory of Spain *in* the Basque Country. Most of the symbology of the Franco-era, including street names, was removed from the public eye during the Transition. Despite its strong Catholic foundations, during the war, the conservative Basque Nationalist Party remained loyal to the republic and fought alongside the openly anticlerical Communists and anarchists. No one of any significance in the Basque Country expresses publicly any nostalgia for the Francoist past. The Spanish conservative PP tends to be more liberal in the Basque Country than in other Spanish regions. Currently PP is a relatively small party in Basque politics, but they memorialised and remembered the victims of the Civil War and the dictatorship when they were the biggest party in the province of Araba and the city of Vitoria-Gasteiz in the 2000s.

However, the Basque society is still working out a public memory about the violence experienced over the three decades that followed the Transition. (About the significance of violence in the politics of Basque nationalism, see section 3.4.) Victims of ETA's cruel violence have received recognition from public institutions, but social recognition has been much slower and more timid. In towns and communities where independence was the preferred political choice, for many years ETA suspects and torture victims were treated like heroes while the Spanish government maintained that the allegations of torture were simply lies. ETA and its supporters justified the use of violence because in their view there had been no interruption in the State's undemocratic nature since Francoism. They said they were 'Eusko gudariak' ('Basque warriors'), the term reserved for the men, Basque nationalist or not, who fought against Franco's troops during the Spanish Civil War. According to Aguilar, ETA tried to give a new meaning to the Spanish Civil War as a conflict between two sides equally foreign to the Basque Country, a conflict that resulted in the military occupation of their nation; the new so-called *gudaris* of ETA saw themselves as the political descendants of those who had fought Franco in Basque land in the 1930s.[60]

ETA caused fear, but for too long it also enjoyed enough social support, particularly in the form of relatively low-intensity uprising in the streets, led by the youth, who set buses and rubbish containers on fire and confronted the police in what was known as 'kale borroka' ('street fight'). In the 2000s, ETA was being cornered by the police, and the decline in popular support was a key reason why ETA stopped for good in 2011. In previous decades, ETA benefited from long periods of silence of large parts of the Basque society who believed their silence would keep them away from the attention of ETA and their informers. Marvellous exceptions must be noted. It is the case, first and foremost, of 'Gesto Por la Paz' ('Gesture for Peace'), an organisation that

---

[60] Paloma Aguilar, "The Memory of the Civil War in the Transition to Democracy: The Peculiarity of the Basque Case," *West European Politics* 21, no. 4 (1998), 16–17.

convened silent concentrations the day after each murder and on a weekly basis for 25 years, starting in 1986. It was a modest gesture that nonetheless required a high dose of bravery particularly in its beginnings.

Over time, the Basque society empowered itself to make clear that ETA did not represent them. The sociological survey of the Basque Country Euskobarometro shows that less than 25% of the people rejected ETA totally in 1981, but that number went up to 60% in 2000 and remained at that level for 10 more years; explicit ideological support for ETA was minimal.[61] Together with police actions, this message significantly contributed to persuade the political movement closest to ETA, 'Ezker Abertzalea' ('Nation-loving or Nationalist Left'), that the threat of armed violence had to end once and for all. Since its inception in the 1960s, ETA had been seen in those political circles as a thermometer, not as an illness per se. For them, ETA was an expression of a deeper political problem, not a problem in itself. The day ETA finally made the announcement, 20 October 2011, is marked as a day of liberation, especially for those whose lives were at risk. When asked what freedom would mean to him, one local politician said on television, 'Freedom for me means the freedom to eat *pintxos* in the Old Town' of Donostia-San Sebastian, my home town. The old town was a neighbourhood that had been a no-go area for him and thousands more for decades.

A number of laws and policies have been adopted at the Spanish and the Basque level to provide economic compensation and to honour victims of terrorism with symbolic memorialisation. The Basque Act 4/2008 and the Spanish Act 29/2011 are noteworthy in this regard.[62] This legislative framework to provide truth, justice and reparation extends not only to victims of ETA but also to victims of other groups considered 'terrorist', including right-wing armed groups from the late 1970s, and GAL.

GAL, the 'Antiterrorist Liberation Groups', were death squads and mercenaries illegally funded by the Spanish government under PSOE that operated on both sides of the French–Spanish border between 1983 and 1987. ETA members took refuge in the French Basque Country in the 1980s, a time when French and Spanish authorities seldom collaborated on anti-terrorism matters. GAL kidnapped, tortured and murdered at least 27 people, including bystanders who they mistook for ETA members. In 1998, José Barrionuevo, former minister of Interior, and his deputy, Rafael Vera, were imprisoned for their responsibility in funding and supporting GAL's criminal activities. GAL followed ETA's years of most intense activity. As recalled by Woodworth, in

---

[61] Archivo online sobre la violencia terrorista en Euskadi: Fondo Euskobarometro.
[62] Basque Act 4/2008, of 19 June, on the Recognition and Reparation of Victims of Terrorism; Act 29/2011, of 22 September, on the Recognition and Comprehensive Protection of Victims of Terrorism.

the 1980s, Barrionuevo and Vera 'found that hardly a week passed without their having to attend a funeral, face to face with officers furiously demanding a harder line against the terrorists'.[63] In 1998, a then retired Felipe González walked both men to the jail's gate, where he was photographed hugging them goodbye. Much has been speculated about the former prime minister's involvement in GAL, but so far nothing sufficiently definitive has been proven. Yet, according to a secret U.S. Central Intelligence Agency memo, dated 1984 and approved for release in 2011, 'González has agreed to the formation of a group of mercenaries, controlled by the Army, to combat the terrorists outside the law.'[64] In an interview in 2010 González declared cryptically, 'I had to decide whether to blow up the leaders of ETA. I said no. And I do not know if I made a mistake.'[65]

GAL was another consequence of the pact of silence. It uncovered the structural inabilities of the most senior figures in the Spanish home office to deal with the threat of terror in a democratic way and in compliance with the rule of law. The emergence of GAL's death squads was 'a continuation rather than a departure of the state's counter terrorism strategies' after Franco.[66] GAL were the result of a less than perfect Transition, where institutions were not cleaned up, resulting in the lack of democratic control over the police, the militarised Guardia Civil and the military intelligence. GAL's existence also emboldened ETA, giving them discursive ammunition to dispute the democratic character of Spain, and offering them the chance to present themselves as victims of State-sponsored repression.

GAL ended in 1987, but the illegal actions in the fight against terror did not end. Combining archival work and interviews – email, face to face and by post – the Basque Institute of Criminology gathered information of more than 4,000 individuals who claimed to have suffered torture between 1960 and 2014. Most allegations took place in 1975 (265). After a sharp decline in the late 1970s, the number of claims was consistently high in the first half of the 1980s (between 113 and 168 per year). They reached a relatively low point in 1990 (22), but remained high between 1991 (51) and 2003 (59), with peaks in 1992 (139) and 2002 (113). Between 2004 and 2010, allegations came down significantly below 50, and they were anecdotal between 2012 and 2014 (1–3), last reported year. The low points of torture allegations coincide with the attempts of dialogue between ETA and the Spanish government in

---

[63] Paddy Woodworth, "Using Terror against Terrorists: The Spanish Experience," in Sebastian Balfour (ed.): *The Politics of Contemporary Spain* (Abingdon: Routledge, 2005), 69.
[64] Central Intelligence Agency, "Terrorism Review," (19 January 1984), 19.
[65] Juan José Millás, "Tuve que decidir si se volaba a la cúpula de ETA. Dije no. Y no sé si hice lo correcto," *El País* (7 November 2010).
[66] Omar G. Encarnación, "Democracy and Dirty Wars in Spain," *Human Rights Quarterly* 29, no. 4 (2007), 952.

Algeria (1987–1989), as well as with ETA's ceasefires of 1996, 1998 to 1999 and 2006. The Basque Institute of Criminology identified only 21 condemnatory rulings confirmed by the supreme court until 2003, with 32 victims and 50 people sentenced in relation to events that took place between 1979 and 1992. The records and forensic psychological analysis suggest that torturers changed their methods in the 1990s, making it more difficult to prove the existence of torture: choking and suffocation, physical extenuation, waterboarding and threats became increasingly common.[67]

In the few cases where there were prison sentences for torturers, the sentence was generally low, inconsistent with the gravity of the crime, and they were followed by official pardons.[68] In 1995, PSOE's government, with Juan Alberto Belloch as minister of Interior, pardoned two members of Guardia Civil who had been condemned for torture. The government argued that the decision was taken to avoid 'discrimination' with similar cases where police officers had been pardoned in the 1980s and early 1990s.[69] In a television interview in 2013, Belloch said he did not recall the pardons but explained them referring to the 'complicated moment' and the 'global climate' in the Basque Country of the time.[70] By April 2017, the conservative PP and the social-democratic PSOE had used the prerogative of executive pardon in no less than 39 occasions to release of criminal responsibility police officers who had been condemned for torture by the courts.[71]

The maximum period of incommunicado detention was extended in 2003 from 5 to 13 days. In the case of incommunicado detention the individual is denied access to family, a lawyer of their choice and an independent doctor, all of which increases the risk of torture and impunity. Between 2010 and 2018, the European Court of Human Rights condemned Spain at least eight times for the failure to investigate claims of torture made by alleged ETA members detained incommunicado.[72] Also at least on eight occasions between 2008 and 2016 the constitutional court ruled that there had not been

---

[67] Instituto Vasco de Criminología, *Proyecto de investigación de la tortura en el País Vasco (1960–2013) Memoria-Resumen de la actividad realizada* (Vitoria-Gasteiz: University of the Basque Country and Basque Government, 2016), 13–38.
[68] Amnesty International, *Acabar con la doble injusticia: Víctimas de tortura y malos tratos sin reparación* (Madrid: Amnesty International, 2004), 22–4.
[69] Jesús Duva and Aurora Intxausti, "El Gobierno indulta por segunda vez a un guardia condenado por torturas y a otro compañero," *El País* (6 May 1995).
[70] La Sexta "Salvados" programme (12 May 2013).
[71] Público, "España, tierra de impunidad para torturadores" (24 April 2017).
[72] European Court of Human Rights, *Argimiro Isasa v. Spain* (Judgment of 28 September 2010), *Beristain Ukar v. Spain* (Judgment of 8 March 2011), *Otamendi Egiguren v. Spain* (Judgment of 16 October 2012), *Etxebarria Caballero v. Spain* (Judgment of 7 October 2014), *Ataun Rojo v. Spain* (Judgment of 7 October 2014), *Arratibel Garciandia v. Spain* (Judgment of 5 May 2015), *Beortegui Martínez v. Spain* (Judgment of 31 May 2016) and *Portu and Sarasola v. Spain* (Judgment of 13 February 2018).

a full and an effective investigation after an allegation of torture in an incommunicado detention.[73]

Despite the evidence, the Spanish government and senior political figures held a firm position of denial of any wrongdoing, claiming that the allegations of torture were part of a strategy of ETA suspects and the Basque pro-independence movement to discredit the image of Spain and its democratic institutions. With the exception of the left-leaning Podemos, none of the other four main parties in Spain – conservative PP, social-democratic PSOE, economically liberal Ciudadanos and, obviously, far-right Vox – has moved from that position so far.

When *Euskaldunon Egunkaria* ('The Basques' newspaper') board members were detained and denounced having been tortured in 2003, the minister of Interior Ángel Acebes (PP) warned of possible 'legal actions' against anyone accusing Guardia Civil officers of torture.[74] Acebes brought a case against Martxelo Otamendi, *Egunkaria* editor, which was eventually shelved by the court. Acebes said in 2003, 'neither the Guardia Civil nor the Policía Nacional use torture. That accusation is absolutely intolerable. . . . The detainees have applied ETA's handbook, . . . which requires them to denounce torture falsely.' In response to a Basque member of parliament who had given credibility to Otamendi's allegations, Acebes said that 'these false accusations deserve the greatest personal and political contempt, (and) they are indecent and despicable.'[75] In 2010, Spanish judges dismissed the claim that *Egunkaria* board members had collaborated with ETA, but it was seven years too late to reopen the newspaper, the only one published entirely in Basque at the time of its closure. In 2012, the European Court of Human Rights condemned Spain for not having investigated the allegations of torture against Otamendi.[76]

In October 2003, the then UN special rapporteur on torture, Theo van Boven, carried out an official mission to Spain. His report was received with an aggressive reaction from the Spanish government. The introductory paragraph gives a good sense of the tone of the 81-page response: In the opinion of the Spanish government, van Boven's report 'contains so many major

---

[73] Constitutional Court, Judgments 52/2008 (14 April), 69/2008 (23 June), 107/2008 (22 September), 63/2010 (18 October), 131/2012 (18 June), 153/2013 (9 September), 130/2016 (18 July) and 144/2016 (19 September).

[74] El País, "Interior anuncia 'acciones legales' contra quienes acusan de tortura a la Guardia Civil" (27 February 2003).

[75] El País, "Acebes: 'Mi mayor desprecio político y personal'" (27 February 2003): "*Ni la Guardia Civil ni el Cuerpo Nacional de Policía torturan. Es absolutamente intolerable esa acusación . . . Los detenidos han aplicado el manual de ETA, . . . que les ordena que denuncien torturas falsamente*"; "*Estas acusaciones de tortura me merecen el mayor desprecio personal y político, . . . estas falsas acusaciones, que son una indecencia y una indignidad.*"

[76] *Otamendi Egiguren v. Spain* (2012).

factual errors that the conclusions drawn by the Special rapporteur are seriously undermined, with the result that the report is virtually unacceptable in its entirety, being unfounded and lacking in rigour, substance and method'.[77] In an unprecedented way, the Spanish delegation left the session while van Boven was presenting his conclusions in front of the UN Commission on Human Rights. With a generous dose of diplomacy, van Boven later said not to have recollections of any other government reacting 'as strongly' as the Spanish one did on that occasion.[78]

Soon after the detention of ETA members Portu and Sarasola in January 2008, the then minister of Interior Alfredo Pérez-Rubalcaba (PSOE) publicly denied that they could have been tortured by the police: 'That's what they always say when they are detained.'[79] Ten years later, the European Court of Human Rights condemned Spain for torture in that case.[80] The Spanish government played down the importance of the ruling saying that the court 'had only appreciated the insufficiency of the evidence about the causes of the injuries that healed after a short period of time and with no consequences or scars'.[81]

Coronel Manuel Sánchez Corbí was condemned for torture in 1997 for events that took place in 1992, but he was pardoned in 1999 and later decorated by the Spanish government. Between December 2015 and August 2018, Sánchez Corbí led the central operative unit of the Guardia Civil, a specialised division in charge of investigating the most serious forms of organised crime, including but not only terrorism. In a radio interview in November 2017, Sánchez Corbí tried to excuse his actions this way: 'The bad guys have tried to put the mistakes of the good guys at the same level of cruelty of the bombing attacks; they are incomparable.'[82]

Policing is an ungrateful job. Spanish police – Guardia Civil and Policía Nacional – and Basque police – Ertzaintza – were in ETA's line of fire. Officers and bodyguards were unjustly killed, and for too long the Basque society remained silent. Healing the wounds of the recent past will require repairing morally that long-lasting indifference. At the same time, however,

---

[77] Government of Spain, *Response to the Special Rapporteur on Torture*, UN doc: E/CN.4/2004/G/19 (4 March 2004), 1.
[78] Teresa Whitfield, *Endgame for ETA: Elusive Peace in the Basque Country* (London: Hurst & Company, 2014), 127–8.
[79] El País, "Rubalcaba: 'Los miembros de ETA aducen siempre que son torturados,'" (9 January 2018).
[80] European Court of Human Rights, *Portu and Sarasola v. Spain* (Judgment of 13 February 2018).
[81] Público, "El Gobierno resta importancia a las condenas de Europa por no investigar torturas: 'Son solo nueve,'" (28 March 2018): "*Sólo se ha apreciado la insuficiencia de las pruebas sobre las causas de unas lesiones que curaron en breve periodo de tiempo sin dejar ninguna secuela.*"
[82] Cadena Ser, "Manuel Sánchez: 'Fuimos aprendiendo a base de muertos,'" (30 November 2017), on demand radio min. 11:10: "*Los malos han querido colocar los errores de los buenos al mismo nivel de la crueldad de los atentados; es incomparable.*"

public authorities have a long way to go to recognise that torture and ill-treatment were an obnoxious part of the anti-terrorist strategy. These practices harmed the credibility of the police as a fully democratic institution, and made life even more difficult for the officers who respected the rule of law. In recent years, the legislative bodies of the Basque Country and Navarra have adopted laws to recognise and repair the damage suffered by 'victims of acts of political motivation', since 1950 in the case of Navarra, and between 1960 and 1999 in the case of the Basque Country.[83] Among others, victims of torture, even with no judicial ruling to prove it, are protected by these laws. This is a potentially important step in the process of historical memory *of* the Basque Country *in* the Basque Country. As far as I know, nothing remotely similar is being considered by Spanish authorities, where public discourse is still heavily based on denial, Manichaeism and demonisation.

More encouraging are the meetings and conversations in the past decade between ETA victims and repented ETA members, in some cases bringing murderers face to face with their victims' loved ones. These meetings are held in private, but some of the participants are talking about their experience in schools, and conveying their emotions in public events, making it therapeutic not only for them but for society at large. Other events have brought together victims of ETA, GAL and police torture. It is also helpful that some Ezker Abertzalea politicians have apologised for the damage they caused with their decades-long thunderous silence. Little by little, these steps are contributing to heal social divisions, to discover the human dimension of the conflict from those who suffered the most, and to make people aware of the fact that they have much in common despite politics. The initiatives took years of preparation and were conducted discreetly away from the public eye until participants felt comfortable to share. Some of these projects were supported by the Basque government, which also edited Herenegun ('Day before yesterday'), an educational guide for schools about violence in the Basque Country since the 1960s. These guides cover Franco-era repression, ETA, GAL and torture during the democratic era. The coverage of all these topics in one volume has not been exempt of controversy, because some consider it apologetic of one form of violence or another. Working out the past in a plural, inclusive and respectful way will take time, and the Basque Country only recently got rid of ETA's yoke. Born after 1995, so-called Generation Z does not know what was like to live under ETA and other forms of violence. Historical memory is a powerful reminder that freedom should not be taken for granted. As my mum once said to me when talking about this, it's shocking how quickly one gets used to normality.

---

[83] Basque Decree 107/2012, of 12 June, for the period 1960–78; Basque Act 12/2016, of 28 July, for the period 1978–1999; and Navarrese Act 16/2019, of 25 March, for events since 1950.

4.5 UNINTENDED CONSEQUENCES AND NEW OLD PLAYERS

One of the lessons from the historical memory *of* the Basque Country is that families should not be forced to bury their relatives next to the man who murdered them. Measures were taken to ensure that ETA victims did not have to share a cemetery with the ETA members who had killed them. Bearing this principle in mind, there was no way to justify keeping Franco in the Valley of the Fallen, next to more than 30,000 other men, thousands of them unidentified partisans of the republic Franco staged a coup against.

The Spanish government disinterred Franco's body from the Valley on 24 October 2019. To provide legal coverage to the exhumation, the Historical Memory Act was amended to say that only people who had died in the Civil War could be buried in the Valley of the Fallen.[84] That is why José Antonio Primo de Rivera is still there: he was executed on 20 November 1936, while Franco passed in bed the very same calendar day but in 1975. In October 2019, Franco was reburied in the family's vault in a municipal cemetery in Madrid. The family opposed the move to the last minute, as did the Valley's abbot. The Spanish far-right organised an online campaign under the hashtag #ElValleNoSeToca ('Do Not Touch the Valley'). Fascism sympathisers and Franco nostalgics concentrated at the gates of the public cemetery and greeted enthusiastically an 87-year-old feeble man called Antonio Tejero, the coronel who took a small group of *guardias civiles* and held all deputies to ransom on 23 February 1981.

Nostalgia plays a dangerous role in politics. Anthony D. Smith wrote that 'our blueprints for the future are invariably derived from our experiences of the past, as we travel forward, we do so looking backwards to a past that alone seems knowable and intelligible and which alone can "make sense" of a future that is forever neither'.[85] Spain's troubled relationship with its twentieth century is entering a new phase with the return of the far-right. Vox is the new old player of Spanish politics. In 2019, they signed confidence and supply arrangements with regional right-wing coalition governments of conservative PP and Ciudadanos. Vox became the third largest party in the Spanish parliament in the November 2019 elections, with 15% of the votes and 52 of the 350 seats. They shy away from endorsing Francoism explicitly, but party leaders refer to him as 'the General', never 'the dictator', and they oppose all attempts of memorialisation, because, they say, historical memory goes against the Transition's spirit of reconciliation. As soon as Vox spokespersons insist that Spaniards should not talk about the Civil War and Francoism

---

[84] New Article 16(3), introduced by Royal-Decree law 10/2018, of 24 August.
[85] Anthony D. Smith, *The Ethnic Origins of Nations* (Oxford: Blackwell Publishing, 1986), 177.

anymore, they rant against leftist politicians of the 1930s, and they slander the '13 Roses', a group of young Communist and Socialist women executed by firing squad in Madrid soon after the Civil War ended in 1939. In October 2020, Vox leader Santiago Abascal said in parliament that the left-leaning coalition of PSOE and United Podemos was the worst government Spain had had in 80 years, which necessarily meant that in his mind this democratically elected government was worse than Franco's dictatorship.[86]

Encarnación observes that, for now, 'when it comes to handling the issue of the past, (the left) has the public on its side'.[87] Whether this will be the case in the future, that remains to be seen. In September 2020, the left coalition announced a new bill on 'democratic memory' that would turn the mausoleum of the Valley into a civil cemetery, remove the remains of José Antonio Primo de Rivera from the altar, and establish that it is the State's responsibility to locate the whereabouts of the victims of extrajudicial executions.[88] Given the political fragmentation in the legislative chamber, the fate of this draft piece of legislation is uncertain. A sceptic would point out that the announcement was primarily an appeal to the core values of traditional PSOE and United Podemos voters at a time when their handling of Covid-19 was seriously under question.

Since the early 2010s, new narratives are confronting ever more forcefully the virtues of the Transition carved out by the generation of the 1970s. One of the most famous lines chanted by the 'Indignados' ('Outraged') anti-austerity movement that emerged in 2011 was 'They call it a democracy but it is not so' ('Lo llaman democracia y no lo es'). If 6 in 10 Spaniards were 'satisfied' or 'very satisfied' with how democracy worked in 2008,[89] the proportion went down to 43% in 2018.[90] Founded in 2014, Podemos is the political party that most successfully capitalised the outrage against austerity policies and corrupt politicians, criticising the compromises made in the 1970s and 1980s. The Transition, wrote Podemos founder Pablo Iglesias, 'left the Francoist economic elites untouched and helped to recycle a good part of the political and administrative leadership'.[91]

While the Catalan question is rooted in history, the political contention has been particularly vivid since 2010, as discussed in section 3.3. A number of

---

[86] Euronews, "Spanish MPs Vote Down Far-Right Vox Party's No-Confidence Motion in PM Sanchez" (22 October 2020).
[87] Omar G. Encarnación, "Memory and Politics in Democratic Spain," in Diego Muro and Ignacio Lago (eds.): *The Oxford Handbook of Spanish Politics* (Oxford: Oxford University Press, 2020), 59.
[88] Sam Jones, "Spain Plans to Turn Franco's Former Burial Site into Civil Cemetery," *The Guardian* (15 September 2020).
[89] CIS, *Barómetro de noviembre 2008, Estudio 2778* (Madrid: CIS, 2008).
[90] CIS, *Barómetro de septiembre 2018, Estudio 3223*, 7.
[91] Pablo Iglesias, "Understanding Podemos," *New Left Review* 93 (2015), 10.

Catalan pro-independence politicians have questioned the democratic nature of Spain in recent years. On 14 October 2019, the supreme court sentenced nine leaders to prison for sedition and other offences for having led a process that ended up in the unconstitutional referendum of 1 October 2017. The hashtag #SpainIsAFascistState, in English, was trending topic on social media the day after the ruling. Leading figures in Catalonia and other parts of Spain called for an amnesty to get the nine leaders out of prison. Such amnesty would also mean that former Catalan premier Carles Puigdemont and other escapees could be free to return to Catalonia. Since the Transition, up until recently, the word 'amnesty' was hardly ever heard outside the Basque Country, where the Ezker Abertzalea campaigned for a 'full amnesty' ('amnistia osoa') for ETA members in prison or hidden abroad.

The patchy way in which Spain has worked out its recent history has had unintended consequences that frame Spanish politics to this day. The country never experienced atonement or liberation after Franco. The regime transformed, transitioned through a very narrow corridor from dictatorship to democracy. There is a significant generational gap in the understanding and remembrance of Francoism and the Transition. Whatever happens in the years to come, the story of Spain in the past four decades shows that it is possible to have peace without justice. But, if not justice, what else can democracy be built on? The outcomes of Spain's epoch-marking challenges are linked to the country's ability to read its recent history. This can affect a political solution for Catalonia, a democratic response to the far-right, the building of trust in the Basque Country, and so on. I dare say those of us with ancestors on the winning side of the Civil War have something to say in this regard. After all, my great-grandfather died conquering Castellón for Franco and is buried in the Valley of the Fallen. Why would I be motivated by revenge?

Confronting the past does not mean perpetuating identities and ideological positions within the political parameters of the 1930s or 1970s. Historical memory is not about Franco, but about the future. A previous generation agreed to let the past go. But it looks like the pact of silence had an expiry date, and the current generation does not feel bound by the Transition's agreements, not at least the way their parents and grandparents did. Spain's difficult relationship with its past is one of Spain's Achilles' heels, but it doesn't have to be a weakness. The Spanish society is mature enough to look in the mirror with honesty and generosity. The future may depend on this.

Chapter 5

Who Weaves the Social Safety Net?

5.1 THIRTY YEARS LATE

Between 2014 and 2017, I worked as a research consultant for the Spanish Section of Amnesty International on housing law and policy in Madrid and Catalonia. Spain was in the midst of an acute economic crisis that, among many troubling consequences, resulted in about 60,000 evictions on average every year. Low-income households in the largest cities were being disproportionately affected. Amnesty International called for greater investment in social housing, a change in the civil procedural code to require a proportionality test of all evictions on a case-by-case basis, better cooperation between social services and the judicial system to ensure nobody would be rendered homeless as a result of an eviction, and the consideration of survivors of domestic violence as a priority group in accessing public social housing.

Between 2015 and 2019, the city of Madrid was governed by a left-leaning coalition with Podemos as a driving force. This was the first time the left was in control of Spain's capital since 1991. As one of its flagship projects, the local government adopted a human rights plan in February 2017. The detailed and ambitious plan was rather prominent in the local council's self-portrait, and that may explain why it was so swiftly abandoned by the right-wing Popular Party (PP) when they got back to power in 2019.

I recall a conversation back in 2017 with one senior official in Madrid's council. He was a civil servant who had worked with politicians both on the left and the right, but he was politically sympathetic to the agenda of Podemos and the coalition. With the left in power, he had management responsibilities in a working-class district, and his job included the allocation and supervision of public housing. We were discussing Amnesty International's recommendations as well as the council's new human rights plan. 'It's all very good,' I remember him saying with these or similar words, 'but we don't have the resources. It's not only that the budget is tightly controlled under the central government's financial rules and regulations. The main problem is that Madrid barely has publicly owned social housing.' He did have a point. Human rights-based recommendations only go so far when there is a structural problem of lack of resources available to the local authority. Spain's social housing for rental purposes accounts for 1.1% of all dwellings, compared to 29% in the Netherlands, 24% in Austria, 17% in Sweden or 16% in France (data from 2019 to 2020).[1] The transformative potential of human rights is debatable when the structural conditions are so limiting. The best human rights plan is a good budget, but there is only so much progressive budgets can achieve in a short time frame. And the pressure to avoid any deficit while keeping taxes down makes the task even more challenging.

Spain has a serious problem: its welfare state is underdeveloped.[2] This is the result not only of insufficient social investment, but also of a late start. Neighbouring countries in Western Europe created and developed their welfare state during Les Trente Glorieuses (The Glorious Thirty) after 1945. But during that time, Spain lived in a dictatorship that swanked about their resolve to combat anything remotely sounding like Socialism. Trade unions and political parties were not allowed, there was no free press, and dissidents were persecuted. World War II started only five months after the Spanish Civil War ended. Many on Spain's democratic front had high hopes that the allies would liberate Spain in 1945. But Franco's anti-Communist fixation made him a loyal ally in the Cold War. Spain's geographical position was also strategically important, on the Atlantic coast of Europe, as the entry point to the Mediterranean, and 12 miles away from Africa across the Strait of Gibraltar. Those who did not agree with Franco's regime would have to wait three decades to return from exile and make the case for democratic institutions. Meanwhile, the country's economy paid a hefty price for the two devastating armed conflicts, the internal and the international one. It took several years for the regime to gain international legitimacy, which meant the country missed on the financial benefits of the Marshall Plan. Politically isolated, underindustrialised, with a seriously deteriorated infrastructure, and in a profound recession, the economy relied on autarchy until the mid-1950s. It took Spain 17 years to recover the per capita income it had had right before the Civil War in 1936.[3]

---

[1] Housing Europe, *The State of Housing in Europe 2021* (Brussels: Housing Europe).
[2] Vicenç Navarro, *El subdesarrollo social de España: Causas y consecuencias* (Madrid: Diario Público, 2009), 23.
[3] Soler, "The New Spain," 4.

Francoism pretended to be an alternative to both liberalism and Socialism, with a disingenuous plan to pursue capitalism while avoiding class conflict. Following Mussolini's Italy, the dictatorship institutionalised a corporatist understanding of labour relations handled with false harmony through the so-called vertical union, which included businesses and workers. Social protection, public investment and social security were valuable discursive tools for the regime, but there was a big gap between promise and reality. With contempt for Socialist or social-democratic policies, and with the opposition decimated, gagged or in exile, Franco's Spain drifted further apart from Western Europe missing an opportunity to resurge with a more egalitarian economy and with universal public services. Much of Spain was still at an early stage of capitalist development, a context in which lack of growth and inexistent welfare policies resulted in capital accumulation and the widening of inequalities.[4] More than half of the labour force worked in agriculture in the 1940s and 1950s, when a rapid and large migration wave ensued from rural areas in Andalusia, Extremadura and Castilla towards the economic poles in Madrid, Catalonia and the Basque Country: In 1965, two-thirds of the new industrial workers would be employed in Madrid, Barcelona and Bilbao.[5] But the living conditions of the working class both in agriculture and in industry were dire. Between 1940 and 1955, the cost of living rose 1.7 times faster than average wages in agriculture and industry, with the corresponding loss of purchasing power.[6]

In the 1960s, Spain discovered the economic attractiveness of tourism, a sector that public authorities continue to treasure to this day. The economy took advantage of tailwind in the 1960s and 1970s, when Spain's GDP grew an impressive 7% average per year.[7] The labour market produced apparent full employment, thanks to the small presence of women in the workforce and to the hundreds of thousands of workers who migrated initially to Latin America and later to Western Europe. Remittances contributed to boost Spain's economy until the oil crisis hit Europe and much of the world in the early 1970s. Before the international crisis, Spain did reasonably well for a number of reasons, one of them being that many Spaniards were not there. Through internal and external migration, rapid industrialisation and a

---

[4] Walter Scheidel, *The Great Leveler: Violence and the History of Inequality from the Stone Age to the Twenty-First Century* (New Jersey: Princeton University Press, 2017), 204–5.
[5] The volume of the streamflow had never been seen before, but internal migration was not a new phenomenon. My grandfather moved from rural Castilla to my home town in the Basque Country in the 1920s. He got there with very limited resources and worked his way up starting as a shop assistant for one of his cousins, who had arrived 10 years before him.
[6] Soler, "The New Spain," 5–6 and 17.
[7] Tusell, *Spain: From Dictatorship to Democracy*, 271.

growing tertiary sector, principally tourism, by the mid-1970s, in aggregate terms Spain achieved an advanced economy.

Despite economic progress, the country lagged far behind Western Europe in relation to welfare state: In 1975, Spain spent 14% of its GDP on social protection, when the Western European countries that would later be known as the EU-15 spent 22%.[8] It was also a profoundly unequal society, both between social classes and in geographical terms. Per capita income in Madrid and Catalonia was close to 40% higher than Spain's average, and in the industrial Basque province of Bizkaia that figure could reach 50%.[9]

Spain joined the club of European democracies in the 1970s, but it was 30 years late for its welfare state. The global neoliberal turn of the 1980s put an end to the relative understanding between labour and capital regarding the need for public investment, social justice and moderate egalitarianism. Instead, advanced economies started to implement ideologically driven policies of deregulation, privatisation, lesser protection for unions, and lower taxes for the wealthy. Spain caught the neoliberal wave late, in the 1990s, but the global economic crisis of the 1970s and the industrial conversion of the 1980s created difficult economic conditions. Furthermore, as explained in the previous chapter (section 4.2), politicians and society in general put faith in consensus-seeking at the expense of other political considerations. After four decades out of the system, illegal or in exile, the left prioritised being seen as moderate and pragmatic.

Spain never caught up with other European countries in terms of investment in social protection, and the continuation of underinvestment had profound implications for housing and social assistance, as we will see later in this chapter (sections 5.3 and 5.4). In the 2000s, about 6% of Spain's workforce was employed in health, education or social care, for 11% in the EU-15; less than 20% of the GDP was spent on public welfare, for 27% in the EU-15.[10]

The gap had narrowed down slightly in the 1980s, when other Western European states began to implement neoliberal policies while Spain was being governed by PSOE, a centre-left party for the first time since 1936. The 1980s is also the decade when Spain successfully moved to a national healthcare system as a universal public service, not based on a national insurance model but financed out of the general public accounts. As observed by Guillén, 'achieving the creation of a national health service was seen at the time as a way of "becoming Europeans".'[11] The health reform began when PSOE got to power in 1982, and it was articulated with legal changes in 1984

---

[8] Navarro, *El subdesarrollo social de España*, 36.
[9] Fraser, "Spain on the Brink," 4, 10 and 17.
[10] Navarro, *El subdesarrollo social de España*, 34–5.
[11] Ana M. Guillén, "The Politics of Universalisation: Establishing National Health Services in Southern Europe," *West European Politics* 25, no. 4 (2002), 49.

and 1986, and through a process of decentralisation that took nearly two decades to complete. Public and social investment decreased again in 1993, when PSOE lost its absolute majority in parliament, and the descent accentuated when the conservative PP won the general election in 1996.

The 1990s is also the time when the so-called Maastricht convergence criteria kicked in, setting strict limits on the ability of European Union (EU) Member States to run deficits – must not exceed 3% – and to borrow from financial markets – 60% debt-to-GDP ratio. With structurally high unemployment and an economy exposed to the ups and downs of international markets, Maastricht set limits to what was financially doable in terms of social expenditure. At the same time, however, Maastricht accelerated Spain's economic growth starting in the late 1990s.[12] Up to the financial crash of 2008, Spain complied with the convergence criteria resolutely, more resolutely than other European countries. Taking the years 2000 and 2005 as reference points, Spain ran a 1.2% deficit and a 57.8% debt ratio in 2000, with PP's José María Aznar as prime minister, and a 1.2% surplus and a 42.4% debt ratio in 2005, with PSOE's José Luis Rodríguez Zapatero. Truth be said, Rodríguez Zapatero had just arrived to power right after eight years of austere spending by PP governments. Germany's numbers were 1.6% deficit and 59.1% public debt in 2000, but 3.3% deficit and 67.3% public debt in 2005, breaching both Maastricht variables. In 2000, France had 1.3% in deficit and 58.9% debt-to-GDP, but 3.4% deficit and 67.4% public debt in 2005, exceeding the two thresholds as well.[13]

Spain had weaknesses but, contrary to the widespread myth, in 2008 the financial health of its public accounts was not one of them. Financially speaking, Spain lived within its means. However, with an economy heavily reliant on construction, Spain would discover in 2008 that it had a big problem with private debt. When the housing bubble burst, hundreds of thousands of Spaniards lost their jobs and, with it, the ability to pay back their loans. An overwhelming number of households lost their homes and fell onto negative equity with little or no expectation of finding another source of income in the foreseeable future. Many suffered for the first time the direct consequences of the structural underdevelopment of the welfare state. In the words of Del Pino, the financial crisis, and the corresponding recession and socio-economic crisis, 'demonstrated the system's limited ability to combat the growing problem of precarious work, poverty, and inequality'.[14] As a last

---

[12] Isidro López and Emmanuel Rodríguez, "The Spanish Model," *New Left Review* 69 (2011), 9.
[13] Eurostat, *Government Finance Statistics – Summary Tables. Data 1995–2019. 1/2020* (Luxembourg: Publications Office of the European Union, 2020), 46, 62 and 66.
[14] Eloísa Del Pino, "Welfare State," in Diego Muro and Ignacio Lago (eds.): *The Oxford Handbook of Spanish Politics* (Oxford: Oxford University Press, 2020), 526.

resort, Spaniards turned to one of this society's strongest suits, intergenerational solidarity. Elderly men and women shared their more or less humble pensions with their children and grandchildren, in many cases hosting them in their homes as well. The 'colchón familiar' ('family mattress') managed to prevent some households from falling into destitution.[15] But the family mattress was not squashy enough for Spain's chronic pain: The welfare state had not developed sufficiently when it needed to.

5.2 AUSTERITY AND OUTRAGE

Spain experienced steady growth for more than 10 years before the economic crisis. Progress seemed natural, caution unnecessary. As late as January 2007, Prime Minister Rodríguez Zapatero predicted that the country would 'match or overtake Germany' in per capita income by 2010.[16] Even when the sub-prime mortgage crisis had erupted in the United States, Rodríguez Zapatero still claimed that Spain played in the 'champions league of world economies'.[17] The economy had been booming thanks to construction and a housing bubble that no one appeared to see coming, or at least willing to do something about (more on this in section 5.3). Unemployment level ranged from 8% to 9% in 2007, which would be high for many advanced economies, but was historically low for Spain's standards. Banks were happy lending money and people were happy borrowing it.

And then everything collapsed. The financial crisis made investors lose confidence in the sustainability of real estate. Construction stopped and, with it, so did the rest of the economy. The popular but often politically influenced saving banks ('cajas de ahorro') were overexposed to the global financial crisis and were hit hard when developers defaulted. Unemployment went up to 14% by the end of 2008, 19% in 2009, 23% in 2011 and 26% in 2013; for those under 25, unemployment reached 56% at its peak in early 2013.[18] The effects of the crisis would soon be visible in public accounts. According to

---

[15] There are important differences between and within Southern European countries, but in general the literature describes the supporting role of family in providing resources as one of the defining features of Mediterranean welfare systems. Maurizio Ferrera, "The 'Southern Model' of Welfare in Social Europe," *Journal of European Social Policy* 6, no. 1 (1996); Martin Rhodes, "Southern European Welfare States: Identity, Problems and Prospects for Reform," *South European Society and Politics* 1, no. 3 (1996); David Natali and Furio Stamati, "Reassessing South European Pensions after the Crisis: Evidence from Two Decades of Reforms," *South European Society and Politics* 19, no. 3 (2014).

[16] La Vanguardia, "Zapatero asegura que España superará a Alemania en renta per cápita en 2010" (15 January 2007).

[17] El Mundo, "Zapatero afirma que España juega en la 'Champions League' económica," (11 September 2007).

[18] Instituto Nacional de Estadística, "Economically Active Population Survey," online scoreboard.

the prevailing narrative, Spain needed to recover the market's confidence to continue borrowing to pay for present and future spending. The markets, the EU and a number of European governments insisted the Spanish authorities and society had to tighten their belts and swallow the austerity pill.

PSOE's minority government adopted a number of decisions to reduce the deficit. In July 2010, Prime Minister Rodríguez Zapatero told parliament that he would take the measures that he deemed necessary 'whatever the cost, whatever it costs me'.[19] Among other things, the government increased the value added tax (VAT), a highly regressive decision considering that the poorest fifth of the population pays approximately three-and-half times more of their income on VAT and property transfer tax than the richest fifth.[20] The government also raised the retirement age from 65 to 67, increased workers' financial contribution to the public pension scheme, erased the automatic updating of pensions in accordance with the cost of living, introduced liberalising reforms in the labour market and announced further cuts to public spending.[21] As a result, a crisis in the financial sector became a crisis for families, who had to face the consequences while they kept losing their jobs and their homes. In summer 2011, PP and PSOE, which accumulated 90% of the seats in the lower chamber, agreed a constitutional reform to appease international investors. The new Article 135 would set in stone that the repayment of public debt would take priority over any other public expense, including, needless to say, health, housing, education, social security and other essential services. That was the second and, so far, only change ever made to the constitution since 1978.[22]

Meanwhile, something extraordinary happened in May 2011. One week before local elections, hundreds of young people gathered and camped in Puerta del Sol in Madrid and other emblematic squares around the country. They quickly grew in number and refused to vacate the public space. In an improvised camp they met and debated ideas. They did not represent any organisation, political party or ideology. They only represented themselves, and they were 'outraged', *indignados*. It is probably reasonable to say that, within the heterogeneity of the movement, two ideas were common: Austerity policies were unfair, because those who had caused the crisis were not paying the price, and the system was not democratic, because austerity

---

[19] Session's Record of Congress, Plenary ("*Diario de Sesiones del Congreso, Pleno y Diputación Permanente*"), 14 July 2010, no. 178, 20: "*Cueste lo que cueste, cueste lo que me cueste.*"

[20] Julio López Laborda, Carmen Marín González and Jorge Onrubia, *Observatorio sobre el reparto de los impuestos y las prestaciones monetarias entre los hogares españoles. Cuarto informe – 2016 y 2017* (Madrid: FEDEA, 2019), 18.

[21] Royal Decree-law 8/2010, of 20 May, to adopt extraordinary measures to reduce public deficit; Act 27/2011, of 1 August, to update, adapt and modernise the social security system.

[22] Article 12 was modified in 1992 to allow EU citizens the right to be elected in local elections, in accordance with the then new Maastricht Treaty of the EU.

was being imposed from the outside by the EU, by other governments, by the financial markets and so on. A new motto was coined in May 2011: 'They call it a democracy, but it is not so' ('Lo llaman democracia y no lo es'). This was a time of active participation, engagement and revolt around the world. Protests had erupted in Greece a year before, Tunisia kicked off the Arab Spring in December 2010, Chilean students marched to defend their right to education in June 2011 and New Yorkers occupied Wall Street in September of the same year (figure 5.1).

The *indignados* eventually broke camp and vacated the squares, but they quickly became a feature of Spanish politics. On the one hand, their horizontal organisational structure made it very hard, if not impossible, to come up with strategic or operational decisions; the outraged did not and could not speak with one voice. On the other hand, at a time when there were no jobs for more than half of the younger population, their energy could not be ignored by the institutions and by politicians of all political parties.

But the *indignados* did not run for office, not yet. In the general election of December 2011, Mariano Rajoy's PP obtained a comfortable majority. The conservatives were back in power after seven years in opposition, but the circumstances were totally different this time. Banks' financial crisis was now a sovereign debt crisis, and some countries were looking down the cliff, Spain

Figure 5.1 *Indignados* demonstrating in Puerta del Sol, Madrid, May 2011. Source: Wikimedia Commons: https://commons.wikimedia.org/wiki/File:Go_Spanish_revolution_-_Indignados.jpg

among them. The breakdown of the Euro area was a real danger; the Euro itself was at risk. The European Commission, the European Central Bank and the International Monetary Fund had approved bailout funds for Greece, Ireland and Portugal in 2010 and 2011. Italy and Spain were next in line, but unlike the other three, these two were too big to fall. If they did fall, they would be forced to leave the monetary union. European governments could not find an agreement to funnel grants or loans to the struggling economies, let alone to mutualise countries' debt. Compromises were reached at the eleventh hour. The Eurozone countries created a new international organisation, the European Stability Mechanism (ESM). Parallel to the EU, acting as an institutional firewall, the ESM was called to centralise the financial assistance to markets in need of support. Spain was one of these markets. But the help would not be free. Further austerity measures were going to be required, some of which were specified in the memorandum of understanding signed between the EU and Spain in summer 2012, through which the Spanish banking sector received 41 billion euro for its restructuring and recapitalisation.[23]

Not all the austerity policies were in black and white in the memorandum with the EU. Neither did they have to, because some of them had been adopted by Spanish authorities beforehand. With no time for negotiation between unions and business associations, within weeks of returning to power, the new conservative government decreed a very significant liberalisation of the labour market.[24] The reform reduced the compensation in case of unfair dismissal from 45 to 33 days of salary per year of work, up to a maximum of 24 months instead of 42. Less protective training or internship-type contracts were further normalised. The number of low-quality and temporary contracts increased notably after this reform. Unions lost bargaining power, and salaries remained stagnated over the course of the crisis.

Spain had established a universal and public healthcare system in the 1980s, which was funded directly by the general treasury and managed by the regional self-governing authorities. Despite all the difficulties, Spaniards have generally been proud of their healthcare system, which they see as one of the reasons why the country has a high life expectancy. However, austerity measures had a heavy toll on public healthcare. A legal reform in 2012 restricted access to healthcare for undocumented migrants,[25] a restriction that several regions refused to implement because they considered it discriminatory, as well as a public health risk. It was eventually lifted in 2018.[26] The

---

[23] European Commission, *Spain: Memorandum of Understanding on Financial-Sector Policy Conditionality* (20 July 2012).
[24] Royal Decree-law 3/2012, of 10 February, and Act 3/2012, of 6 July.
[25] Royal Decree-law 16/2012, of 20 April, of urgent measures to guarantee the sustainability of the National Health System and to improve the quality and safety of its benefits.
[26] Royal Decree-law 7/2018, of 27 July, on the universal access to the National Health System.

2012 reform also introduced user co-payment for certain services and goods, in particular in pharmaceutics, which had been free at the point of delivery before; about 400 products were removed from the list of medicines covered by the public healthcare system. Public spending on health decreased by 11.5% between 2010 and 2013,[27] all of which resulted in significant delays in waiting times, a reduction in the amount of time patients could spend with healthcare professionals, and an overall deterioration of the accessibility, affordability and general quality of healthcare.[28] Public healthcare has the potential of being the most redistributive benefit in kind,[29] but the regressive measures diminished the State's ability to reduce inequalities.

Between 1998 and 2005, the price of land increased fivefold, the price of housing by 150% and the total value of mortgages multiplied by 10.[30] None of that seemed to be a problem at the time because the economy was prosperous, and banks and middle-class families were cheerful. The circumstances changed drastically very quickly. An economy that was supposed to be made of bricks turned out to be less stable than a house of cards. More than 600,000 foreclosure procedures were initiated between 2008 and 2014, with 60,000 evictions every year on average, half of them emerging from foreclosures the other half from the rental sector.[31] Starting in 2012, the Spanish government adopted limited measures to suspend evictions of households considered 'especially vulnerable', and created a voluntary code of good practice for creditors, which included payment in kind (*datio in solutum*) to avoid negative equity, reduction of the interest rate and extension of the term of contract. Virtually all banks subscribed the code. However, with distressing images of evictions on television and social media on a daily basis, and reporting of cases of people that killed themselves under pressure, public opinion now had the banks in the spotlight, the same banks that were recipients of the 41 billion euro worth bailout from the EU. As a result of a series of condemnatory rulings from the European Court of Justice, legal changes introduced in 2013 and 2014 allowed households to defend themselves in case of foreclosure by arguing that they had been forced to accept unfair terms to secure their loans. However, the legislation did not envision a proportionality assessment of all

---

[27] Ministerio de Sanidad, Servicios Sociales e Igualdad, *Estadística de Gasto Sanitario Público 2014: Principales resultados* (Madrid: Ministerio de Sanidad, 2016), 2.

[28] Amnesty International, *Wrong Prescription: The Impact of Austerity Measures on the Right to Health in Spain* (London: Amnesty International, 2018).

[29] Luis Ayala and Olga Cantó, "Los efectos redistributivos de las prestaciones sociales y los impuestos: un estado de la cuestión," *Observatorio Social de la Caixa* (Palma: Fundación La Caixa, 2020), 10.

[30] Special rapporteur on adequate housing as a component of the right to an adequate standard of living, Miloon Kothari, *Mission to Spain*, UN doc: A/HRC/7/16/Add.2 (2008), para. 40–4.

[31] Consejo General del Poder Judicial, "Datos sobre el efecto de la crisis en los órganos judiciales: Desde 2007 hasta 2016" (12 December 2016).

evictions on a case-by-case basis; the Spanish government was criticised by international human rights bodies for the lack of coordination between courts and social services to offer adequate protection and accommodation to persons at risk of falling homeless as a result of an eviction.[32]

Underlying all this, in any case, there was a structural problem of lack of resources. As indicated earlier, Spain's social housing stock was very limited, and austerity policies only made things more complicated. General public spending on housing halved between 2009 and 2012, and housing benefits went down by about 30% over that course of time. In addition to reducing public spending on housing and social protection, in 2013 the regional and the local authorities of Madrid sold together 4,800 apartments, parking slots and storerooms to real estate investment trusts.[33] A UN committee that monitors States' compliance with international law on socio-economic rights criticised heavily that decision because the authorities had 'not convincingly explained why it was necessary to adopt (such) retrogressive measure, . . . which resulted in a reduction of the amount of social housing precisely at a time when demand for it was greater owing to the economic crisis'.[34]

While Madrid was getting rid of much of its very limited public housing stock, other regions chose a different course. Starting in 2011, Catalonia, Andalusia, the Basque Country, Navarra, the Canary Islands and other self-governing regions and nationalities adopted decrees and laws to impose temporary dispossessions of properties that were being left empty for a relatively long time. When PP was in power in the central government, between 2011 and 2018, they systematically brought these laws to the constitutional court arguing that the laws posed a threat to financial stability and to the unity of the internal market, and were therefore contrary to the 1978 constitution. In September 2018, however, the court declared that important elements of the 2015 Housing Law of the Basque Country were constitutionally admissible in light of the social function of the right to private property, proclaimed in Article 33(2) of the Spanish constitution.[35] The constitutional court thereby recognised the regions' power to establish that an empty dwelling may not meet the social function of housing when it is kept unoccupied for more than two years with no valid justification. In accordance with the legislation in place in the Basque Country and other regions, keeping a property empty can

---

[32] Committee on Economic, Social and Cultural Rights, *Concluding Observations: Spain*, UN doc: E/C.12/ESP/CO/6 (2018), para. 38.

[33] Koldo Casla, "The Rights We Live In: Protecting the Right to Housing in Spain through Fair Trial, Private and Family Life and Non-Retrogressive Measures," *International Journal of Human Rights* 20, no. 3 (2016), 288, 290 and 292.

[34] Committee on Economic, Social and Cultural Rights, *Ben Djazia v. Spain (Communication 5/2015)*, UN doc: E/C.12/61/D/5/2015 (Views of 20 June 2017), para. 17.6.

[35] Constitutional Court, Judgment 97/2018 (19 September).

be socially irresponsible. In that case, public authorities are allowed to take action that ultimately can lead to the temporary dispossession of the property to make it available for rental purposes, with the owner being entitled to fair compensation. In the spirit of greater protection of tenants' rights, the 2015 Housing Law of Catalonia,[36] reformed several times since then, imposed additional responsibilities on large-scale real estate holders, namely, corporate or private landlords that owned more than a certain number of apartments, currently 15.

Despite the austerity measures, the progressive law and policy achievements at the regional level were the direct consequence of effective lobbying and campaigning by local and community groups, particularly the stop evictions movement of the Platform of People Affected by Mortgages ('PAH, Plataforma de Afectados por las Hipotecas'). Formed in Barcelona in 2009, the PAH was an organised and housing-specific manifestation of the outrage expressed in the squares in and after May 2011. Similar initiatives were formed in relation to healthcare and education. Some of that outrage was later on funnelled through the ballot box. In early 2014, a group of lecturers in politics at the Complutense University of Madrid launched the political party Podemos ('We can') with an anti-austerity ticket. They obtained 8% of the vote in the European elections three months later. PAH's founder and most visible figure, Ada Colau, became mayor of Barcelona in 2015 as the leader of a local and diverse coalition where Podemos played a central role. As part of a broad church to the left of PSOE, Podemos obtained nearly 21% of the vote in the general election of 2015, with 69 of the 350 seats. Voter behaviour analysis by Orriols and Cordero suggests that the political crisis, more than the economic situation, explains why millions of voters switched to Podemos: it was particularly due to lack of confidence in political institutions and dissatisfaction with how democracy was working.[37] However, in November 2019, Podemos and its partners only managed to persuade 13% of the electorate and went down to 35 seats. The far-right had just arrived at the lower chamber with Vox and 15% of the vote. The far-right had been missing or hiding for more than three decades. Some would say that they were under a more presentable guise within the ranks of the conservative PP. Be that as it may, unlike France, Austria, Italy, Germany or Scandinavian countries, Spain's extreme right missed their chance to weaponise the economic crisis. Vox's emergence on the political chessboard in 2019 had more to do

---

[36] Catalan Act 24/2015, of 29 July, of urgent measures to tackle the emergency on housing and energy poverty.
[37] Lluis Orriols and Guillermo Cordero, "The Breakdown of the Spanish Two-Party System: The Upsurge of Podemos and Ciudadanos in the 2015 General Election," *South European Society and Politics* 21, no. 4 (2016), 485–6.

with the situation in Catalonia, even though Vox would quickly position itself in relation to other issues, particularly against migration, feminism and historical memory. The far-right was late and incoherent in relation to the socio-economic crisis, its causes and possible solutions. Spain's anti-austerity movement did not have all the right answers, but they framed their politics in the language of democracy and social justice, not hatred and xenophobia. Most of Spain's neighbours in Europe cannot say the same.

5.3 THE HOUSING BUBBLE AND WEALTH INEQUALITY

Spain's economy was too reliant on construction, and that is one of the primary reasons why the country fared so badly in the 2010s. Up to the crisis, Spain was a country of homeowners, but it had not always been that way. Homeownership was the goal of decades of public policies that began during the dictatorship and remained largely unquestioned when democracy was restored. There is a myth, widely spread, according to which expanding residential private property would result in greater egalitarianism in society. Spain's history since the 1950s shows this is not necessarily how things turn out to be. Despite the stubbornness about the virtues of private property as the preferable form of tenancy, shared by politicians on the left and the right and appreciated by the banks, homeownership-prone policies did not result in a fairer distribution of wealth.

'We do not want a country of proletariat, but a country of homeowners,' announced José Luis de Arrese, Spain's first housing minister, in 1959.[38] Arrese chose a clever play on words because the terms 'proletarian' and 'homeowner' rhyme in Spanish, 'proletario' and 'propietario'. In the 1950s, Spain was a country of renters. By the 2000s, Spain had become one of the European countries with the highest rates of households living in dwellings they owned. Following the same trend of other countries in the continent, the proportion of homeowners went down during the economic crisis, returning in 2019 to levels slightly below those of 1991, 76.1% and 77.8% respectively.[39] In the deepest moments of the real estate dream, around 2001, 82.2% of families were homeowners.[40]

---

[38] José Luis Arrese, "No queremos una España de proletarios, sino de propietarios," *ABC* (2 May 1959), 41–2.

[39] Instituto Nacional de Estadística, *Encuesta Continua de Hogares 2019. Nota de prensa* (2 April 2020), 5.

[40] Observatorio de Vivienda y Suelo, *Boletín especial: Alquiler residencial* (Madrid: Ministerio de Fomento, 2017), 5.

The real estate market grew at a breakneck speed in the three decades prior to the economic crisis. The price of housing doubled in real terms between 1976 and 2002,[41] and again between 2002 and 2008, entirely decoupled from the evolution of wages.[42] Between 1997 and 2004, in Europe, only Ireland experienced a housing price increase higher than Spain's.[43] After his official mission to the country, in 2008, the UN special rapporteur on adequate housing, Miloon Kothari, expressed his concerns about the affordability of housing: 'Among developed countries, Spain has experienced one of the highest increases in housing prices in recent years. During the last five years, housing prices have increased in real terms at an average annual rate of almost 10 per cent.'[44] Spain built as though there were no tomorrow. In 2005, the country built as many residential units as the UK, France and Germany together.[45] Houses were being built for the mere purpose of selling and owning them, not to live in them. In 2011, 3.68 million houses (14.6% of all) were second residences or were only used during vacation; 3.44 million (13.7%) were simply left empty.[46]

We have already pointed out that Spain has not always been a country of homeowners. More than 4 in 10 families rented their homes in 1960, a similar proportion to that of the Netherlands, France, UK or Sweden at the time, and not far from West Germany.[47] Unlike those countries, however, Spain lacked policies to ensure a minimally adequate standard of living for the working class and to advance towards a more egalitarian society. Capital accumulation of the post-War era resulted in wider inequalities of income and wealth.[48] In the 1950s, out of a confluence of interests, the real estate sector and the industrial sector jointly demanded cheap accommodation for the hundreds of thousands of internal migrants who moved from rural areas to the more

---

[41] Jorge Martínez Pagés and Luis Ángel Maza, *Análisis del precio de la vivienda en España, Documento de Trabajo no. 0307* (Madrid: Banco de España, 2003), 7.

[42] Ministerio de Fomento, *El ajuste del sector inmobiliario español* (Madrid: Ministerio de Fomento, 2012).

[43] Sebastian Dellepiane, Niamh Hardiman and Jon Las Heras, "Building on Easy Money: The Political Economy of Housing Bubbles in Ireland and Spain," *Paper Presented at the 7th ECPR General Conference* (2013).

[44] Special rapporteur on adequate housing, *Mission to Spain*, para. 14.

[45] Observatorio Estatal de la Sostenibilidad, *Cambios de ocupación del suelo en España: Implicaciones para la sostenibilidad* (Alcalá de Henares: Universidad de Alcalá de Henares, 2006), 15.

[46] Instituto Nacional de Estadística, *Censo de población y viviendas 2011. Nota de prensa* (18 April 2013).

[47] Carme Trilla, *La política de vivienda en una perspectiva europea comparada* (Barcelona: Fundación La Caixa, 2001), 58.

[48] Leandro Prados de la Escosura, "Inequality, Poverty and the Kuznets Curve in Spain, 1850–2000," *European Review of Economic History* 12, no. 3 (2008), 301.

prosperous cities.⁴⁹ Businesses' concurring interests required new policies to favour homeownership.

The privatisation of public housing was one of those policies. As mentioned earlier, with less than 2%, Spain has one of the lowest social housing rates in Europe, for 29% in the Netherlands, 24% in Austria, 17% in Sweden and 16% in France. These striking differences, however, are not simply due to the neglect of duties by Spanish authorities. In other words, it is not because Spain has not spent public resources on housing; it is because of the way those resources, as limited as they were, have been spent. In fact, Spain's government reports that of all the houses built between 1951 and 2015, more than a third (6.3 million, 36.8%, to be more precise) were or had been at some point 'protected housing units' ('viviendas protegidas').⁵⁰ In administrative parlance, protected housing means that property developers received financial incentives to sell them at a more affordable price to first buyers, keeping the price fixed and relatively low for a limited period of time. Spain's peculiar public housing model, created during the dictatorship and retained in the democratic era, was defined by two unique features. Firstly, in most cases people enjoyed the legal title of leasehold property over their homes; not in the form of long-term rental tenure, but as nearly full property rights, only limited *for some time* by the impossibility of transferring the property for more than a set price. And that was indeed the second abnormal feature: The set price of these privately owned but publicly protected housing units was automatically lifted after a few years, when the house could be sold and purchased freely.⁵¹ This in effect meant that developers could sell a house or an apartment to a buyer who could have the reasonable expectation of selling it at a free price sometime later. Only a small number of the protected housing units, built with a public or social purpose and with an affordable price, remain social and publicly owned. Government's data shows that, between 1981 and 2019, more than 2.36 million protected houses were completed, which equates to 21.6% of all houses built in that time. However, in 2019 the total social housing stock was only 290,000 units, three-fifths of which were owned by regional governments and the other two-fifths by local authorities.⁵² Developers of social or publicly protected homes could be public or private companies, and in the latter case they could be charities, or they could

---

⁴⁹ Aitana Alguacil et al., *La vivienda en España en el siglo XXI: Diagnóstico del modelo residencial y propuestas para otra política de vivienda* (Madrid: Foessa, 2013), 11.
⁵⁰ Dirección General de Arquitectura, Vivienda y Suelo, *Agenda Urbana Española 2019* (Madrid: Ministerio de Fomento, 2018), 33.
⁵¹ Joris Hoekstra, Iñaki Heras Saizarbitoria and Aitziber Etxezarreta Etxarri, "Recent Changes in Spanish Housing Policies: Subsidized Owner-Occupancy Dwellings as a New Tenure Sector?," *Journal of Housing and the Built Environment* 25, no. 1 (2010).
⁵² Ministerio de Transportes, Movilidad y Agenda Urbana, *Observatorio de Vivienda y Suelo. Boletín especial vivienda social 2020* (Madrid: Ministerio de Transporte, Movilidad y Agenda Urbana, 2020), 4–5.

act for profit. Often these residential units were built on publicly owned land, resulting in an even coarser manifestation of the denationalisation of public resources. Property developers were financially compensated by the State for the construction and sale of housing that was affordable at first but was bound to become less so in time. For more than a century, Spain's public housing construction strategy resulted in the progressive privatisation of a resource that otherwise could have served a public purpose, namely, the purpose of satisfying the right to adequate housing of those who could not afford it on their own in the private sector.

Alongside the peculiar public housing model, the regulatory framework of the residential rental sector was the second policy instrument that contributed significantly to the general shift towards the homeownership paradigm. The 1964 Urban Rental Act established the principle of the indefinite nature of lease contracts and allowed closest relatives – children, mostly – to inherit the tenancy in the same conditions enjoyed by tenants. Rent increases were practically impossible, which meant that the passing of time and inflation made rents obsolete. This very protectionist legislation demotivated landlords from making their properties available in the rental market. PSOE's government moved to the opposite end of the policy spectrum with a liberalising reform in 1985. The new law put an end to the automatic renewal of leases, giving landlords and tenants nearly absolute freedom to set the conditions of their contractual relationship. In many cases, tenants were left unprotected vis-à-vis the generally more powerful other side. A new reform was introduced in 1994, tempering some of the defencelessness in which tenants found themselves. In particular, it established a general five-year-long rule, mandatory for the landlord, but with an exit clause for the tenant. This five-year term, as well as court deadlines for evictions, would be shortened during the economic crisis in 2011 and 2013, diminishing security of tenure.[53] Before the crisis, the 2005–2008 Housing Plan, adopted by PSOE's government with José Luis Rodríguez Zapatero as prime minister, tried to give a boost to the rental sector. But there was very little time for the plan to unfold before the financial crash and the beginning of the economic crisis.

Like other European countries, Spain's housing rental sector has walked towards greater deregulation, resulting in the progressive shrinking of the sector. Including Spain, four of the five European countries that most decisively bet for deregulation in the last decades of the twentieth century experienced a significant diminution of this form of tenancy until around 2012. The other three countries were Norway, Denmark and Finland. Of the five, England

---

[53] This tendency would be reversed in 2019 with a reform that was much more protective of tenants' interests: Royal Decree-law 7/2019, of 1 March, of urgent measures on housing and renting.

was the only jurisdiction where renting remained an option for a significant number of people, due to the general unaffordability of housing in London.[54]

Public authorities' disinterest for the rental sector was also reflected in fiscal policies. In addition to a lower VAT for the purchase of apartments in new buildings, between 1978 and 2013 there was a tax deduction in place intended to boost the homeownership market. In 2010, this deduction figured in nearly seven million income tax statements – 38% of all – and was approximately equal to 10% of all the money collected through income tax.[55] The tax deduction for purchasing a new residential property that would be used as primary residence disappeared in 2013. This had been part of the 2012 memorandum of understanding between the European Commission and the Spanish government, which made clear, among other things, that Spain had to take measures to 'ensure less tax-induced bias towards indebtedness and home-ownership'.[56] If we consider the money the State did not collect due to tax deductions – leaving tax evasion and avoidance out – the extent of the public policy support for homeownership becomes overwhelming. For example, if the mentioned tax deduction had not been in place in 2008, the central government would have collected 3.33 billion euro extra; as a point of comparison, the central government's 2013–2016 Housing Plan was allocated 2.42 billion euro.[57] In other words, the amount of money that the central government did not collect from new homeowners in the year when the housing bubble burst was approximately 37% more than what the government expected to spend on housing rehabilitation and rental support over four years during the peak of mortgage and rental evictions. Tax deductions increased households' ability to borrow, and it has been estimated that they could explain about one-third of the significant growth in the price of housing in the 2000s.[58] Research has also shown that tax deductions appreciably enlarged income and wealth inequalities.[59] For decades, Spain's housing policy was actually a sort of tax policy and a policy to keep the economy rolling, but it definitely was not a social policy.

We have discussed the privatisation of public housing, the deregulation of the rental housing sector and the generosity of the tax system with

---

[54] Christine Whitehead et al., *The Private Rented Sector in the New Century: A Comparative Approach* (Cambridge: University of Cambridge, 2012), 67.
[55] Amadeo de Fuenmayor Fernández and Rafael Granell Pérez, "Evaluación de la desgravación fiscal a la adquisición de vivienda," *Presupuesto y Gasto Público* 59 (2010), 173.
[56] European Commission, *Spain: Memorandum of Understanding*, para. 31.
[57] Statistics of income tax statements since 2003; Central Government's Housing Plan 2013–16 (Royal Decree 233/2013, of 5 April).
[58] Cinco Días, "Los incentivos fiscales inflaron más de un 30% el precio de las casas" (16 March 2016).
[59] Magdalena Rodríguez Coma, "Incidencia distributiva de la política de gasto en vivienda en el IRPF 2006," *Papeles de Trabajo del Instituto de Estudios Fiscales* 59 (2010).

homeowners. Apart from these three, the availability of mortgage loans was the fourth key driver of the big private over-indebtedness of the economic crisis 2008 onwards. The economic and monetary union converged interest rates within the EU, which benefited investors, including those investing in housing, who saw how interest rates declined five- or sixfold in the 2000s compared to the 1980s. One could conceivably argue that the tax deductions mentioned earlier were helpful in allowing middle-class households to access the homeownership market when interest rates were so high and voluble. However, these deductions lost any justifiable sense when the EU's economic and monetary union was set in place in the 1990s. And yet, they lasted until 2013. The economic and monetary union contributed to make the country's finance sector look stable, which in turn helped to make mortgage loans widely available and rather flexible. Before the crash, both the demand and the supply of these loans were considered low-risk operations in a context of economic growth, manageable unemployment and ever-growing housing prices. In the early 2000s, investing in housing appeared to make sense financially speaking, even when the investment was often intended for pure speculative purposes, not to actually live in the premises. The radical change in the perception of risk followed the dire economic and labour prospects after 2008, in turn becoming a self-fulfilling prophecy. But by then not all investors had the same tools to face the new crisis situation. Already in 2002, the official but independent Economic and Social Council spoke of a 'crisis of accessibility', warning that those who were not homeowners, particularly younger people, were being forced to devote a large share of their income to housing costs, reducing their ability to save, invest or consume essentials; often they needed to incur in further debt, putting them at risk of poverty.[60] In 2010, the Bank of Spain documented that the number of households with private debts above 75% of their assets rose from 11.1% to 14.8% between 2005 and 2008, and the most concerning forms of over-indebtedness affected particularly younger families and families with one or more members unemployed.[61]

One might think, and it is widely assumed, that increasing the number of homeowners is an effective way of reducing inequalities in wealth distribution. Spain's recent history shows that, at least for this country, this has not been the case. Due to the out-of-control pace at which prices went up in the decade prior to the crash, cheaper loans and tax deductions did not translate into more affordable housing for lower income households. Those who

---

[60] Consejo Económico y Social, *La emancipación de los jóvenes y la situación de la vivienda en España* (Madrid: CES, 2002), 57 and 72.
[61] Banco de España, *Encuesta Financiera de las Familias 2008: Métodos, Resultados y Cambios desde 2005* (Madrid: BDE, 2010), 57.

accessed homeownership in the 2000s subscribed long-term loans backed by mortgages over their newly acquired properties. The banking crisis, the economic slump, the massive job losses and austerity-driven policies led to thousands of evictions, on average 60,000 every year of the economic crisis. In the early 2010s, most of these evictions were the result of foreclosures; after 2014 to 2015, the number of evictions due to the lack of payment of a lease became higher than the number of mortgage-related evictions. Each eviction had its own personal and family story of pain and sorrow. In the case of foreclosures, evictions were also accompanied by the loss of many families' only wealth asset. Between 2008 and 2014, households' median wealth fell by 37%.[62]

Until the financial crash, wealth concentration had remained more or less stable since the mid-1980s. The country's economy grew notably due to construction and real estate investment. Between 1982 and 2005, average wealth per household grew twice as much as the average income, 315% for 160% respectively. Real estate accounts for four-fifths of that growth, and rising prices of housing and land explain the increase in the average family wealth. Even the wealthiest in society invested heavily on real estate: 60% of the wealth of the bottom half of the top 1% – namely, the second richest family every 200 – was in construction.[63] Research carried out under the World Inequality Database estimates that 85% of Spain's capital gains between 1950 and 2010 were linked to housing.[64] Over a long period of time, and since homeownership began to be actively promoted as a public policy in the 1950s, Spain's wealth concentration was based on capital gains derived from blind faith on the unlimited growth of real estate value.

Wealth inequalities have risen in Spain as they have in all other advanced economies since the 1980s. According to the World Inequality Report of the Paris School of Economics, in the middle of the economic crisis, in 2013, Spain's wealthiest decile accumulated 57% of the country's wealth, while the bottom half owned less than 7%. The concentration of wealth in the three decades prior to the crash was the result of a number of causes, including the construction and purchase of second and third residences, an estimated 146 billion euro worth investments in tax havens, and the relative ease with which the wealthy diversify their assets to maximise their benefits.[65] Upper

---

[62] Banco de España, *Encuesta Financiera de las Familias 2014: Métodos, Resultados y Cambios desde 2011* (Madrid: BDE, 2017), 6–7.
[63] Facundo Alvaredo and Emmanuel Sáez, "Income and Wealth Concentration in Spain from a Historical and Fiscal Perspective," *Journal of European Economic Association* 7, no. 5 (2010), 1156–7.
[64] Miguel Artola Blanco et al., "Wealth in Spain, 1900–2014: A Country of Two Lands," *WID.world Working Paper Series*, no. 5 (2018), 4.
[65] World Inequality Lab, *World Inequality Report 2018* (Paris: Paris School of Economics, 2017), 230.

and middle classes, as well as working-class families trying to climb up the ladder, invested unwaveringly on private property when the economy was doing well. When it stopped going well, the wind of the financial meltdown did not blow away all those investments equally. The Bank of Spain's data shows that wealth inequality kept going up during the economic crisis. The amount of wealth of the richest decile was 16 times greater than that of the poorest half in 2002 (642,000/40,000 euro), but the ratio increased to 21 times in 2011 (1,268,600/61,500 euro), and 38 times in 2017 (1,354,400/35,700 euro).[66] In other words, the wealth gap between the top 10% and the bottom 50% more than doubled in 15 years; half of those years were spent in a dream made of bricks and the other half in a demolition site with broken bricks around.

Drafters of the 1978 constitution declared in Article 47 that 'all Spaniards are entitled to enjoy decent and adequate housing', and that 'public authorities shall promote the conditions and shall establish appropriate standards in order to make this right effective'.[67] However, the pledge is yet to be fulfilled, and generally speaking the policies implemented in the past four decades did not cruise in that direction. Instead, public resources were used to support homeowners as a State policy at least since the 1950s. With the privatisation of public housing, subsidies for property developers, deregulation of the rental sector and tax deductions, public authorities treated housing as a real estate investment asset, not as an essential good to ensure the right to adequate housing. The price was paid by young people and low-income families struggling to find suitable and affordable accommodation in the private sector.

5.4 THE GENERAL FAILURE OF REGIONAL MINIMUM INCOME SCHEMES

A sixteenth-century Spanish humanist, Juan Luis Vives, played a critical role in the conception of social assistance as a public duty. In *De Subventione pauperum*, published in 1526, Vives argued that the social salvation of the poor was more important than the spiritual salvation of the rich, and that non-religious public institutions ought to be in charge of poverty alleviation.

---

[66] Banco de España, *Encuesta Financiera de las Familias 2017: Métodos, Resultados y Cambios desde 2014* (Madrid: BDE, 2020), 8; Banco de España, *Encuesta Financiera de las Familias: Descripción, Métodos y Resultados Preliminares* (Madrid: BDE, 2004), 67.

[67] "*Todos los españoles tienen derecho a disfrutar de una vivienda digna y adecuada. Los poderes públicos promoverán las condiciones necesarias y establecerán las normas pertinentes para hacer efectivo este derecho, regulando la utilización del suelo de acuerdo con el interés general para impedir la especulación.*"

Hitherto, wherever it existed at all, poor relief had been a matter of beneficence. Vives's writing inspired a whole range of welfare interventions managed by local authorities in what we now know as Germany, Belgium, Switzerland, the Netherlands and France. Over time, these initiatives would go national with so-called poor laws all over Europe.[68]

Vives spent most of his adult live in Flanders and the Netherlands, but he was born and grew up in Valencia. There is a saying in Spain, borrowed from the Bible (Luke 4:24): 'No prophet is accepted in his own country.' And the saying applies to Vives seamlessly. His vision was one of the earliest precursors of twentieth century welfare state. His impact was visible and credited all over Western Europe, but it was meagre in Spain. A number of factors contributed to prevent the emergence and expansion of public social protection: Historic reliance on charity managed by the Catholic Church, late capitalist development in the nineteenth century, Francoism and the illegalisation of unions during the dictatorship in the twentieth century, and so on.

Social assistance is a central component of a strong welfare state. By social assistance I mean specifically non-contributory cash transfers to households outside other social insurance schemes – pensions, including the non-contributory one; unemployment benefits; disability benefits and so on – particularly when those or other sources of income, from capital or labour, are insufficient to cover basic needs. In other words, I am talking about minimum income schemes, the last resort to alleviate the worst forms of poverty. The way the European Committee of Social Rights defines it, social assistance is the collection of 'benefits for which individual need is the main criterion for eligibility, without any requirement of affiliation to a social security scheme aimed to cover a particular risk, or any requirement of professional activity or payment of contributions'.[69]

Other Western European countries set up minimum income schemes in the 1950s, 1960s or 1970s, but Spain did not. And the return of democracy did not make a big enough difference. All European countries have one form or another of minimum income scheme; the last two to set up their own were Greece and Italy, in 2017 and 2018 respectively.[70] As I proceed to show, the redistributive capacity of Spain's *programmes* is very limited. And we are talking about *programmes*, plural, because Spain has a

---

[68] H. C. M. Michielse and Robert van Krieken, "Policing the Poor: J. L. Vives and the Sixteenth-Century Origins of Modern Social Administration," *Social Service Review* 64, no. 1 (1990), 2.
[69] European Committee of Social Rights, *Digest of Case Law* (Strasbourg: Council of Europe, 2018), 143.
[70] Hugh Frazer and Eric Marlier, *Minimum Income Schemes in Europe: A study of national policies 2015* (Brussels: European Commission, 2016); Manos Matsaganis, "Safety Nets in (the) Crisis: The Case of Greece in the 2010s," *Social Policy Administration* 54, no. 4 (2020); Matteo Jessoula and Marcello Natili, "Explaining Italian 'Exceptionalism' and Its End: Minimum Income from Neglect to Hyper-Politicization," *Social Policy Administration* 54, no. 4 (2020).

regionally fragmented system of social assistance, utterly insufficient, and with enormous differences between regions in terms of coverage, adequacy and conditionality.

The 1978 constitution established that social security should be maintained 'for all citizens (to) guarantee adequate social assistance and benefits in situations of hardship'.[71] Social security had been central to the Moncloa pacts of 1977 between the governing party and opposition, as well as unions and business representatives. In the middle of a global oil crisis and in parallel to the constitutional drafting process, unions swallowed the pill of austerity in the form of structural reforms. They signed off on wage rise ceilings 8 to 10 points below the rocketing inflation rate, which bordered 30%, and accepted that employers would have more leeway to lay off their staff. In addition to that, the Moncloa pacts settled that a new social security system would include national healthcare – later separated from social security in the 1980s – public pensions and unemployment benefits. Both the Moncloa pacts and the constitution envisioned that the implementation of social security could be decentralised, but the constitution also made clear that it would be financed centrally.[72]

Over time, the new democratic regime developed a social security system with public pensions, including non-contributory pensions, unemployment protection and other economic benefits for those temporarily unable to work for different reasons. But with hundreds of thousands of workers in long-term unemployment or in precarious jobs, too many people were being left behind or simply excluded from the system. A complementary non-contributory mechanism was necessary to respond to the urgent needs of people in poverty, too often ignored by the labour market. The constitution simply stated that the regions and nationalities would set up complementary social assistance schemes.[73] All of them assumed such responsibility in their respective statutes of self-government in the 1980s. Inspired by the French *revenue minimum d'insertion* of 1988, the Basque social assistance scheme was set up in 1989, followed by all other Spanish regions by 1995.

Comparative research from different countries shows that social assistance and minimum income schemes tend to have a positive impact on consumption, which in turn results in wider benefits for the local economy. Given the

---

[71] Article 41: "*Los poderes públicos mantendrán un régimen público de Seguridad Social para todos los ciudadanos que garantice la asistencia y prestaciones sociales suficientes ante situaciones de necesidad, especialmente en caso de desempleo. La asistencia y prestaciones complementarias serán libres.*"

[72] Article 149(1)(17): "*El Estado tiene competencia exclusiva sobre las siguientes materias: . . . Legislación básica y régimen económico de la Seguridad Social, sin perjuicio de la ejecución de sus servicios por las Comunidades Autónomas.*"

[73] Article 148(1)(20): "*Las Comunidades Autónomas podrán asumir competencias en las siguientes materias: . . . Asistencia social.*"

limited amounts and recipients' urgent needs, money transferred via minimum income schemes is money that is spent immediately, not invested or saved for the future. Economic benefits do trickle down creating new opportunities for businesses, for job creation and for tax collection.[74]

Between 1977 and 1980, Spain signed and ratified a number of international human rights treaties that had been ignored during the dictatorship. This includes two treaties by which the State committed to develop policies to fulfil the human right to social security, including social assistance. These are the International Covenant on Economic, Social and Cultural Rights, which recognised the right to social security in Article 9, and the European Social Charter, in Articles 12 and 13. Compliance with this charter is overseen by the European Committee of Social Rights. Based on the purpose of the norm and decades-long continuous assessment of policies across the continent, this independent body under the umbrella of the Council of Europe, which is different from the EU, has established a few criteria to determine the adequacy of social assistance: (a) The individual need must be the main criterion for eligibility, with no other requirements of affiliation or professional activity, although it is possible to require that the beneficiary receives training or seeks employment opportunities. (b) It must be an individual right supported by an appeal mechanism. (c) The right must have a universal scope, and the entitlement must be determined purely by the existence of need. (d) The adequacy of the amount depends on the composition and size of the family, but as a general principle the benefit should not go below 50% of the median income, a standard often used to draw the relative poverty line – sometimes set at 40% or at 60% of median income. (e) The assistance must not be time-limited, and it must be provided for as long as the need exists. (f) Sanctions that result in the suspension or reduction of the benefit are only acceptable as long as the recipient is not deprived of the means of subsistence, and always provided there is a justification for it and an appeal mechanism in place.[75] If we take this committee's analysis as an authoritative interpretation, as shown next, it is clear that the Spanish model of social assistance is far from meeting the human right to social security, which includes social assistance.

In the opinion of the independent authority for fiscal responsibility (AIREF), created in 2013 in application of the memorandum of understanding between Spain and the EU, minimum income schemes are potentially a key policy instrument to protect against poverty, but due to their fragmentation

---

[74] Nicholas Mathers and Rachel Slater, *Social Protection and Growth: Research Synthesis* (Canberra: Department of Foreign Affairs and Trade Australian Government, 2014); Naila Kabeer and Hugh Waddington, "Economic Impacts of Conditional Cash Transfer Programmes: A Systematic Review and Meta-Analysis," *Journal of Development Effectiveness* 7, no. 3 (2015).

[75] María Dalli, "The Content and Potential of the Right to Social Assistance in Light of Article 13 of the European Social Charter," *European Journal of Social Security* 22, no. 1 (2020), 10–13.

and generally low amounts of the social benefits, too many people remain inadequately covered or not covered at all.[76] The number of recipients went up from one to three million between 2007 and 2016, but this number is partly misleading due to its uneven territorial distribution. The three regions that already had the highest coverage in 2007 – the Basque Country, Asturias and Navarra – are the very same ones that increased the coverage the most in the following decade: 5.2% more households in Navarra, 4.1% more in the Basque Country and 3.3% in Asturias. Catalonia, and the more impoverished Andalusia and Castilla-La Mancha experienced the smallest growths, with less than 1%.[77] Furthermore, within this period there were two moments when progress stopped or even reversed. The second one was in 2015, precisely when progressive forces and unions started to consider more seriously the possibilities of a central scheme of social assistance for the whole of Spain, which would see the light in June 2020 (discussed in the next section). The first stop, indeed retrogression, happened at the peak of the economic crisis, in 2011 to 2012. At a time of rocketing redundancies and diminishing unemployment benefits, regional authorities followed the austerity agenda and introduced legal changes imposing more sanctions and making accessibility of benefits contingent upon a stricter set of requirements.[78] During the years of crisis, several regions – Basque Country, Navarra, Murcia, Catalonia, La Rioja and Madrid – made access more difficult by hardening the residency requirement to request the benefit, and a number of them – Valencia, Cantabria and Catalonia, among others – introduced benefit cuts of more than 5%.[79] Furthermore, the cuts were being applied on benefits that were, with the exception of Navarra and the Basque Country, 'manifestly insufficient', to echo the conclusion of the European Committee of Social Rights in 2014.[80] Spain's Ministry of Health acknowledged in 2013 that the minimum income schemes did not reach far enough to cover the minimum needs of at least two-thirds of the more than 700,000 families that had no income whatsoever.[81]

The different regional schemes vary substantially in terms of coverage, adequacy and governmental effort. For example, Madrid and the Basque Country are two of the richest regions, with similar levels of GDP per capita.

---

[76] AIREF, *Los programas de rentas mínimas en España* (Madrid: AIREF, 2019), 82–94 and 98.
[77] Manuel Aguilar Hendrickson and Ana Arriba González de Durana, "Crisis económica y transformaciones de la política de garantía de ingresos mínimos para la población activa," *Panorama Social* 29 (2019), 95–6.
[78] Casla, "The Rights We Live In," 292–3.
[79] Noemi Bergantiños, Raquel Font and Amaia Bacigalupe, "Las rentas mínimas de inserción en época de crisis. ¿Existen diferencias en la respuesta de las comunidades autónomas?," *Papers: Revista de Sociología* 102, no. 3 (2017), 415.
[80] European Committee of Social Rights, *Conclusions XX-2: Spain* (2014), 26.
[81] Ministerio de Sanidad, Servicios Sociales e Igualdad, *El Sistema Público de Servicios Sociales: Informe de Rentas Mínimas de Inserción – Año 2012* (Madrid: Ministerio de Sanidad, 2013), 45.

The Basque Country has one-third of Madrid's population and half the level of poverty: 6.4% of the population in the Basque Country, 12.3% in Madrid, are below 40% of the median equivalised disposable income. Yet, the Basque scheme reaches 2.3 times more people and public expenditure is 2.6 times greater. With just over 8% of the country's population, nearly 38% of recipients of a regional minimum income live in the Basque Country, Navarra or Asturias, and the three regions accumulate 43% of all of Spain's public spending on minimum income. For example, despite having a similar population in terms of size, for every household receiving a minimum income in Castilla-La Mancha, 18 people receive it in the Basque Country, where the benefit is between 25% and 50% higher depending on the family size. If we use a single benchmark for the whole of Spain, the Basque programme covers 88% of those in greatest need, for 23% in the case of Madrid. With the exception of Navarra, La Rioja and the Basque Country, the vast majority of regions leave out at least half of the population meeting the objective criteria, that is, people who theoretically are entitled to this form of social assistance. Almost 8 in 10 people in Spain are unable to get the economic support they need.[82]

In light of all this, in 2018 the European Committee of Social Rights reiterated the conclusions of their previous report and found Spain in non-conformity with the European Social Charter on the grounds of the excessively burdensome requirements of length of residence in the region, the arbitrary age restrictions, the time limit of the benefit in a number of regions and the general inadequacy of the amounts.[83] In a nutshell, as observed by research from the International Monetary Fund, Spain's minimum income schemes fail to reduce the risk of poverty, inequality and social exclusion due to a series of bureaucratic hurdles and big gaps in terms of adequacy and coverage.[84]

Addressing these gaps would certainly be no small challenge for any progressive party, let alone for the first ever coalition government since 1936.

---

[82] All the data of this paragraph is from 2018. Adrián Hernández, Fidel Picos and Sara Riscado, "Moving towards Fairer Regional Minimum Income Schemes in Spain," *JRC Working Papers on Taxation and Structural Reforms* (Brussels: European Commission, 2020), 12.

[83] European Committee of Social Rights, *Conclusions XXI-2: Czech Republic, Denmark, Germany, Poland, Spain, UK* (2018), 147.

[84] Svetlana Vtyurina, "Effectiveness and Equity in Social Spending – The Case of Spain," *Working Paper 20/16* (Washington, DC: IMF, 2020), 21.

5.5 GOVERNING IN TIMES OF CORONAVIRUS, AND AFTERWARDS

In January 2020, PSOE and United Podemos finally managed to join forces in government. United Podemos includes Podemos, United Left – a coalition in its own right, where the Communist Party remains predominant – and sister parties of the two in Catalonia and Galicia. The previous year had seen two general elections because PSOE and United Podemos had failed to agree, not so much about policy, but about the distribution of ministries between them. Between the two polling days, seven months apart, PSOE and United Podemos lost 10 seats and 1.3 million votes overall. Meanwhile, the far-right Vox rocketed to third place with 3.6 million votes and 52 deputies. Around Christmas time of 2019, the left and the centre-left still did not trust each other but the circumstances had changed drastically. Virtually inexistent one or two years before, extreme right populism was suddenly surfing the wave of widespread frustration with the political situation in Catalonia. A number of people outside Catalonia thought that the Spanish government had been too lenient with the pro-independence process, and the criticism was directed towards the two main parties and their prime ministers, Mariano Rajoy (PP) and Pedro Sánchez (PSOE), before and after June 2018.

PSOE and United Podemos spoke harshly of each other in summer 2019, as they had done many times before, particularly when the two parties competed for the same electorate in 2015 to 2016 and again in 2019. But after the November 2019 election, the fear of the potential outcome of a hypothetical third snap election was greater than their reciprocal apprehension. They bit the bullet and swiftly agreed a programme for a new coalition government. There had been several regional coalitions before, but this was the first experiment in central government.

PSOE and United Podemos pledged to implement a series of socio-economic reforms with a progressive agenda to increase public spending and to reverse austerity. Much of the discussion dealt with the extent of a potential reversal of the liberalisation of the labour market implemented by Mariano Rajoy in January 2012; United Podemos wanted to scrap it entirely, PSOE wanted another reform instead.[85] One other point of contention was the regulation of housing. United Podemos wanted to emulate policies that had been tested in some regions since 2013, including sanctions to homeowners that keep houses empty, a mechanism to cap rent increases, and stricter regulation of corporate landlords; PSOE preferred stimulating the private rental sector with tax deductions, promoting affordable housing through financial

---

[85] Iñigo Aduriz and Laura Olías, "Iglesias dice que la derogación de la reforma laboral debe ser total como se firmó con Bildu después de que el PSOE limitase su alcance," *eldiario.es* (20 May 2020).

incentives for promoters, and encouraging greater coordination between courts and social services when dealing with evictions.[86]

Internal disagreement aside, the coalition would need to fight every vote in parliament, where the executive was 21 seats short of an absolute majority. That, plus the demands of the financial markets, the EU rules and businesses' interests, meant that it was bound to be extremely difficult to fulfil their promises.

Spain did have a significant margin for improvement in terms of social protection. Despite being the fourth largest economy of the EU, in 2019 Spain spent on social protection less than the EU average, 17.4% of its GDP for 19.3%. The gap was also noticeable when we look at the number of people at risk of poverty: 20.7% in the case of Spain, 16.5% for the EU. Other than pensions, social transfers – social protection, health and education – had a much more limited impact on poverty reduction: 23.05% in Spain, 32.38% in the EU. Income inequality was also higher than the European average: the difference in income between the top fifth and the bottom fifth was 5.94, for 4.99 in the EU's average.[87]

Part of the problem is structural and rooted in history, as we saw earlier in this chapter, but part of it is simply that the tax revenue is not high enough and that the tax pressure is not fairly distributed. The tax-to-GDP ratio was 35.4% in 2018, five and six points lower than in the EU and the Euro area respectively (40.3% and 41.7%); in fact, the tax revenue decreased two points in Spain during the economic crisis of the 2010s, while it went up slightly in the EU.[88] The redistributive effect of household taxation is also much lower: Spain's ability to reduce the income gap between the richest and the poorest fifths of the population is approximately one-third of that of other EU countries on average.[89] In fact, most of the redistribution of income comes from public pensions, not from taxes. Considering the design of direct and indirect taxes as well as unemployment benefits, tax deductions and public pensions, the bottom 20% of the population are net losers while the top 40% are the ones who benefit the most out of it.[90] According to OECD data from 2014, Spain's poorest 20% should receive twice as much in cash transfers just to keep the system even in relation to the rest of the population.[91] In other

---

[86] Aitor Riveiro, "Las negociaciones por la ley de vivienda revelan profundas diferencias entre el PSOE y Unidas Podemos," *eldiario.es* (2 February 2021).
[87] Eurostat, Social scoreboard of indicators (data from 2019).
[88] Eurostat, "Taxation in 2018: Tax-to-GDP ratio up to 40.3% in EU," press release (30 October 2019).
[89] European Commission, *Country Report Spain 2019* (2019), 32.
[90] Laborda, Marín González and Onrubia, *Observatorio sobre el reparto de los impuestos y las prestaciones monetarias entre los hogares españoles*, 4–5.
[91] Orsetta Causa and Mikkel Hermansen, "Income Redistribution through Taxes and Transfers across OECD Countries," *Economics Department Working Papers no. 1453* (Paris: OECD, 2017), 18.

words, it is not only that most people in poverty and at risk of poverty are not adequately covered by the regional public assistance schemes (section 5.4); it is also that they are actually net contributors, not net recipients, if we take both taxes and cash transfers into account.

The coalition between PSOE and United Podemos raised high expectations among those who believe the State should play a greater role in addressing material inequalities. I think it is fair to say that many progressive people were hopeful, even if not necessarily optimistic about what the new coalition could achieve. There was much room for upgrading in social investment after decades of structural underdevelopment, accentuated by the austerity policies of the 2010s. At the same time, however, the government was fragile, and they would need to operate within a set of institutional, financial and political constraints.

And then, weeks after their arrival to government, a lethal coronavirus spread quickly from China to the rest of the world. A state of alarm was declared in mid-March and was in force for months. Covid-19 killed tens of thousands of people and tested the resilience of the public health system and care homes like nothing else in living memory. Besides the epidemiological contagion, it quickly became clear that the virus was also going to have significant effects in terms of public debt, employment and the socio-economic conditions of particularly vulnerable people. In this context, with three months in office PSOE and United Podemos pushed forward a policy that had been in the government's programme but probably was not intended to be put in place so quickly. Starting in June 2020, Spain implemented a *national* or central 'minimum vital income' scheme that would complement the regional ones. It was meant to ensure a basic floor – between 469 and 1,033 euro in 2021, depending on the size and composition of the household – on top of which the regional authorities could provide additional benefits.[92] With one in four children living in households below 60% of the country's median income, Spain has the dishonour of having one of the highest child poverty rates in the EU.[93] Far from being a revolutionary measure, social assistance schemes exist in other European countries, and in fact Spain's regions have had them since the 1990s, albeit not always with satisfactory result, as shown in section 5.4. Provided it was set up as complementary to existing regional programmes, a centrally managed minimum income scheme had the potential of helping out many people and alleviating the most severe forms of poverty and social exclusion.

At the point of writing, approximately one year after its implementation, the minimum income scheme has fallen way short of expectations. The

---

[92] Royal Decree-law 20/2020, of 29 May, to establish the minimum vital income.
[93] Eurostat, Children at risk of poverty or social exclusion (data extracted in 2020).

administration only dealt with 34% of the nearly one million applications received between June and October 2020, approving 14% and rejecting the other 20%.[94] By the end of 2020, only 460,000 people were beneficiaries,[95] still far from the one- to two-and-half million that had been initially estimated. According to Oxfam, in June 2021, more than 1.5 million people living in poverty did not have access to the minimum income scheme, with nearly 600,000 households with no reliable income at all.[96] Numbers aside, a number of issues remained unclear and were concerning. For example, the coverage was rather arbitrarily limited to people between 23 and 65 years of age. Considering that most disadvantaged families find themselves at the lower end of the digital divide, many did not have the means to claim the benefit online without assistance face to face at the local level. It also remains to be seen what effects the central scheme will have on regional programmes, as some regional authorities might feel tempted to ignore the constitution and simply defund their benefits altogether letting the central government assume the cost instead. Needless to say, should that happen, it would result in little or no gain for people that need the State's support the most.

We shall see if and how these and other questions are answered, and what impact the minimum vital income has in the mid- and long-term. When the initiative was debated in parliament in the middle of the pandemic in June 2020, the right-wing PP voted in favour and even the far-right Vox abstained. They did this despite having publicly spoken against the scheme with hyperbolic allusions to the nanny-State and referring to this new social entitlement as 'little pocket money' ('la paguita'). No deputy voted against it. After a long decade of austerity policies, the initiative was a victory for the left, possibly the most significant victory since equal marriage (2005), the Social Care Act (2006) and the Historical Memory Act (2007). But, as well as a victory, it was also the expression of a huge policy and political failure. As we have seen, the regions and nationalities had had the power and the responsibility to protect the most vulnerable for more than three decades. However, by and large they failed to do so.

This does not mean, to put it in simple terms, that federalism or decentralisation are bad for the welfare state. First of all, while one should never be complacent when talking about structural poverty, some regions have provided a relatively adequate response. It is the case of the Basque Country and Navarra, and to a lesser extent Asturias. The inadequate regional minimum

---

[94] María Zuil, "El IMV sigue sin llegar a los hogares: solo lo recibe un 6% del millón que lo ha pedido," *El Confidencial* (21 October 2020).

[95] Cinco Días, "Los 460.000 beneficiarios del ingreso mínimo estarán obligados a presentar declaración del IRPF" (24 March 2021).

[96] Oxfam Intermón, *Armando el Puzle: Avanzando hacia el sistema de garantía de rentas que deberíamos tener* (June 2021).

income schemes do not represent the failure of federalism, but the failure of the State in responding to the needs and rights of some of the most vulnerable people in society. It is a failure of public accountability. The way decentralised social assistance has ignored those who are economically worst off has been sadly consistent with tax and social security policies that had equally harmful effects and that were managed by the central government. Also, as we saw in section 5.3, in some of the worst moments of the crisis, and against the wishes of the central government when PP was in power, between 2013 and 2017, regions learned from each other's experiences and attempted to implement innovative policies with limited resources to provide some protection for tenants. That was an example of how multilevel governance could contribute to explore and test new social policies.

Time will also tell if the structural changes promised by the PSOE-United Podemos coalition will ever see the light of day. On the one hand, one might think that the austerity of the 2010s was a reaction, obsessive or not, to a specific crisis, and that it will not go on in the 2020s. Political discourse appears to have changed direction in European politics, with a generally more permissive approach to public spending. On the other hand, the 1992 Maastricht criteria remain in place, as does the 2011 constitutional reform according to which the repayment of public debt trumps social or any other form of public expenditure – new Article 135. Despite the reddish colour of the coalition, in June 2020, the *Financial Times* reported that, due to the fiscal constraints, Spain was being 'less generous than other European states in its way out' of the Covid-19 crisis, adding that it would take balanced budgets between 2030 and 2040 simply to return to the debt-to-GDP ratio of 2019.[97] Financial markets will follow their own rules about what is deemed acceptable and what not, and countries seeking funds via public debt will not be able to ignore them. This question matters greatly not only in Spain's context, but in relation to global political economy. Since the early 1980s, governments in advanced economies have increasingly relied on public debt at the expense of taxation, lowering the pressure on the wealthiest strata while diminishing the size of the welfare state.[98] With historically low interest rates, in 2020, governments around the world incurred into huge debt to pay for the emergency and palliative measures during the pandemic and its aftermath. Governments are accountable to those they rely on for revenue. That is one of the reasons why it is so important for a healthy democracy that people sustain their government through a fair tax system. Otherwise, creditors call the shots about what governments should be spending taxpayers' money on. However, it

---

[97] Daniel Bombey, "Spain's Tight Budget Puts Squeeze on Coronavirus Response," *Financial Times* (24 June 2020).
[98] Wolfgang Streeck, "How Will Capitalism End?," *New Left Review* 84 (2014).

would be adventurous to suggest that a radical change in the tax strategy will follow Covid-19. The former European commissioner in charge of budgeting, Günter Oettinger, admitted that the EU's coronavirus recovery plan for 2021 to 2024, which Oettinger himself contributed to bring to life, is 'unfair (to) future generations', because the debt is meant to be paid off between 2028 and 2058, 'when we all will have passed away'.[99]

Let us end this chapter by returning to the minimum vital income scheme. The policy was championed by then deputy prime minister and Podemos founder and leader, Pablo Iglesias, and by the social security minister, José Luis Escrivá. Escrivá had been the chair of the independent authority for fiscal responsibility (AIREF) between 2014 and 2020. AIREF was created in application of the EU-Spain 2012 memorandum thanks to which banks were recapitalised with taxpayers' money from all over Europe. Days after Iglesias and Escrivá announced the plan to set up a central minimum vital income scheme, in an online press conference the spokesperson of the Episcopal Conference, the board of directors of the Catholic Church in Spain, expressed that 'help for those who need it is indispensable, but to make it permanent, to let them live subsidised, would not be a desirable horizon for the common interest'.[100] The press conference was intended to convey a message of condolence and hope on behalf of Catholic bishops in one of the most difficult moments in the country's recent history, when hundreds of people were dying every day with Covid-19 symptoms, and hospitals were seriously struggling to cope. In those extremely difficult circumstances, why did the representative of the Catholic Church express such a negative opinion about a social policy that some might say was very Christian in spirit? That is a question for the next chapter.

---

[99] Politico, "Brussels Playbook" (15 June 2020).
[100] Conferencia Episcopal Española, "El secretario general de la CEE apela a trabajar por el bien común," press release (20 April 2020): *"Ayudas a quienes lo necesitan es indispensable, pero pensar en una permanencia, que vivan de manera subsidiada, no sería un horizonte deseable para la organización del común."*

Chapter 6

'It's the Church We Have Lit Upon, Sancho'

Catholicism and Conservative Politics

6.1 A DISPLAY OF EMPTINESS

When I was a child, my parents used to stop the car by an old cooperative winery on the way to Ayegui, in Navarra, where we spent many of our summer vacations and other breaks. They would purchase bulk wine, half red, half rosé, as my dad enjoyed bottling it in the garage at home, to make sure they had enough provisions for a few months. Back then, I could not grasp adults' obsession with that then unappealing liquid, but there was something oddly attractive about the place. It may be the intoxicating aroma, perhaps the massive size of the barrels, or the winemaker's demeanour, sparing in words, as I remember him. The winery was a pit stop 20 kilometres before our final destination. It was conveniently located near the highway, so there was no need to enter the village. From time to time, however, we would extend our stay for a few hours to visit my dad's cousins and their families. My dad's mum was born in the village in question, Cirauqui, or Zirauki in Basque spelling. Basque is a language increasingly used in the area, a language that nonetheless my grandma never heard in her home town. She left around 1930.

It was during one of those slightly longer stays when I saw it for the first time. I must have been eight or nine years old. My dad took me to the front of the church, the main one of the existing two in the village. To the left of the main entrance, I encountered a long list of names engraved on the wall, right behind a large stone cross. One of them was Daniel Araiz Caro. Daniel was 16 years old when the Civil War began in July 1936. Franco's coup, led in Navarra by General Emilio Mola, triumphed in the region from the beginning. Navarra was not on the battlefront at any point, which did not stop Mola and his followers from retaliating and executing about 3,000 republican, liberal and Socialist opponents in the rearguard. A regiment of traditionalist

Christians arrived in the village one morning that summer. Known as *requetés*, they were recruiting volunteers to join Franco's and Mola's army. A devout Christian, like so many Navarrese young men and women of his generation, Daniel raised his hand and jumped onto the truck. 'Tell mum I'm going to the war,' he yelled at one of his friends while the truck was leaving. Daniel was too young, but nobody checked his age. Sometime later, he would be badly injured in battle and died on the operating table months after the end of the war. Around the same time Daniel became a soldier, his sister was expecting the more or less imminent entry of Franco's troops where she lived, around 120 kilometres north, in San Sebastian. One can imagine her chubby two-year-old boy playing blissfully unaware in the background while soldiers marched by. That boy was my father.

My dad told me about Daniel many times. In my recollection the first time was in front of that church in Zirauki. By then, Franco had been dead for two decades. Daniel's name was one of many who, the engraving of the church said, fell for God and for Spain. I naively assumed that these were the local men who died in the war. But in time I would discover that other men were killed in action, or simply executed treacherously and in the dark in the vicinity. Their names were nowhere to be found, and the reason for their absence was that they had dared to act, speak or simply be against Franco's eventually victorious coup.

As pointed out earlier (section 4.3), the Historical Memory Act 2007 established that Francoist symbols and monuments had to be removed from public display. However, the act introduced an exception for expressions that could have special artistic, architectural or religious significance.[1] For the first time in about two decades, I visited Zirauki again in summer 2018. I had a vague memory of the church, the cross and the inscription. Would had it fallen under the exceptions of the 2007 act? Would the engraving and the stone cross be considered exceptionally significant from an artistic, architectural or religious perspective? Would I still be able to find the name of my father's uncle, as well as others who fought and died for God and for Spain? I would not be. That sizzling morning of July, I walked up the beautiful pedestrian road to the top of the hillside where Zirauki is situated, and there I found the church of San Román. On the left of the façade, I encountered a display of emptiness where 25 years before I had read Daniel's name behind a big cross. The local authority of Zirauki informed me via email that the Francoist symbology had been removed in 2007, and that there had not been any complaint or protest as far as they knew. The monument in remembrance of the men who died on Franco's side is no longer visible in the church, but it was there for the greatest part of last century and most of the first decade of the present one (figure 6.1, figure 6.2).

---

[1] Article 15(2) of the Historical Memory Act 57/2007.

Figure 6.1 Façade of the church of San Román in Zirauki, Navarra in 1979. Source: Catalogue of Monuments of the Arts Department of the Archbishopric of Pamplona

Figure 6.2 Façade of the church of San Román in Zirauki, Navarra in 2020. Source: Mónica Casla

6.2 FRANCO UNDER THE LITURGICAL CANOPY

The Catholic Church was one of the three pillars of Franco's regime, together with the Army and the Fascist party Falange. Suspicious of Falange's politics and faith, or lack thereof, the Church provided moral respectability to the coup of July 1936 and actively supported the regime in the following decades. After the defeat of fascism in Europe, Falange's latent anticlerical tendencies were contained, and the Church secured a hegemonic position as the main provider of moral and ideological legitimacy. For the regime it was absolutely irrefutable that being a good Spaniard required being a good Catholic.[2] During his four decades in power, Franco enjoyed the privilege of walking under liturgical canopy, a privilege generally reserved to religious icons and most senior figures of the Church.

Catholics' support for Franco was not univocal, however. The then profoundly Catholic Partido Nacionalista Vasco (PNV), the Basque Nationalist Party, lined up with Socialists and Communists in defence of the Spanish republic, and much of the Basque clergy did not endorse Franco's ambitions.

Franco and a number of bishops referred to the coup as a 'crusade'.[3] Pope Pius XI fell short of using that word, but his speeches were used by Franco to legitimise the military punch. This was the case, in particular, of a speech the pope delivered in Castel Gandolfo in September 1936, as well as his *Divini Redemptoris* encyclical of March 1937, where the pope denounced the 'horrors' under Communism, which have 'scourged (. . .) our beloved Spain'.[4] Franco and his allies framed the Civil War as a conflict between the advocates of the immutably Catholic nature of the true Spanish identity and its demonised, barbarian, foreign and anti-Spanish opponents. Franco saw himself and his regime as the sentinel of the West and the defender of Christendom in front of the threatening Soviet Communism and the moral decay of Western Europe. When Franco declared himself victorious in April 1939, Pius XII, who had been appointed pope only one month before, congratulated him with a telegram that was widely circulated in the country by Franco's propagandists:

> Lifting our heart to the Lord, we sincerely give thanks, with Your Excellency, for the desired victory of Catholic Spain. We make solemn vows because

---

[2] Juan J. Linz, "Religion and Politics in Spain: From Conflict to Consensus and Cleavage," *Social Compass* 27, no. 2–3 (1980), 257; Eusebio Mujal-León, "The Left and the Catholic Question in Spain," *West European Politics* 5, no. 2 (1982), 34–5.
[3] Enrique Moradiellos, "Ni gesta heroica ni locura trágica: nuevas perspectivas históricas sobre la guerra civil," *Ayer* 50 (2003), 15.
[4] Pope Pius XI, *Divini Redemptoris: Encyclical on Atheistic Communism* (March 1937), para. 18 and 20.

this beloved country, on achieving peace, takes up its ancient Christian traditions with renewed vigour. With these sentiments, we effusively send to Your Excellency and to all the Spanish people our Apostolic blessing.[5]

To understand the church's endorsement of Franco's uprising and dictatorship one needs to acknowledge the general anticlericalism of the left during the republic, anticlericalism that, at the same time, was a reaction to the conservatism and elitism of the Catholic hierarchy, as well as to the national Catholicism prevalent on the right (more on this in section 6.3). The republican constitution of 1931 established the separation of Church and State declaring for the first time in Spain's constitutional history that there would not be an official religion. The Catholic Church had been an ever-present reality in Spain's politics and social and cultural life for more than four centuries. However, the new constitution announced that from then on education would be secular ('laica'), and the church would only be allowed to teach religious doctrine in their own establishments. The constitution also declared the dissolution of the Jesuit order and the nationalisation of their properties. Any public expression of worship would now require prior authorisation from the government, no religion would be financially supported by the State and they would be required to pay taxes. On top of this, the constitution recognised the right to divorce for the first time.[6]

The Catholic question was one of the most divisive issues from the very beginning. In a fervent parliamentary speech during the drafting of the constitution, the president-to-be Manuel Azaña boasted that 'Spain is no longer Catholic'.[7] The church was politically reactionary and conservative, closely associated with the aristocracy, high-bourgeoisie, landowners, the Army and the powerful in general. From their position of dominance, the church was perceived as the most influential voice trying to preserve and legitimise the status quo the new republic was so determined to break with. Left-leaning deputies were adamant to reverse centuries of privilege and influence, influence that was extraordinary in political, cultural and economic terms. In their parliamentary interventions, however, some of the politicians went as far as to question Catholic morality and the intellectual acceptability of the gospel as interpreted by the Catholic Church, discourses that nowadays would be deemed contrary to freedom of conscience. For the most enthusiastic, limiting not only the Church's powers but also the collective dimension of worship was necessary in order to protect the republic from the overwhelming

---

[5] Hilari Raguer, *Gunpowder and Incense: The Catholic Church and the Spanish Civil War* (London: Routledge, 2006), 313–14.
[6] Constitution of 1931, Articles 3, 48, 27, 26 and 43.
[7] Session's Record of the Constitutional Assembly (*"Diario de Sesiones de las Cortes Constituyentes"*), 13 October 1931, no. 55, 1667: *"España ha dejado de ser católica."*

power of the Church.[8] The Catholic question fractured the republican political front very early on in 1931, when some moderate republicans felt that the left was going too far in its anticlericalism.[9] The fracture became intractable and contributed to turn the scales in the 1933 general election, in which a right-wing coalition became victorious. The new very conservative executive skilfully exploited the anger at a moderate agrarian reform advocated by the left, reform that was considered detrimental to the Church's interests. Anticlericalism would only grow stronger as time went by: unruly mobs burnt down churches and convents, and priests and nuns were assassinated in republican zones during the Civil War. If one intends to understand and critique Catholicism's official support for Franco, his coup and his regime, one must not ignore the victimisation suffered by many decent Catholic men and women in the 1930s.

Franco was appointed generalissimo, chief of government and 'caudillo' by his military board at the beginning of the war, in September 1936. 'Caudillo' was to Spain what 'Duce' was to Italy and 'Führer' to Germany. The full denomination would become 'Caudillo of Spain by the Grace of God' ('Caudillo de España por la Gracia de Dios'). The 1947 Act on the Succession to the Head of State made clear that Franco would appoint his successor in due course – he chose Juan Carlos in 1969[10] – and established that Spain was a 'Catholic State' and a 'kingdom' with no king (yet), because the head of State would be Franco, 'Generalissimo of the Armies' and 'Caudillo of Spain and of the Crusade'.[11] The 1947 Act was only derogated with the 1978 constitution.

Due to Franco's sometimes explicit and sometimes implicit support for Hitler's Germany, Spain underwent a period of political isolation after World War II. However, Franco's unreserved anti-Communism soon won him the diplomatic support of the United States, with which Spain signed a defence agreement in 1953. That year marked Spain's return to the international diplomatic arena, followed by the country's acceptance as a member of the UN in 1955. To endorse Catholic Spain's reappearance in international affairs, the Vatican was no less important than the United States. Spain and the Holy See signed their third concordat in 1953, the previous two dating from 1753 and 1851. With the legal status of an international treaty, the 1953 concordat formalised the regime's disposition to validate the Church's extraordinary privileges based on the premise that Catholicism would 'continue to be the

---

[8] Abraham Barrero, "Sobre la Libertad Religiosa en la Historia Constitucional Española," *Revista Española de Derecho Constitucional* 21, no. 61 (2001), 167.
[9] Joan Oliver Araujo, "La cuestión religiosa en la Constitución de 1931: Una reflexión sobre un tema clásico," *Revista de Estudios Políticos (Nueva Época)* 81 (1993), 179.
[10] Act 62/1969, of 22 July, whereby it is decided on the succession to the head of State.
[11] Act on the Succession to the Head of State, of 26 July 1947, Articles 1 and 2.

sole religion of the Spanish State'. Such privileges included exemptions from taxes; the teaching of Catholic morality and dogma in all schools, public and private; the direct civil execution of decrees and judgements issued within the Church in application of Canon Law; and the State's commitment that media would favour the 'exposition and defence of the religious truth'. The State also promised to contribute to 'an appropriate Church patrimony to ensure a fitting endowment for the worship and the clergy'. Among other things, this meant that the State would allocate funds to the Church on an annual basis 'by way of compensation for previous confiscations of the Church's properties and as a contribution to the work of the Church in favour of the Nation'.[12]

Despite their intricate bond, the relationship between Church and State began to deteriorate in the 1960s as a result of a multiplicity of reasons, starting with changes within the Church itself. And that's a significant difference with the history of other European countries. In the case of Spain, the distancing between Church and State was not the result of a revolutionary process in the State, as had been generally the case in the continent in previous centuries, but of a slow but steady introspection and evolution in the Church.[13] The liberalising Second Vatican Council of 1962 to 1965 reflected a profound change in perspectives about the appropriate relations between Church and State. John XXIII's encyclical *Mater et Magistra* of 1961 raised the issues of just wages, humane working conditions, redistributive taxes and union rights, and *Pacem in Terris* in 1963 spoke in favour of human rights and the freedoms of association, expression and political participation.[14] The regime was forced to adapt to the changes in the Church. As a direct result of the conclusions of the Vatican Council, a new piece of legislation was adopted in 1967 to recognise the private practice of other faiths, but the exercise of freedom of religion had to be made compatible with the confessional nature

---

[12] Concordat between Spain and the Holy See, 27 August 1953, Articles 1, 20, 26, 27, 24, 29 and 19. Article 1: "*La Religión Católica, Apostólica, Romana sigue siendo la única de la Nación española y gozará de los derechos y de las prerrogativas que le corresponden en conformidad con la Ley Divina y el Derecho Canónico.*" Article 29: "*El Estado cuidará de que en las instituciones y servicios de formación de la opinión pública, en particular en los programas de radiodifusión y televisión, se dé el conveniente puesto a la exposición y defensa de la verdad religiosa por media de sacerdotes y religiosos designados de acuerdo con el respectivo Ordinario.*" Article 19: "*1. La Iglesia y el Estado estudiarán, de común acuerdo, la creación de un adecuado patrimonio eclesiástico que asegure una congrua dotación del culto y del clero. 2. Mientras tanto el Estado, a título de indemnización por las pasadas desamortizaciones de bienes eclesiásticos y como contribución a la obra de la Iglesia en favor de la Nación, le asignará anualmente una adecuada dotación.*"

[13] Juan J. Linz, "Church and State in Spain from the Civil War to the Return of Democracy," *Daedalus* 120, no. 3 (1991), 169.

[14] Pope John XXIII, *Mater et Magistra: Encyclical on Christianity and Social Progress* (May 1961), para. 13, 48 and 132; Pope John XXIII, *Pacem in Terris: Encyclical on Establishing Universal Peace in Truth, Justice, Charity and Liberty* (April 1963), para. 23, 61, 73 and 75.

of the regime.[15] Spain would remain Catholic, and the Vatican Council was not going to alter that.

Change surfaced from within society as well. The rapid modernisation and urbanisation contributed to the progressive secularisation of society. In the 1960s, Spain was very different from her old self of three decades before. A movement of so-called grassroots Christians and Socialist Christians appeared in the 1960s and 1970s, opposing the dictatorial regime and backing a democratic turn for the country. A new subgroup of young clergy emerged known as worker-priests. Committed to improving the living conditions in the working-class communities they were part of, many of them were ideologically aligned with Socialism and Communism. Being as they were the only civic institution that enjoyed limited freedom under the dictatorship, churches located in neighbourhoods of low-income families became the meeting point of political groupings, trade unions and cultural associations that were still illegal. Such was the problem posed by this new generation of leftist clergy that in 1968 the regime opened a prison exclusively for dissident priests in the small city of Zamora. The Basque clergy had a close connection with a Basque national identity and many young priests expressed their support for a growing political and cultural movement in the region.

Meanwhile, the ultra-conservative Opus Dei prelature was reinforced with an increase in important ministerial positions in 1969, which created discomfort both within and outside Catholic circles. Over time, change reached the top of the hierarchy of the Church. Cardinal Tarancón, president of the Spanish Conference of Bishops between 1971 and 1981, wrestled with the regime until Franco's death. Tarancón officiated the State funeral of Prime Minister Carrero Blanco, killed by Euskadi Ta Askatasuna (ETA) in December 1973, and upon arrival to Madrid's cathedral he was harassed and insulted by right-wing fanatics shouting 'Tarancón al paredón' ('Tarancón to the firing line'). Particularly significant was the case of the bishop of Bilbao, Antonio Añoveros. Añoveros issued a homily in defence of Basque culture in 1974, quoting the late pope John XXIII. Franco and some of his ministers were adamant to expel the bishop from the country, but Cardinal Tarancón did not let it happen. Among other things, Tarancón threatened members of Franco's executive with excommunication.[16] This was unprecedented for a regime that had relied on the Church as one of its three pillars, a regime whose leader was supposedly so by the grace of God, a regime that nowhere

---

[15] Barrero, "Sobre la Libertad Religiosa," 178–9; Act 44/1967, of 28 June, about the exercise of the civil right of freedom of religion in education centres, Article 1.

[16] Stanley G. Payne, *Spanish Catholicism: An Historical Overview* (Madison: University of Wisconsin Press, 1984), Chapter 8.

else but in a concordat with the Holy See had established that Catholicism was the only true religion.

After more than three decades of continuous support, in the final stages of the regime the Church as an institution facilitated the end of Francoism. Some within it at a more grassroots level risked their freedom and personal integrity by involving themselves in political and pro-democracy movements, including Socialist and Communist groups and unions. At the same time, the leadership of the Communist Party understood that the anti-religious and anti-clerical positions of the past were no longer fair or at least not strategically wise.[17] Communist leaders believed that more than a few Catholics suffered from a 'guilt complex' due to the close identification between the Church and the dictatorship, and that bridges could be built with worker-priests and with grassroots Catholics.[18] In the 1970s, Spain was still a largely Catholic country, but society was much more secular, and the Church did not hold sway the way it used to. To a great extent, anticlericalism had disappeared on the left. Progressive and democratic forces were willing to find an understanding with the Catholic Church, and in fact many of their members and some of their leaders were practising Catholics, which would have been inconceivable in the 1930s. In the 1970s, the Church concluded they did not need Francoism anymore; as far as the Catholic leadership was concerned, the country was ready for democracy. The time of National Catholicism was over.

6.3 NATIONAL CATHOLICISM

Looking under moonlight for the imaginary palace of beautiful Dulcinea in El Toboso, Don Quixote and his squire came up against another building instead: 'It's the church we have lit upon, Sancho,' said the hidalgo. Over time this line from Cervantes's most famous novel would become a metaphor of the sense of helplessness and frustration when challenging an all-embracing power. The Catholic Church has been that power at least since the late fifteenth century. As a common thread in Spain's history, religious unity had a decisive influence on the unity of the different political structures. Catholicism also played a central role in internal security and international relations. The Inquisition was only disbanded in the 1830s, and the defence of the Catholic faith provided an aureole of legitimacy both to colonial adventures in the Americas and to Spain's ambitions within Europe's balance of power in the fifteenth, sixteenth and seventeenth centuries.

---

[17] Linz, "Religion and Politics in Spain," 258.
[18] Mujal-León, "The Left and the Catholic Question in Spain," 40.

A product of the nineteenth century, the political project of National Catholicism sought the instrumentalisation of the faith to consolidate the idea of a nation and to preserve the predominance of the Catholic Church in the country's political and economic system. As observed by Linz, National Catholicism was based on the idea that 'the greatness of a nation, its historical success, is linked with its loyalty to the faith and the church'; therefore, 'secularization becomes a threat not only to the church but to the nation'.[19] National Catholicism entailed the indissoluble marriage of Church and State, an anachronism in twentieth-century Western Europe, but a core claim in Franco's regime. It was a symbiotic relationship. Spanish nationalists obtained the benefit of the transcendence and morality of their political ambitions, and the defenders of the faith secured the political and material backing of State institutions.

Catholicism's institutional predominance is reflected in Spain's constitutional history. As shown in the previous section, the 1931 constitution of the Spanish republic was the first one to separate Church and State, and it did so in a controversial and perhaps disproportionate way as a sort of sudden divorce of what had been a long-lasting marriage of convenience.

The country alternated moderately liberal and conservative-leaning constitutions in the nineteenth century. The constitution of 1812, the first one in the country's history, despite being supposedly liberal, made clear in Article 12 that the Roman, Catholic and apostolic religion was the only true one and was and would always be the religion of all Spaniards; the text gave the State the responsibility to protect the Church and to make sure that no other religion could be practiced. This happened a generation after the American and French revolutions, and by then a number of European countries had decades if not centuries of religious diversity and tolerance. Spain itself had experienced a much greater degree of plurality and faith interchange before the expulsion of the Jews and the conquest of the remaining Moorish kingdom in Al-Andalus in January 1492.

The conservative constitutions of 1837 and 1845 unabashedly reiterated the confessional nature of the State, based on the principle that both monarchy and Church trumped the will of the people. Religious tolerance was perceived as alien and a sign of weakness in faith. While holding other religions was no longer prohibited as long as it was kept private, in the second half of the nineteenth-century Catholicism would remain the official religion and the State would assume the cost of sustaining its operations as well as the wages of the clergy. Religious doctrine was taught in all schools, public or private, and in any case the Catholic Church held a nearly perfect monopoly in education.

---

[19] Linz, "Church and State in Spain," 163.

The liberal and short-lived constitution of 1869 recognised individual rights and freedoms, including private or public worship primarily for non-nationals but also for any Spaniard who might profess a religion other than the Catholic one (Article 21). The 1869 constitution avoided taking a position about whether the State should have an official religion, but it confirmed that the State's treasury would fund the Church. This constitution lasted barely four years. Apart from the republican period of the 1930s, this was the only interruption in five centuries to the confessionalism of the Spanish State.

The conservative constitution of 1876, however, went back in time to declare in Article 11 that the state's religion is the Catholic, apostolic and Roman one, and that the nation is obliged to sustain worship and clergy; other religious beliefs and practices would be tolerated only insofar as they did not clash with so-called Christian morality; and no public manifestation or ceremony would be allowed other than the Catholic ones. After the radical shift of the 1931 constitution, Franco borrowed the wording of 1876 for his 'Fuero de los Españoles' of 1945, one of the fundamental laws of the regime, which would remain in force until 1978.[20]

The Church was Spain's largest landowner in the nineteenth century. It is estimated that the Church owned 24% of the agricultural land and 30% of all properties around 1750.[21] In the 1830s, 1840s and 1850s, a number of 'disentailments' ('desamortizaciones') took place, by which the State seized and sold land and real estate that had been owned by the Catholic Church. As observed by Payne, the government had three objectives with the disentailments: firstly, to secure funds to continue the Civil War against the Carlistas in the north and north-east; secondly, to make sure the Church depended financially on the State; and thirdly, to create a new social class of landowners loyal to the centralised state that was being developed.[22] In practice, the State did not obtain much benefit from the disentailments in terms of public resources. Land was sold at a lower price than the market value and rural areas became even poorer in the southern provinces, which contributed to increase wealth inequalities. By 1875, three quarters of the disentailed land had been privatised for the benefit of rich landowners. Their reinvigorated position of strength in turn neutralised the slow process of industrialisation in much of Spain. Many of these landowners became the local caciques who made possible the rigged elections that sustained the non-aggression pact of the so-called Restoration of monarchy (1874–1923), a pact by which moderate liberals and conservatives took turns to govern the country unopposed.[23]

---

[20] Barrero, "Sobre la Libertad Religiosa," 144, 148–50 and 157.
[21] Piketty, *Capital and Ideology*, 90.
[22] Payne, *Spanish Catholicism*, 84–5.
[23] Preston, *A People Betrayed*, 13 and 22–5.

Catholicism cannot be dissociated from the formation of the national spirit in the nineteenth and twentieth centuries. Initially, and particularly in the periphery, the Church identified itself with the traditionalist anti-liberalism of Carlism in the succession war of the 1830s. Over time, however, Catholicism and the triumphant branch of the Bourbonic family made peace and found a mutually advantageous understanding. Throughout the nineteenth century, Catholicism was established as the defining feature of the idea of Spain, where religion supposedly identified and brought together all of the members of the single political community that was meant to be Spain.[24] The Church was going to provide the necessary moral legitimacy to the centralised State and to the nation-building exercise. National symbols and celebrations would be associated with Catholic rites and traditions, for example, with the remembrance of victims of the Napoleonic war in Spain – 'Independence War' – as martyrs of nation and religion. This was also expressed, as we saw in section 3.1, with the choice of 12 October as a *national* bank holiday to honour the apparition of the Lady of the Pillar to Saint James the Apostle, patron of Spain, which conveniently was made to coincide with the arrival of Columbus's fleet to the Americas. This bank holiday was sometimes referred to as the Day of the 'Race' or Day of the 'Hispanicity' ('Hispanidad'), a concept that supposedly keeps Spain close to its former colonies in Latin America.

At the same time, as said earlier, the State was going to support the Church financially, making it exempt from taxes, reserving the delivery of education to the Church with little or no competition, and keeping Catholicism as the only true religion of all Spaniards. As pointed out by Quiroga, the influence of the Catholic Church in education constituted an obstacle to the promotion of civic, liberal and republican values,[25] not to speak of Socialism and anarchism, which became popular among working-class communities in industrial Europe in the later decades of the nineteenth century. For Colomer, 'like in other aspects of the frustrated modernization of Spain, there was too little religion to unify the population and too much to permit the success of an alternative cultural cosmovision'.[26] Spain's schools made Catholics, not citizens. The Church had no reason to change the status quo. They made their choice by siding with the rich in a country and at a moment in which the distance between rich and poor was gigantic. The English Hispanist Gerald Brenan observed in 1943 that, 'had the Church been drawn into serious support of the working classes, they would undoubtedly have seen the greater

---

[24] Álvarez Junco, *Spanish Identity in the Age of Nations*, 216–17.
[25] Alejandro Quiroga, *Making Spaniards: Primo de Rivera and the Nationalization of the Masses, 1923–30* (London: Palgrave, 2007), 12.
[26] Colomer, *The Spanish Frustration*, 88.

part of their present allies, the *gente de orden*, leave them'.[27] The Church lost any remaining touch with much of the peasantry and working-class communities,[28] and they opposed minimally liberalising reforms framing them as foreign and alien to the country's culture, history and identity, all of which contributed to develop the links between nationalism, traditionalism and anti-liberalism.[29] Shielding an infantilised society from foreign influence was a central goal of religious unity.

If the connection between Spain's nation-building and Catholicism began in mid-nineteenth century, such connection turned into an ever more conservative project in the first two decades of the twentieth century, specifically between the so-called Disaster of 1898 and the year 1923. In 1898, Spain lost its remaining colonies in Cuba, Puerto Rico and the Philippines, and in 1923 King Alfonso XIII handed the keys of power to General Miguel Primo de Rivera, who presented himself as the saviour of the nation after six decades of fictitious democracy where two parties rigged the elections to take turns in power.[30] In a way, Primo de Rivera's promise was not that different from Vox's pompous entrance in parliament in 2019, only for the fact that Spain was a democracy in 2019, but far from it in 1923. With Miguel Primo de Rivera, Spain's right-wing conservatism became more martial, clerical, antiliberal and nationalistic, increasingly hostile to Catalan and Basque nationalisms and to the political demands of the surfacing working class. Quiroga writes that 'most of the ideas that would eventually constitute the official ultra-nationalist discourse of the *primorriverista* regime were first formulated during the last years of the Restoration',[31] in the late 1910s and early 1920s. Primo de Rivera's dictatorship, which ended in 1930 to 1931, was also a training ground for men that would become towering figures in Spain's right and far-right politics the following decade. This includes his son José Antonio, founder of Fascist Falange; his finance minister, José Calvo Sotelo, whose assassination by leftist mobs in July 1936 was used as an excuse to justify Franco's coup; and José María Gil-Robles, who would lead the largest right-wing coalition, CEDA, in the 1930s.

Religion and clergy played a different role in the Basque Country. As covered in section 3.4, after the triple defeat of Carlism in the nineteenth century, the Basque provinces lost the remaining fueros and a new financial settlement, known as the economic concert, was put in place. The economic concert would allow Basque authorities to levy and manage taxes locally. In the last quarter of the century, much of the remaining traditionalist Carlism in

---

[27] Brenan, *The Spanish Labyrinth*, 86.
[28] Payne, "Spanish Nationalism in the Twentieth Century," 406.
[29] Álvarez Junco, *Spanish Identity in the Age of Nations*, 220–1.
[30] Preston, *A People Betrayed*, chapter 7.
[31] Quiroga, *Making Spaniards*, 30.

the Basque Country evolved towards a new political movement led by Sabino Arana. That was the beginning of Basque nationalism, which progressively seduced a number of representatives of the industrialist bourgeoisie interested in making the most of the economic concert. Besides advocating for self-government, Basque nationalism was unapologetically Catholic when it was born and for much of the twentieth century. In fact, as noted in chapter 3, the party founded by Arana, PNV-EAJ, hegemonic for a long time in Basque politics, has two different names in Spanish and Basque. While the Spanish acronym PNV means 'Basque Nationalist Party' ('Partido Nacionalista Vasco'), the Basque EAJ can be translated as 'Basque Party fond of God and the old laws' ('Euzko Alderdi Jeltzalea'). For most of the twentieth century, religion was used by conservative voices in Basque nationalism to oppose external influences considered incompatible with some immutable version of the Basque culture and identity. The suspicion of the influence that the Catholic Church could have on Basque nationalism was such during the 1930s republic that some on the left feared that a self-governing statute could result in a 'Vaticanist Gibraltar'.[32] This is one of the reasons why Catalonia's statute was adopted in 1932 and the Basque one had to wait until 1937, when Franco's troops had already engulfed half of the Basque territory. As a collective, the left-leaning and Marxist pro-independence movement that emerged in the 1950s and 1960s, on the contrary, adopted a more agnostic or even atheist position towards religion, and this approach would continue under democracy. Having said that, religious establishments harboured some of ETA's assemblies and other important meetings in the 1960s, and once democracy was established, the Basque Church offered its services to mediate between the Spanish government and the armed group.

To echo Boyd's words, more than a formal ideology, National Catholicism was a 'mentality (that) blended the reactionary cultural values of traditional Spanish Catholicism with strident authoritarian nationalism', legitimising 'the authoritarian state as the form of political organization best equipped to defend the economic interests and religious and cultural values associated with national unity and power'.[33] Together, Tarancón, young priests and a modern and secular society moved National Catholicism to the history books in the last years of Franco's dictatorship. But the Church was going to continue influencing conservative politics in the decades to come.

---

[32] Frances Lannon, "Modern Spain: The Project of a National Catholicism," *Studies in Church History* 18 (1982), 581.

[33] Carolyn P. Boyd, *Historia Patria: Politics, History, and National Identity in Spain, 1875–1975* (Princeton: Princeton University Press, 1997), 168.

6.4 THE CATHOLIC CHURCH AND THE DEMOCRATIC ERA

There were Democratic Christian candidates in the ballot papers, and some of them were very well known, but their parties fared badly in the general election of 1977. Under that specific name, Christian Democracy obtained less than 2% of the vote. Irrespective of denomination, within the broad church of Christian Democracy, the Democratic Union of Catalonia and the Basque Nationalist Party obtained respectable results in their territories. Yet, in the rest of Spain, in a context of growing secularisation, political fragmentation seriously damaged the electoral prospects of the Spanish Christian Democratic ticket. The silence of the Catholic Church was deafening, as the Conference of Bishops very consciously decided not to endorse any candidate or party. The conference did not express an official position about the constitution, but during the referendum campaign, 60 of the 80 bishops made clear that they favoured an affirmative vote, and only 9 spoke against it.[34] After more than one century of close association between nationalism and Catholicism, and at the end of a dictatorial regime that had relied on Catholicism to legitimise their political cause, the Spanish Church made the strategic choice of abstaining from siding with one or another option in electoral politics. This, however, did not mean that Catholicism was going to disappear from the political arena, as future laws and policies would retain a prominent role for the Church in the lives of all Spaniards.

Only months after Franco's death, Spain and the Holy See signed an agreement where both parties pledged 'to undertake in common the study of matters of common interest that require a new order according to the new circumstances arisen after the signature' of the 1953 concordat.[35] It was summer 1976, a time when it was still uncertain what sort of country Spain was going to become. The first free and fair elections had not yet taken place, parties and unions were illegal and dissidents were still in prison. It remained to be seen whether Spain would manage to become a democracy altogether. The government was being led by Carlos Arias Navarro, who had been appointed by Franco to replace Carrero Blanco in 1973. Arias Navarro's executive agreed to revise and amend the 1953 concordat, and the mission was executed by his successor, Adolfo Suárez. Under Suárez's leadership, the Spanish government negotiated four international agreements to update the concordat. The

---

[34] Payne, *Spanish Catholicism*, 214–16; Linz, "Church and State in Spain," 171–2.
[35] Instrument of Ratification of the Agreement between the Holy See and the Spanish State, held in the Holy See on 28 July 1976, published in the Official Gazette (BOE) no. 230, of 24 September: "*Se comprometen, por tanto, a emprender, de común acuerdo, el estudio de estas diversas materias con el fin de llegar, cuanto antes, a la conclusión de Acuerdos que sustituyan gradualmente las correspondientes disposiciones del vigente Concordato.*"

negotiation with the Church and the Vatican lasted no less than two full years, time during which deputies were drafting and debating the future constitution in parallel. The four agreements with the Catholic Church were formally subscribed in January 1979, less than a week after the promulgation of the constitution, and a month after the constitution was endorsed by the people in referendum. With the negotiation timetable and the overall strategy, before and after the first free elections, the conservative government was making clear that, as far as they were concerned, the Catholic question would remain a matter of international relations and largely beyond democratic control. Political representatives in the constitutional assembly were informed of the ongoing negotiations with the Holy See. However, the four agreements were presented as a fait accompli before knowing for sure what place the constitution would reserve to the Catholic Church in the budding democracy, and whether the Spanish people would at all support the constitution in referendum. While the ruling party and other right-wing forces did not use the word 'Christian' as part of their names, the leaders of the Church knew they could rely on their support.

The four agreements covered legal matters, education, religious assistance in hospitals, army barracks and other institutions, and economic and financial issues.[36] The agreements gave special protection to places of worship, as well as registries, archives and other documents owned and managed by the Church. The state pledged to consult with the Church about bank holidays, and committed to recognise immediate legal effects to religious marriages and to decisions of the ecclesiastical jurisdiction on their nullity or dissolution. The agreements ensured that Catholic education would be offered in publicly funded schools (more on this later), making clear that in any case the education imparted in public schools would 'respect the values of Christian ethics'.

The economic agreement included tax exemptions for the Church in relation to income, wealth, consumption, gifts and inheritance. On top of that, until 2006, the State continued funding the Catholic Church through an unconditional allowance in the general State budget. Gift and inheritance deductions, as well a specific tax designation scheme in annual income statements, contribute to finance the Catholic Church's laudable charitable initiatives. But they also pay for the maintenance of the clergy and for their very legitimate but partisan activities of proselytism. More questionable from a moral standpoint is the use of the Church's privileged financial position to create and sustain two of the most conservative and Spanish nationalistic media platforms in the country, COPE Radio and TRECE TV. Particularly this second one has served as a platform for the far-right party Vox. With

---

[36] Instrument of Ratification of the Agreements between the Holy See and the Spanish State, held in the Holy See on 3 January 1979, published in the Official Gazette (BOE) no. 300, of 15 December.

Prime Minister Rodríguez Zapatero in office (PSOE), in 2006, the percentage of the personal contribution in the designation scheme of income statements increased by approximately 50% to compensate for the mentioned loss of the unconditional allowance in the State budget. Favouring the Catholic Church in the designation scheme is voluntary, and approximately one in three taxpayers choose to do so. They tick a box to express that they would like the Catholic Church – and/or NGOs and socially conscious causes – to receive an amount equivalent to 0.7% of their taxed income. It is important to note that such choice is cost-free for them, they do not pay any more, which means the money eventually comes from all taxpayers, irrespective of whether they have ticked the box in their income statement or not.

The agreements envisioned that the Church should be able to fund its own activities, but not enough progress has been made since 1979. According to the information gathered and made public by the Catholic leadership, the Church is still financially dependent on the State, with the designation scheme making 23.1% of its income in 2017 to 2018, 224.88 million euro, which went up to 285.12 million euro in the definitive settlement of 2018 to 2019.[37] After several months of delay due to lack of agreement within its plenary, in summer 2020, the Court of Auditors (Tribunal de Cuentas) published its first ever report on the Church's accounts. The Court of Auditors is the statutory body that audits the bookkeeping of political parties and monitors revenue and expenditure in public accounts. The Court of Auditors denounced the lack of clarity in the Church's finances, the discrepancy between supposedly corresponding items, and the general lack of interest of the State in keeping track of the use of taxpayers' money and of the destination of the Church's surplus of recent years, all of which could breach European Union Law on State aid.[38] More than four decades after the agreements subscribed with the Holy See, the evidence provided by the Church is insufficient to establish the needs the State is being required to sustain, and many questions remain unanswered about the Church's capacity to self-finance. In the meantime, Spaniards of all faiths and of no religious affiliation continue funding the Catholic Church with their taxes.

The Church is also exempt from any sort of wealth or capital gains tax, which could make a significant difference considering that it has been estimated that they own about 100,000 properties, including apartments, office space,

---

[37] Fernando Giménez Barriocanal, *Principales cifras de la economía de la Iglesia Católica en España: Año 2018* (Madrid: Edice, 2020), 49 and 17.

[38] Tribunal de Cuentas, *Informe no. 1382 de fiscalización sobre las actuaciones desarrolladas por la administración general del estado en materia de cooperación económica con las confesiones religiosas a través de los programas de ingresos y gastos contenidos en los presupuestos generales del estado, ejercicio 2017* (July 2020).

places of worship and acres of land.[39] A legal reform introduced by José María Aznar's (Popular Party (PP)) government in 1998 allowed the Catholic Church to claim private property in the Land Registry over places of worship by simply declaring they were theirs. This was a prerogative that the Francoist mortgage legislation had granted the Church in relation to all other properties, and the 1990s reform simply lifted the exception for places of worship.[40] In February 2021, the Spanish government revealed that, making use of this new privilege, between 1998 and 2015 the Catholic Church registered as their own 34,961 estates, 20,014 of which were temples and units attached to them.[41]

Article 16 of the 1978 constitution was ambivalent about secularism. The first two paragraphs proclaimed freedom of ideology, religion and worship 'with no other restriction on their expression than what may be necessary to maintain public order as protected by law', adding that 'no one may be compelled to make statements regarding their religion, beliefs or ideology'. However, the third paragraph, after declaring that the State would not have an official religion, added that 'public authorities shall take the religious beliefs of the Spanish society into account and shall consequently maintain appropriate cooperation with the Catholic Church and the other faiths'.[42] As has just been seen, the legal basis of such cooperation was no other than an international treaty negotiated in the Vatican City while the deputies were drafting the constitution in Madrid. Less generous agreements of cooperation were subscribed with the representatives of the Evangelical, Jewish and Muslim communities in 1992, agreements that were adopted and published as acts of parliament.[43] These three religions do not receive economic aid from the State, and doctrinal education is only imparted in public schools whenever there is sufficiently large demand for it, not as a default option, as is the case with Catholicism.

Article 27 of the constitution deals with the right to education, which 'shall aim the full development of the human character with due respect for the democratic principles of living together and for the basic rights and freedoms'. While about two-thirds of school-age children attend public schools,

---

[39] José Manuel Vidal, "El IBI y la Iglesia católica," *El Mundo* (20 May 2012).

[40] Decree of 14 February 1947, Mortgage Regulation, Articles 5 and 304. The exception for places of worship was lifted with a modification of Article 5 via Royal Decree 1867/1998, of 4 September.

[41] Ministerio de la Presidencia, Relaciones con las Cortes y Memoria Democrática, "Estudio sobre la inmatriculación de bienes inmuebles de la Iglesia Católica en el Registro de la Propiedad desde el año 1998 en virtud de certificación del diocesano respectivo" (February 2021).

[42] "*1. Se garantiza la libertad ideológica, religiosa y de culto de los individuos y las comunidades sin más limitación, en sus manifestaciones, que la necesaria para el mantenimiento del orden público protegido por la ley. 2. Nadie podrá ser obligado a declarar sobre su ideología, religión o creencias. 3. Ninguna confesión tendrá carácter estatal. Los poderes públicos tendrán en cuenta las creencias religiosas de la sociedad española y mantendrán las consiguientes relaciones de cooperación con la Iglesia Católica y las demás confesiones.*"

[43] Acts 24/1992, 25/1992 and 26/1992, of 12 November.

the constitution allows the existence of publicly funded but privately owned education institutions, known as 'concerted schools' ('escuelas concertadas'). The constitution also guarantees the right of parents to ensure that their children receive religious and moral instruction in accordance with their own convictions.[44] Approximately one in four children attend a concerted school, not all but most of which are Catholic. Concerted schools enjoy significant support from the State. While public funding for public education decreased by 7.5% between 2011 and 2016, it went up for concerted schools, and the growth is even higher when dating it back to 2006: 28.4% increase in funding for privately owned schools from taxpayers over those 10 years. Defenders of concerted education argue that their model is more cost-effective for the State, because they receive less than 13% of all public expenditure on education but serve 25% of the students.[45] However, one should also bear in mind that students in concerted education tend to come from families that are socio-economically more privileged, families that top up the concerted school's resources with the payment of fees, and whose children may have fewer educational needs than those in public schools. Furthermore, the model appears to contribute to concentrate – therefore, segregate – students based on their socio-economic status: Within the OECD, only Turkey and Lithuania have higher levels of socio-economic segregation in primary education.[46]

Introduced by the left-leaning coalition of PSOE and United Podemos, a new Education Act was adopted in late 2020, intending to keep a better balance between the number of students from relatively poor backgrounds in public and in concerted schools; religion would still be offered but the grade would not be recorded for official purposes and for the final qualification.[47] The new law was supported by small nationalist and regionalist parties, but it was strongly opposed by right-wing parties, as they deemed it contrary to personal liberty and to the unity of Spain due to the alleged protection of Catalan at the expense of Spanish in Catalan schools. This suggests that a future conservative government would probably be keen to come up with a

---

[44] "*1. Todos tienen el derecho a la educación. Se reconoce la libertad de enseñanza. 2. La educación tendrá por objeto el pleno desarrollo de la personalidad humana en el respeto a los principios democráticos de convivencia y a los derechos y libertades fundamentales. 3. Los poderes públicos garantizan el derecho que asiste a los padres para que sus hijos reciban la formación religiosa y moral que esté de acuerdo con sus propias convicciones. . . . 6. Se reconoce a las personas físicas y jurídicas la libertad de creación de centros docentes, dentro del respeto a los principios constitucionales.*"

[45] Data from: Ministerio de Educación y Formación Profesional, *Sistema estatal de indicadores de la educación* (Madrid: Ministerio de Educación, 2019), 64–6.

[46] Álvaro Ferrer and Lucas Gortazar, "Diversidad y libertad: Reducir la segregación escolar respetando la capacidad de elección de centro," *EsadeEcPol Insight* no. 29 (April 2021), 4–5.

[47] Ignacio Zafra, "Estos son todos los cambios en la escuela que trae la nueva ley educativa," *El País* (19 November 2020).

new law on education, as has been traditional in Spain's democracy whenever there is a change in central government.

In entirely publicly funded schools, parents can choose between Catholic education and secular ethics. According to the Spanish Conference of Bishops, in 2019 to 2020, 52% of students in public education opted for Catholic religion, 63% when including concerted and private schools.[48] Religious education in Spain is confessional and doctrinal. Non-partisan teaching of religion as a social, historical or cultural phenomenon is not part of the curriculum, although teachers, Catholic or not, may very well choose to impart their classes in this way. While Catholic religion must always be offered in public schools in conditions equivalent to the other subjects, Jewish, Islamic and Evangelic teaching is only available upon request. Other religions have not concluded any agreement with the State, and therefore they do not need to be taught. Teachers of Catholic religion in public schools are appointed and paid by the State, but they are selected and dismissed by the local diocese in accordance with their own criteria and Canon Law, which includes 'witness of a Catholic life'.[49]

In addition to these privileges recognised in the 1979 agreements, the Catholic Church resisted liberalising policies in the 1980s. Particularly noteworthy are the legalisation of divorce in 1981 under a conservative government (UCD), and the partial decriminalisation of abortion in 1985 with a social-democratic one (PSOE). Probably the most contentious issue in the last few years was the recognition of same-sex marriage in 2005, with Prime Minister José Luis Rodríguez Zapatero (PSOE). After the Netherlands and Belgium, Spain became the third country in the world to equalise marriage without discrimination on grounds of sexual orientation, and the first one to allow same-sex couples to adopt children together. The legal change had been included in PSOE's manifesto one year before, with an ever more visible and effective LGBTQ+ community campaigning for it. At the other end, the Catholic Church was very vocal in their opposition. The Vatican deemed the reform 'iniquitous',[50] and in an unusual move cardinals, archbishops, bishops and priests led a demonstration convened by the right-wing opposition PP in June 2005. Speaking for *The Guardian*, the archbishop of Madrid, Cardinal Antonio María Rouco Varela, pontificated that 'if it is the state itself that establishes a law which ignores the essence of marriage, then the damage it causes to the true family, to children and society as a whole will be incalculable'; 'we Christians should speak now,

---

[48] Conferencia Episcopal Española, "El 63% de los alumnos eligen religión católica," press release (24 May 2020).
[49] Code of Canon Law, Canons 804 and 805.
[50] BBC, "Vatican Condemns Spain Gay Bill" (22 April 2005).

we must go out on to the street', rallied Cardinal Ricard María Carles Gordó, archbishop of Barcelona.[51] Rouco kept stressing over the years his profound dissatisfaction with same-sex marriage, which he saw as 'man's rebellion against his biological limits'.[52] PP brought the contention to the constitutional court, which confirmed the constitutionality of equal marriage seven years later, in 2012.[53] By then, the issue was not contentious anymore, and leading figures in the conservative PP have used the law to get married themselves.

Equal marriage enjoyed popular support when legalised in 2005, across the political spectrum, but much more on the left. In June 2004, two-thirds of Spaniards expressed the view that homosexual couples should be able to marry whoever they chose, and only one-fourth was against such proposition.[54] Something similar would happen again in early 2021, when Spain became one of the first countries to legalise euthanasia, a legal change supported by seven in ten Spaniards,[55] but opposed by PP and Vox. As had happened with divorce and with abortion in the 1980s, the political controversy around equal marriage in 2004 to 2005 confirmed that the Church's opinions carried little or no weight for most people on the left and centre-left. Neither was the Church trying to reach them. Instead, the Catholic leadership chose to provide a platform to the most ardent defenders of traditionalist politics within Spain's conservatism. PP lost the general election in March 2004, shocking many in their own ranks, and since then the party pursued a line of opposition that focused on the demonisation of PSOE's prime minister, Rodríguez Zapatero. They portrayed him as soft with Catalan nationalists and revanchist about the Civil War and Francoism. The right-wing rallied people in the streets repeatedly between 2004 and 2008 in defence of traditional family, traditional values, leaving the past behind and defending the unbreakable unity of the Spanish nation. In a way not seen in decades, the Catholic Church offered their platforms to legitimise a very conservative political agenda. In turn, the Church could hope to benefit from the rising political temperature in the renegotiation of their financial settlement with the State, which was on the table at the time. A new era had begun, an era in which the Catholic Church would not shy away from politics, and conservatism was once again their choice.

---

[51] Giles Tremlett, "Bishops to Lead Gay Law Protest," *The Guardian* (17 June 2005).
[52] El Mundo, "Rouco: 'El matrimonio gay es la rebeldía del hombre contra sus límites biológicos'" (24 May 2008).
[53] Constitutional Court, Judgment 198/2012 (6 November).
[54] CIS, *Barómetro de junio 2004, Estudio 2568* (Madrid: CIS, 2004), 5.
[55] CIS, *Barómetro de enero 2021, Estudio 3307* (Madrid: CIS, 2021), 20.

6.5 THE CHURCH, HISTORICAL MEMORY AND THE NATION, TODAY

We said earlier that after 25 years of pact of silence, things began to change in the early 2000s with a new wave to recover the historical memory (section 4.3). A new generation felt ready to ask difficult questions that had remained untouched until then. There was a sense of urgency in the air, because those who might have an idea about the whereabouts of people who had been made to disappear in the Civil War were getting dangerously old. Many felt the need to revisit the foundations on which the so-called consensus of the Transition had been built. The political class agreed in the second half of the 1970s that a large dose of compromise, good will, forgiveness and purposeful oblivion was necessary to forge a new democracy in Spain. In the dawn of the new millennium, with a consolidated democracy with its virtues and its flaws, some wondered if it was not the time to evaluate the consequences of that pact, name the crimes and honour the victims.

Much of that new political class had family and ideological ties with the losing side of the Civil War and Francoism, but crucially, they had not experienced the dictatorship and the Transition first-hand. We showed in chapter 4 that the political expression to recover the historical memory was a project of the left. However, as Boyd points out, at the same time an

> increasingly conservative Catholic hierarchy . . . practiced its own brand of memory politics, refusing to allow the eradication of Falangist and Francoist symbols on its property while petitioning the papacy to beatify priests, monks, and nuns who had fallen victim to anticlerical violence.[56]

In March 2001, Pope John Paul II beatified 233 nuns, priests and laypeople who had been murdered in the republican rearguard during the Civil War in the largest collective beatification ever carried out in the history of the Church until then. Such record was broken with the beatification of 498 more clergymen and women from the same time by Pope Benedict XVI in October 2007, and 522 more in 2013 with Pope Francis delivering a video message; in their coverage of this last service the BBC reported that 'the Vatican (had) gone out of its way to stress that Sunday's beatifications were in no way a political endorsement of events during the civil war'.[57] Meanwhile, the Spanish Catholic Church has not yet issued an apology for their support of Franco's

---

[56] Boyd, "The Politics of History and Memory in Democratic Spain," 145.
[57] L.A. Times, "Pope Beatifies 233 Martyrs of 1936–39 Spanish Civil War," (12 March 2001); BBC, "Vatican Honours Spanish War Dead" (28 October 2007); BBC, "Spanish Civil War 'Martyrs' Beatified" (13 October 2013).

uprising and his regime. Their silence does not represent the whole of Spanish Catholicism, and many priests and Christians lament and deplore the past association between their religion and Francoism. In 2009, for example, Basque bishops officiated mass to apologise for the execution of 14 Basque priests by Franco's troops in 1936 to 1937; the Church's muteness had been an 'affront on truth, justice and charity', said their homily.[58] However, it is striking that seven decades after the events the Catholic Church organised some of the largest ever ceremonies of their kind to honour its servants killed in the Civil War but, as an institution, the Church has not yet found the opportunity to acknowledge the full extent of their complicity with Franco, the coup and the regime.

The Spanish Conference of Bishops was headed by Cardinal Rouco Varela between 1999 and 2005, and between 2008 and 2014, a position of power from which he influenced conservative politics assertively. Rouco was one of the leading faces of the demonstration against the government because of the legalisation of same-sex marriages, which he saw, as mentioned earlier, as an expression of 'man's rebellion against his biological limits', and 'incalculably' damaging to the 'true family', children and the entire society. Rouco talked profusely against the historical memory agenda. In his opening remarks of the 2008 annual Conference of Bishops, he said it was necessary to 'forget, . . . forgive, . . . and release the youth from the burdens of the past, from old quarrels and resentment'.[59] Rouco's words resonated clearly with PP's message that the government was reopening old wounds, that pages of history had to be turned and that the Transition's spirit of concord had to be conserved.

The Church's views in relation to historical memory came to the fore again when Spanish authorities, with Prime Minister Sánchez (PSOE), decided to unearth Franco's remains from the Valley of the Fallen in 2019. After intense diplomatic efforts from the Spanish government, the leadership of the Church abstained from expressing any views against it, and declared that they did not oppose the decision. However, the prior of the Benedictine abbey of the Valley, Santiago Cantera, who had been a candidate in a fringe far-right Falange electoral list in the 1990s, opposed Franco's exhumation because Franco's descendants were not in agreement and because, in his view, the

---

[58] RTVE, "Los obispos vascos piden perdón por la ejecución de 14 religiosos a manos del bando franquista," (11 July 2009): *"No es justificable, ni aceptable por más tiempo, el silencio en el que medios oficiales de nuestra Iglesia han envuelto la muerte de estos sacerdotes. Tan largo silencio no ha sido sólo una omisión indebida, sino también una falta a la verdad, contra la justicia y la caridad."*

[59] ABC, "Rouco apela al olvido basado en 'reconciliación y perdón'" (24 November 2008): *"Hay que liberar a los jóvenes de los lastres del pasado, no cargándolos con viejas rencillas y rencores, sino ayudándoles a fortalecer la voluntad plena de concordia y de amistad."*

government's decision breached the sanctity and inviolability of a place of worship.[60] In the end, Cantera was forced to comply with the law. Franco, who obviously did not fall in the Civil War, is no longer in the Valley of the Fallen. In an interview five months later, the prior interpreted the exhumation of the dictator as an expression of the 'sinking of Western civilization' and the 'erosion of values' of the Spanish society, and compared it with the destruction of Buddhas by the Taliban in 2001.[61]

Catholicism is very present in Spain, in its history and its culture. In 2020, 20.5% of Spaniards reported being practising Catholics, and 46.7% more were non-practising Catholics. As a point of comparison, in 1980, 51.8% of Spaniards said they were practising Catholics, and 36% did not practice but saw themselves as Catholics as well. Among Catholics of 2020, practising or not, 62% admitted they never or hardly ever went to church, if not for baptisms, weddings or funerals.[62] Beyond percentages, religion is a less than subtle sociological reality in Spain, even among atheists and non-religious people. This reality is well reflected in arts and culture. When Pedro Almodóvar was awarded the 1999 Academy Award in the category of non-English language film for *All about My Mother*, he felt the need to explain:

> You know, I come from a country, from a culture very different from this. And you know, in that country now is six . . . in the morning, so let me dedicate this to the Spanish people that are watching TV now and they sacrifice their Monday just to look you and me with this. I mean, this is for Spain. I'm going to be very quick. . . . You know, I also want to thank my sisters . . . for the amount of candles [*sic*] that they lit to their favorite saints during the last months. You know, culture different. Thanks to the Virgin of Guadalupe, the Virgin of la Cabeza de Milagros, the Sacred Heart of Mary, Saint Judas Tadeo and El Jesus de Medinaceli.[63]

He managed to sputter this while being pulled away from the stage by Penélope Cruz and Antonio Banderas.

Spain has been a country of immigration since the 2000s, primarily from Eastern Europe, Latin America and North Africa. The country is becoming increasingly multicultural and greater religious diversity is to be expected.

---

[60] Jessica Martín, "Santiago Cantera, de candidato de la Falange a prior del Valle de los Caídos," *RTVE* (9 October 2019).
[61] Religión Digital, "Santiago Cantera: 'Lo que realmente molesta no es Franco, es la Cruz, es la comunidad benedictina'" (5 March 2020).
[62] CIS, *Barómetro de diciembre 1980, Estudio 1258* (Madrid: CIS, 1980), 14; CIS, *Barómetro de enero 2020, Estudio 3271* (Madrid: CIS, 2020), 22.
[63] From the Academy Awards Acceptance Speech Database.

Still, Catholic traditions and symbology are very present in society, and most Spaniards regard themselves as more or less devout followers of that religion. However, the political reach and persuasiveness of the Catholic hierarchy is disproportionately greater on the right than on the left. This is both a historical observation and the result of the strategic priorities of the leaders of the church. Faithful grassroots Christians, many of whom volunteer and contribute to commendable charity causes inside and outside the Church, hold different views and may have different political priorities from those of the leaders.

The defence of the unity of the Spanish nation has been one of the political issues the chiefs of the Church in Spain have focused on in the last 20 years. The national question recalls the historically close association between Catholicism and Spanish nationalism, a partnership to unite the country through religion. Upper echelons of the Church and conservatism appear to share the belief that being a good Spaniard is synonymous of being a good Catholic. In the early days of 2005, a week after the Basque parliament voted in favour of a new political settlement for greater self-government within Spain, the Conference of Bishops responded with a press release that, making a reference to terrorism, drew a link between the demand for self-determination and totalitarianism, and expressed the view that 'the unilateral denial of Spain's sovereignty, with no consideration for the grave consequences that such denial could lead to, would be unwise and morally unacceptable. . . . It is necessary to respect and protect the general interest of a centuries-old society.'[64] A few months later, PP launched a campaign to gather signatures outside Catalonia against the new Catalan statute of self-government (see section 3.3), and some of the party leaders advocated a boycott to the language and to Catalan products. In that context, COPE, the radio station of the Conference of Bishops, provided an extraordinary platform to sound the alarm about the alleged danger that the renewed statute of self-government was going to pose to the unity of the Spanish nation. In a statement in 2012, when the secessionist process had already begun in Catalonia, the Conference of Bishops expressed the view that

> none of the peoples or regions that conform the Spanish State could be understood, the way they are nowadays, if they had not been part of the long history of cultural and political union of the old nation that is Spain. Political proposals

---

[64] Conferencia Episcopal Española, "Sobre nación y nacionalismos," press release (7 January 2005): "*Poner en peligro la convivencia de los españoles, negando unilateralmente la soberanía de España, sin valorar las graves consecuencias que esta negación podría acarrear, no sería prudente ni moralmente aceptable. . . . Es necesario respetar y tutelar el bien común de una sociedad pluricentenaria.*"

headed towards the unilateral disintegration of such union are a cause of great concern for us.[65]

In an opinion piece in June 2018, the vicechair of the conference, Cardinal Antonio Cañizares, after declaring that he did not want 'to get into political considerations, which do not concern me', did exactly that, writing that 'the very unity of our Nation is also a moral question, whatever might be said or desired'. Cañizares went as far as to say that the fourth commandment – honour your parents – 'requires us to honour the Fatherland as well'.[66]

The position expressed many times by the top of the Church and its leaders as regards the unity of the Spanish nation is perfectly acceptable from a political perspective, but it is also hard to justify by reference to the sacred scriptures. The association between faith and nation reached absurdly comical proportions with the large nativity installed for Christmas in Madrid's city hall. It is said that the conservative mayor in the 2000s, Esperanza Aguirre, made her displeasure known because the scene did not have 'the flag' ('la bandera'). The following day, the nativity woke up with a large Spanish flag around it. The mayor expressed her surprise. 'What is the flag doing there?' 'You asked for it, ma'am.' 'The laundrywoman ("lavandera")! Her figurine is what I was asking for!' Apocryphal or not, given the circumstances the story could easily be true, and the fact of the matter is that in 2019 the city of Madrid decorated the nativity of the city hall with a long red and yellow tablecloth.

When PSOE and United Podemos formed their coalition government in January 2020, the chair and the vicechair of the Conference of Bishops shared publicly their concerns and issued a 'call to prayer for Spain'; Carlos Osoro Sierra, Pope Francis's ally and the archbishop of Madrid, quickly responded on social media that he preferred not to be carried away by polarisation, advocating 'working together within the rules we have provided ourselves for the common project that is Spain'.[67] While waning, a sizeable number of people consider themselves Catholic, and Catholic rituals and symbology remain very present in Spaniards' daily lives. This sociological reality is

---

[65] Conferencia Episcopal Española, "Ante la crisis, solidaridad," statement (3 October 2012): "*Ninguno de los pueblos o regiones que forman parte del Estado español podría entenderse, tal y como es hoy, si no hubiera formado parte de la larga historia de unidad cultural y política de esa antigua nación que es España. Propuestas políticas encaminadas a la desintegración unilateral de esta unidad nos causan una gran inquietud.*"

[66] Antonio Cañizares, "Oremos por España," *La Razón* (13 June 2018): "*No entro en ninguna valoración política, que no me corresponde*"; "*de la misma unidad de nuestra Nación, que también es una cuestión moral, se diga lo que se diga, se quiera o no*"; "*como un deber del cuarto mandamiento de la Ley de Dios que nos manda honrar también a la Patria.*"

[67] Religión Digital, "Osoro se desmarca de la cúpula de la CEE y anima al nuevo Gobierno a 'alcanzar acuerdos' por un 'proyecto común'" (7 January 2020): "*Con las reglas de juego que todos nos hemos dado, alcancemos acuerdos y trabajemos por este proyecto común que es España.*"

generally alluded to when trying to justify the Church's privileges in funding, taxes, education and so on, privileges that are unimaginable for other faiths or non-religious institutions. In the first two decades of the twenty-first century, the leaders of the Catholic Church returned to its centuries-old practice of openly cosying up with political and media conservatism in a truly symbiotic relationship. Only time will tell how exactly the Catholic Church will use its cards in the coming years.

Chapter 7

Vulnerabilities Need Not Be Weaknesses

On 11 March 2020, the World Health Organization made it official: Covid-19 was a pandemic. The epidemic had crossed international boundaries affecting large numbers of people worldwide. Spain's government declared the state of emergency three days later, and parliament approved a strict lockdown of the whole population, including children, who were not allowed to leave their homes at all for two months. No other country in Europe went so far so quickly in dealing with this menace. Spain was suddenly experiencing rocketing numbers of infections and the death toll seemed unstoppable. For weeks, Spain was the global epicentre of Covid-19. The fear was palpable in the air, in messaging apps and on media. Why was Spain being hit so hard? Humanity knew very little about this threatening new illness. Epidemiologists expressed tentative hypotheses to explain the particularly rapid expansion of the virus in the country, but one needed not be an expert to have an opinion, and many were prone to share theirs in case there was someone listening. *The Guardian* correspondent in Madrid, Giles Tremlett, asked himself, 'How did Spain get its coronavirus response so wrong?' He summarised some of the existing theories and then added a conjecture of his own:

> The main reason for the quick spread through Spain may be completely mundane. It has been an unusually mild, sunny spring. In late February and early March, with temperatures above 20C (68F), Madrid's pavement cafes and bars were heaving with happy folk, doing what *Madrileños* like best – being sociable. That means hugging, kissing and animated chatter just a few inches from someone else's face.[1]

---

[1] Giles Tremlett, "How did Spain Get Its Coronavirus Response So Wrong?," *The Guardian* (26 March 2020).

A perfect storm ensued on social media first, and radio and television talk shows second. Many people living in the country, and Spaniards living abroad, found the journalist's words distasteful. If one follows Tremlett's work, it becomes apparent that he meant no offence. He seems to enjoy living in Spain, and he has a profound knowledge of the country's history, culture and politics. But none of that mattered in those strange times, the strangest times for many societies in generations. Judging by the noise on the Twittersphere, enough people took the article in *The Guardian* as a personal attack, as if the author was blaming them and their way of life for their own misfortunes. I was not one of them. In my opinion, Tremlett was simply expressing a guess, and not a counter-intuitive or crazy sounding one. In fact, knowing what we learned over time about how the coronavirus spread, speculating about the likely significance of close physical distance, was not baseless at all. But there was something else, one other reason why he did not upset me. Tremlett was writing about a 'sociable' society where people hug, kiss and engage in 'animated chatter just a few inches from someone else's face'. Perhaps he exaggerated the proximity in this last claim, and such characterisation of personal interactions is not uniformly valid everywhere in Spain. But insofar as generalisations are allowed, *many* people in *many* parts of Spain do behave like that. And I think it is wonderful. The journalist was writing about one of the most beautiful things in the society where he lived, and he was well aware that not all countries, starting with the one where he was born – the UK – are equally capable of that form of sociability. It is their loss. Good humour, family spirit, care for the elderly, propensity to get physically close to each other – which, I know, is not for everyone – openness with emotions – at least with the positive ones – and so on, these are *typically* Spanish. I am dangerously bordering the stereotype now, so I will stop here, but the point is this: The Spanish society has virtues that are enviable abroad. These are characteristic strengths that make society more resilient and healthier. Paradoxically, they can become weaknesses when a gravely infectious disease kicks in. And that's when some of the characteristics need to be put temporarily on hold – for example, taking a step back and avoiding physical contact – and others ought to be maximised – like making sure grandpa and grandma have access to good healthcare. But no virus will change the fact that Spain, with its way of life, has many good reasons to be proud most of the time.

Spain is a sociable and friendly place where, notwithstanding socioeconomic inequalities, many people have a reasonable expectation of leading a long and good life, enjoy tasty food and maintain a healthier relation with alcohol than many of their European neighbours. While in monolingual Spain there is a 'widespread belief that Castilian is, and should remain, the dominant and common language',[2] the fact of the matter is that Spain is also a multilingual society where one in four people communicate in one other local language apart from Spanish. Because of its rich history, Spain harbours unique sites, 49 of them recognised by UNESCO as humanity's heritage. One in five organ donations in the European Union (EU) takes place in Spain, 6% of all of the world's donations with just over 0.6% of the world's population.[3] People living in other advanced economies may wish to have access to Spaniards' public health system, with all its limitations and all. None of that should be taken for granted.

And yet, Spaniards frequently compare their problems and their institutions to those in other European countries, and they do not like what they think they see in the mirror. On a good day, this habit is manifested in wit, mockery and self-mockery, in sarcastic and self-deprecating jokes. It is said, for example, that when Prime Minister Antonio Cánovas del Castillo was asked what in his view the 1876 constitution should say about the nation, he recommended they should just write that 'Spaniards are those people who can't be anything else'.[4] That's on a good day. On a bad day, however, the attitude can be defeatist and, worse still, haunted by an impostor syndrome. We cited former *Financial Times* Madrid correspondent, Tobias Buck, in chapter 2: 'Here was a country that . . . never seemed quite sure of its place in the world, a country forever in doubt, always measuring itself against the outside world and more often than not finding itself wanting.'[5] The keenness to look for references and possible good practice elsewhere is praiseworthy. The belief that the issues facing other societies are not as serious, however, is unfounded.

Not unrelated to this inferiority complex is the very present nationalism in much of Spain's society and institutions. The reinterpretation of history in the nineteenth century so as to construct the idea of the Spanish nation as an immanent reality, the loose ideology of National Catholicism, the imposition of cultural homogeneity during Francoism, the recent re-emergence of the far-right Vox in response to the independentist movement in Catalonia and so on have much in common. With their militaristic demeanour, they all have the appearance of strength, when in fact they are expressions of the deepest fears, weaknesses and fragilities. To be clear, nationalist hubris and self-absorption have not been unique to Spain in the last two centuries. Other countries have

---

[2] Xosé-Manoel Núñez Seixas, "Spanish Nationalism since 1975," in Diego Muro and Ignacio Lago (eds.): *The Oxford Handbook of Spanish Politics* (Oxford: Oxford University Press, 2020), 487.
[3] Gobierno de España, "España revalida en España revalida en 2019 su liderazgo mundial en donación de órganos y aporta el 20% de los donantes de la UE y el 6% del mundo," press release (7 September 2020).
[4] Brenan, *The Spanish Labyrinth*, 7.
[5] Buck, *After the Fall*, 10.

had and are having their own difficulties with their national questions. In this book, however, I have argued that one of the characteristic features of Spanish politics is not so much the uncertainty about the number of nations, but the heavy-handed way in which Spain and its nationalities and regions deal with this question. The frustrations and contradictions stemming from the failures to deal with such uncertainty delimit what's politically likely, what would be audacious and what outrageous. It is a political frailty without which it is not possible to make full sense of the country's politics, one of its Achilles' heels.

Achilles' heels are vulnerabilities but need not be weaknesses. Vulnerabilities are only weaknesses when society chooses to ignore them, when it fails to come to terms with them, as if pretending the past is gone and the future is to be written on a blank slate. In the case of Spain, beginning the policy analysis from the Achilles' heels illuminates our understanding of the controversies around the symbolic recognition of territories and the distribution of power between centre and periphery (chapter 3). It also applies to the way the country reads its painful recent history, including the necessary introspection about how the public institutions of the present are linked to the silence of the past (chapter 4). It is an invitation to reflect critically about the remaining privileges of a formerly almighty organisation, the Catholic Church, and the disproportionate influence such organisation may still have due to those privileges (chapter 6). The Achilles' heels are also an appeal to both sides of the political spectrum, left and right, to manage expectations about what is and should be realisable in terms of socio-economic justice within available resources (chapter 5).

Societies have long histories, but nations are a product of the nineteenth century, socially constructed to serve political agendas. In the case of Spain, the idea of the single nation State has faced a tension between centre and periphery, tension sometimes akin to high electrical voltage. The nation-building exercise of the first few decades of the nineteenth century was a liberal and unionist enterprise. Hence, the great interest of the centralising and economically liberal party Ciudadanos to present themselves in recent years as the 'political heirs' of the 'brave' deputies who adopted Spain's liberal constitution of 1812.[6] But in the second half of the nineteenth century a conflict between an old and a new economic class arose from regionally uneven capitalist development. With it, between the two Carlista wars – 1830s and 1870s – and with the loss of the remaining colonies in 1898, a new political cleavage emerged that associated centralisation with nationalism and conservatism, on the one hand, and progressivism with federalism

---

[6] La Vanguardia, "Rivera proclama a C's heredero de los liberales de la Constitución de 1812" (19 March 2017).

and decentralisation, on the other hand. Both Carlista wars and the Civil War of 1936 to 1939 had many causes, but the relationship between centre and periphery was a crucial element in all three conflicts, not the only cause, not necessarily the most important, but one of the most important ones. About the role of violence in the process of formation of the State, the American sociologist Charles Tilly wrote in the late 1960s that 'Spain, as usual, is the significant exception'.[7] Violence is not exceptional in the formation of nation States; Spain's particularity is that violence lived on as a persistent threat and a painful reality. While the threat of violence is now thankfully out of the equation, the political cleavage remains alive in this century. By and large, to this day nationalist and regionalist forces in the Basque Country and Catalonia, but also in Galicia, Valencia and other territories, tend to have a better understanding with Spain's left than with the right.

After Franco, the 1978 constitution managed a nearly impossible juggling act with the recognition of the indissoluble unity of the Spanish nation as well as the right to self-government of regions and nationalities. The constitution did not name the regions, neither did it mandate that all of them had to become self-governing entities. Drafters were purposefully vague but made the option of self-government available should regions choose to go for it. And that is exactly what happened within a few years. In the name of interterritorial equality, a policy of moderate devolution managed from the centre, 'coffee for all' ('café para todos'), was advocated by the Spanish government in the 1980s and 1990s. This progressively resulted in a sense of grievance among Basque and Catalan nationalists, the two territories where decentralisation enjoyed overwhelming support.

Ten years after the end of Euskadi Ta Askatasuna's (ETA) violence, nationalist parties have never been stronger in the Basque Country. Alongside Navarra, the Basque Country enjoys a long-lasting and unique financial settlement that suits its institutional and economic outlook. The pragmatic and *foralista* Basque Nationalist Party remains hegemonic, not only in light of its popular support, but also considering its influence in Madrid. Other parties in the Basque Country often define themselves in relation and relative opposition to *Partido Nacionalista Vasco's* standpoint. At the same time, the pro-independence left is now actively engaged in political debates in the Spanish parliament. While still advocating self-determination and independence, they seem to be less rushed about the speed with which they would want the Basque Country to get there. ETA is still very much part of living

---

[7] Charles Tilly, "Collective Violence in European Perspective," in Hugh Davies Graham and Ted Robert Gurr (eds.): *Violence in America: Historical and Comparative Perspectives: A Report to the National Commission on the Causes and Prevention of Violence*, Vol. 1 (Washington, DC: US Government Printing Office, 1969), 25.

memory, and society is still licking its wounds and learning to deal with a still recent past of violence. Too many people suffered in silence for too long. In this context and at this stage, a hypothetical coalition of pro- and anti-independence parties on the left seems unlikely. However, one should not presume it will remain this way forever. As time goes by, such hypothetical coalition could present a serious and innovative alternative to the currently dominant Basque Nationalist Party.

Catalonia had a very troubled relationship with the rest of Spain and with herself in the 2010s. The two high points were the illegal but widely supported independence referendum of October 2017, and the supreme court ruling that sentenced nine Catalan leaders for sedition in October 2019. Despite what might seem from the past decade, however, if one looks back in history, the relationship between Catalonia and the rest of Spain has not always been of latent war. It would be premature and plainly wrong to believe that the relationship could not be restored. Sociological research shows that, even in the very charged late 2017, Catalans had multiple regional and national identities, and a majority felt *both* Catalan and Spanish, or *more* Catalan than Spanish.[8]

Having said that, Catalonia seems to have outgrown the 'State of self-governing entities' ('Estado de las autonomías') established in the 1978 constitution. At the same time, 'the challenge of Catalan secessionism has given rise to more visible manifestations of Spanish national feeling, as expressed by the displaying of Spanish flags in balconies and shops' around Spain.[9] According to the official Centre for Sociological Research, in December 2018, three in ten Spaniards wanted an entirely centralised system or one where regions had less power than they have now.[10] The far-right Vox, on the political chessboard since 2019, is capitalising that position muscularly. Research has also shown that generally in Spain there has been a 'centralising drift in public perception of central government's responsibilities'.[11] This was likely to be the result of the recentralisation derived from the austerity of the 2010s, with the resulting restriction of regions' budgetary and operational capabilities.[12] It cannot be serendipitous that such recentralisation in the name of economic rationalism coincided in time with deep political tension between Catalan authorities and the central government in Madrid.

---

[8] María José Hierro, "Regional and National Identities in Spain," in Diego Muro and Ignacio Lago (eds.): *The Oxford Handbook of Spanish Politics* (Oxford: Oxford University Press, 2020), 505.

[9] Núñez Seixas, "Spanish Nationalism since 1975," 480.

[10] CIS, *Barómetro de noviembre 2018, Estudio 3231* (Madrid: CIS, 2018), 14.

[11] Sandra León and Ignacio Jurado, "Multilevel Governance in Spain," in Diego Muro and Ignacio Lago (eds.): *The Oxford Handbook of Spanish Politics* (Oxford: Oxford University Press, 2020), 238.

[12] Diego Muro, "When Do Countries Recentralize? Ideology and Party Politics in the Age of Austerity," *Nationalism and Ethnic Politics* 21, no. 1 (2015), 25.

Spanish politics since 2010 has been a reminder that the 1978 constitutional fitting of the territories was a ceiling for some but a floor for others. The decade made clear that there is no more road to kick the can down any further. This is an eminently political question, not a legal one, a political question that affects national identities as well as less symbolic but more practical issues related to taxation and public investment. This is a political question that will not be resolved, in the sense that it will not end, because it is part of what makes Spain different. It is a question that can only be dealt with – or 'brought along', to use Ortega's 'conllevanza' – politically, relying on the rule of law and democracy as equally fundamental pillars in society. The democratic wish of the people is expressed by the combination of all parliamentary assemblies of Spain, not only the lower and upper chambers in Madrid, but also the regional ones. With this point I do not suggest that each region or nationality has equal collective subjectivity in Spain's history and politics; some of them go centuries back while others were set up in the early 1980s. The question about the historical subjectivity of each region remains open but, for now, the distribution of power and representativeness between existing political authorities in Madrid and elsewhere should be the starting point. The law should not be manipulated to stop the debate, and neither should democracy be manipulated to cause political dislocations. The Catalan question will require less involvement from courts, and more responsibility, mutual trust, self-control, generosity and imagination from politicians.[13]

Just one or more? If more, how many more? The disagreement and the uncertainty about the number of nations in Spain need not be a weakness. A difficult question can be answered by providing a response, but sometimes it can be better answered by changing the question. A disagreement can actually be transformed into a source of strength, turning uncertainty into diversity, something to be proud of. In a democratic society, disagreements are not the problem; the problem can be how societies and their leaders deal with disagreements.

Throughout history, at least three times have Catalan authorities expressed a desire to create a political entity partly or totally separate from Spain, four if we remember 1641. The last time so far was in 2017, but there were two more during the second republic. With his declaration in 1931, Francesc Macià was trying to shape the outlines of a baby democracy, and set the ground for the statute of self-government one year later, which in turn would inspire the constitutional fitting of the territories in 1978. With his declaration in 1934, Lluís Companys was responding to a reactionary and militaristic turn

---

[13] Koldo Casla, "La hermana del Estado de derecho," *El Periódico* (29 September 2017).

from the central government in Madrid – and it costed him his life; he was executed in Barcelona in 1940. It is too early to know if the current crossroad is more like the future-defining moment of 1931 or the politically dangerous zero-sum game of 1934. Nations are nostalgic for their imagined golden age, a past that never quite was the way they think they remember it. In 1882, Ernest Renan wrote that forgetting one's history is 'an essential factor in the creation of a nation'.[14] In 1931, 1934, 1978, 2010, 2017 or today, Renan must not be right about that.

Francoism was an extreme representation of nationalist hubris. Not in vain, Franco's side in the armed conflict was known as 'los nacionales', as if the others were aliens. During the dictatorship, republicanism, Marxism, socialism, Masonry, liberal democracy and indeed any position mildly contrary to the regime were not only illegal, but were also considered foreign and contrary not only to Spain's interests, but to Spain's ethos. The Transition to democracy in the late 1970s saw the adoption of a pact of silence. The pact was symbolised in the Amnesty Act 1977, but its effects reached far beyond the official gazette. It was not merely a legal or political agreement. For at least two decades, society as a whole was tacitly imbued by this pact of silence, *amnesia*, a calculated forgetting. In the 2000s, little by little a new generation of Spaniards began to denounce that the amnesia was muting into a sort of *aphasia*, the deliberate obstruction of the production and understanding of speech and discourse, and *agnosia*, the inability to interpret and recognise the external world. This new generation did not feel represented by the compromises made by their parents in the Transition; they demanded a renegotiation of the terms of the contract.

I for one will not try to teach a lesson to the previous generation from the comfort of my lounge. I am in no position to say that they should have known better. The constitution and the Transition were far from perfect, but given the extreme difficulties, the Spanish society and their representatives did what they could with the ingredients at hand. Under the threat of violence from the State and from armed groups, I believe the Transition was, with all its limitations, one of the best things that happened to Spain in the twentieth century. But we are in the twenty-first century now. Recovering the historical memory is not about pointing fingers to our parents. It is about honouring and acknowledging the victims' suffering, and about inquiring self-critically about the consequences of society's past decisions. Now that the Spanish democracy has matured and is consolidated, it is time to embrace the past

---

[14] Renan, *What Is a Nation?*, 251.

and reflect on the possible impact that the difficult compromises had on the robustness of the democratic institutions, including the judiciary, the police and the monarchy. It would be a mistake to assume that historical memory deals only with the past. It is predominantly about the future, about the perspective necessary to learn about oneself.

It is important to admit that, still today, the general opinion about Franco's time is nuanced. The number of people openly nostalgic about the regime may be relatively small, but more would say that the politics of the republic partly provoked the armed conflict, and even more would add that Spain's economy advanced significantly in the second half of the dictatorship. As discussed in this book, the country's starting point in capitalist development was belated, and economic progress seemed a historical inevitability in the mid-twentieth century. The structural conditions were ripe for the country to do much better in the 1950s and 1960s, and it is questionable how decisive the regime actually was in securing such progress. That the economy improved with Franco does not mean it did so because of him. Unemployment got down, and the economy went up partly thanks to low wages, emigration and the exclusion of women from the workforce.

We should not underestimate the effort required to achieve democracy. Spaniards overcame enormous difficulties in the 1970s. The Transition may not have been fair or just, but it worked. However, one should not forget that those placing the hurdles to democracy were Spanish as well, with their constant threats of military retaliation and the pervasive fear that a misstep could be disastrous. There was nothing natural about the risks in that scenario. The impediments were political and man-made. And those who placed the barriers, the men leading the dictatorship, were never held accountable. The older ones left politics entirely, but many found their way into the new democracy, in the political arena and State institutions. There was nothing exemplary about Spain's Transition, and people would do well to avoid self-complacency.

Spain's democracy is not fragile, no more than any other. Eight decades after the end of the Civil War and more than four decades after the constitution, society is ready to examine if and how the past has shaped the present time. But also to put the past into perspective, because not for everything that has happened in Spain since the late 1970s we can find an answer in the dictatorship and the Transition. Spanish politics is much more than Franco and Catalonia. There is no excuse why Spain should not hold its Achilles' heels tight. As observed by the UN special rapporteur on truth, justice, reparation and guarantees of non-recurrence, Pablo de Greiff, after his mission to Spain in 2014, 'The strength of democratic institutions must be measured not by their ability to ignore certain issues, especially those that refer to fundamental rights, but rather by their ability to manage them effectively, however complex and awkward they may be.'[15]

The economic crisis and the austerity of the 2010s showcased the value of intergenerational solidarity and community engagement, two of Spain's most valuable assets. Individuals and community groups around the country organised themselves to demand better public education, healthcare and housing. Outraged and organised civil society put pressure on the political class, and they managed to have some influence on some housing laws adopted at the regional level. However, the Spanish society went through a long and aching time of austerity, with mounting unemployment and a high number of evictions, a time when the worst off suffered the most and inequality went up. The so-called family mattress prevented many from falling into destitution, but the welfare state proved insufficient to cope.

While the rest of Western Europe set the structures of their welfare states in the three decades after World War II, Spain had a dictatorship suspicious of anything that might sound remotely Socialist. While the 30 *glorious* years resulted in greater egalitarianism in much of the continent, income and wealth inequality rose significantly with Franco. Soon after democracy was restored in the late 1970s, the rest of Western Europe began flirting with neoliberalism. On top of the structural gap after 30 years of underinvestment, and despite initial efforts in the 1980s, public spending in welfare state never caught up with the standards of the European Communities – EU since 1992 – with the possible exceptions of unemployment benefits and public pensions, and periodically healthcare.

Privatisation of social housing, subsidies for developers, deregulation of the rental sector, generous tax benefits and policies since the 1950s put public resources at the service of homeownership. Those policies resulted in a crumbly economic substrate that benefited some but did not contribute to reduce inequalities. In the 2000s, Spain got flashed by fast economic growth and missed the opportunity to make the necessary structural changes to the housing market. Instead, the country's economy relied on two pillars, construction and tourism. The former burst like a bubble with the financial crash of 2008. The long-term sustainability of the latter in the era of global warming is very much under question.

Since the 1990s, Spain's regions have had minimum income schemes that were meant to fulfil their constitutional responsibilities in relation to social assistance. Nonetheless, the system has allowed gigantic differences between

---

[15] Special rapporteur on the promotion of truth, justice, reparation and guarantees of non-recurrence, Pablo de Greiff, *Mission to Spain*, UN doc: A/HRC/27/56/Add.1 (2014), para. 102.

regions, and most of the schemes present significant gaps in terms of coverage and adequacy. The result is that most households in poverty or at risk of poverty do not have access to a minimum income necessary to satisfy the most essential needs of clothing, energy, food or housing. In June 2020, the Spanish government put in place a *national* vital income scheme. For now, its effects have been modest, and time will tell if some regions use this as an opportunity to defund their already poorly subsidised schemes.

Society is still suffering the historical consequences of the late development of the country's welfare state. If politics is the art of the possible and the attainable, politicians on the left should be frank with the public and admit that there are certain financial constraints derived from international markets, the EU and the constitution itself. Meanwhile, politicians and commentators on the right should be reminded that, compared with other EU Member States, Spain has a notable margin of improvement in terms of social spending, tax revenue and fairness in the distribution of the tax pressure.

Less than ever before, but the Spanish society is largely Catholic. Some are devout followers, others do not practice rigorously, but Catholicism is very present in culture and society, as well as in Spaniards' daily lives, and that includes believers and non-believers, as well as those having other religions. In the twenty-first century, Spain is still a Catholic-majority country, but religion and religious leaders do not influence society across the board. An international study by Pew Research in 2020 showed that 78% of Spaniards did not think a belief in God was necessary to be a moral person and to have good values, just as many as Dutch and Britons, fewer than in France, but more than in Germany and Italy. The difference was important in the political spectrum: only 8% of people aligned with politics on the left thought God was necessary for morality, but 33% on the right did. According to that study, in no other European country has the share of people for whom God plays an important role in their lives declined so much since 1991.[16]

Since the Visigoth king Recaredo converted in the sixth century, Catholicism has been central in Spain's history, particularly in the last 550 years. Spanish monarchs declared themselves global defenders of the true faith, and much of Spain's international relations over the centuries were framed in religious terms, starting with colonialism and empire. In the nineteenth century, the nation-building project and the defence of Catholicism went hand in hand. Since then, religion has played a central role in the centralising agenda, which in the early decades of the twentieth century became unapologetically conservative as well as nationalist. Partly as a reaction to the real and

---

[16] Pew Research, *The Global God Divide* (July 2020).

perceived anticlericalism of much of the left during the second republic in the 1930s, most of the church supported Franco's side in the Civil War, which was presented as a confrontation between good and evil, believers and atheists, nationals and foreigners – meaning those induced by foreign ideas. The church provided moral legitimacy and a transcendental cause to the coup and the regime that followed. In the decade of the second Vatican Council, in the 1960s, young priests and grassroots Catholics started to demand a change in the Church, a change that reached the top of the institution in the early 1970s. With anticlericalism out of the picture on the left, and in a wealthier, modernised and urban society, the dictatorship was no longer fit for the purposes of the Church. The changes within the Church were a decisive factor in Spain's Transition to democracy after Franco.

The 1978 constitution recognised religious freedom and declared that no religion would be official. However, it also reserved a special place for the Catholic Church in light of its historic and sociological significance. That special place was formalised with four international treaties negotiated in Rome at the same time that the constitution was being drafted in Madrid. The supposed secular nature of the Spanish State is put under question by the privileges that Catholicism enjoys to this day, which derive from those agreements signed with the Vatican in 1979. The church competes on unequal terms in the provision of education, both because of the funding it receives from the State for its private schools, and because no other religion is mandatorily offered in all schools, public and private. Despite their multiple real estate investments, the Church is not financially autonomous from the State. While the Church's accounts have not been cleared by the Court of Auditors, they benefit from a unique tax settlement by which Spanish citizens, regardless of their conscience and convictions, continue funding the Church's operations, and that includes its charities, but also its proselytism.

There are Catholics of all political and ideological orientations, but particularly since 2005 the leadership of the Catholic Church has sided with the right and even the extreme right on a number of political questions. With its public and private resources, the Catholic Church launched and financially supports conservative and far-right media that have a decisive influence on the political environment. Leaders of the Church have openly expressed political views aligned with conservative politics in relation to historical memory and the unity of the Spanish nation. Meanwhile, they have not yet made amends for the Church's support for Franco's coup and Catholicism's prominence in the dictatorship.

Cutting off the umbilical cord between Church and State – which does not mean extirpating Catholicism from society – is proving very difficult with little and slow progress since the late 1970s. The extraordinary privileges of one faith are becoming ever less justifiable in an increasingly secular and multicultural society that proclaims the freedom of religion and the separation between Church and State. If the Catholic Church has so many followers, it should not be that difficult to secure funding for their activities without having to rely on non-religious taxpayers.

The first semester of 2020, there was a profound disagreement between European governments about whether and how the EU could and should respond to the pandemic of Covid-19. The Netherlands led the group of so-called frugal States that were not that keen on sharing a pool of resources. Spain was with France, Italy and Portugal on the other side of the debate arguing the opposite. On 10 April, the Portuguese prime minister António Costa publicly questioned the Dutch commitment to the EU:

> We need to know whether we can go on with 27 in the European Union, 19 (in the Eurozone), or if there is anyone who wants to be left out. Naturally, I am referring to the Netherlands. . . . If there is not enough rational thinking to realize that we need to respond together, if there is no courage to resist populism and you are afraid of next year's elections, (then that raises the question of) whether we can have a Eurozone with these 19, or if we need to have other forms of organization within Europe.[17]

Leaving aside the merits of the case, this was politics, but it was politics of the clever sort. Here was the head of government of a small-sized country from the south questioning the credentials and the commitment to the common project of one of the richest nations from the north, a nation that had co-founded the European Communities back in the 1950s, while Portugal was only allowed to join the club in 1986, alongside Spain. Costa was reclaiming centre stage for his country while trying to displace one that had played a key role in the show from the beginning. Whether one government or the other was in the right is beside the point. The anecdote is a good example of a leader unafraid of taking the bull by the horns, ready to present his country as no less European than anyone else. Costa knew other countries were richer and more powerful, but he believed his society was not inferior to any other. He was not going to belittle himself or his people. He showed intelligence and confidence, but not arrogance.

We live in times of rising xenophobia and nationalist hubris, but self-confidence is in much shorter supply. Confident is that who does not look away in front of a mirror. A confident society is one that is courageous to acknowledge its historical flaws, one that is willing to grow into its vulnerabilities,

---

[17] Ivo Oliveira, "Portugal's Costa questions Dutch commitment to EU," *Politico* (10 April 2020).

to learn, examine and deal with the strong foundations of its weaknesses. The rising scapegoat nationalism of our times, in Spain and elsewhere, is an expression of the exact opposite. They manipulate the symbols of the nation for their political agenda, and they try to confiscate the commons by excluding a supposedly undeserving *other* from society's protection.

In the 12th scene of Bohemian Lights, written in the early 1920s, Ramón María del Valle-Inclán makes Max Estrella say in his last breaths:

> The tragic sense of Spanish life can only be rendered through an aesthetic that is systematically deformed. . . . Spain is a grotesque deformation of the European civilization. . . . The most beautiful images on a concave mirror are absurd. . . . Distortion ceases to be distortion when subjected to a perfect mathematic. My present aesthetic approach consists in the transformation of all classical norms with the mathematics of a concave mirror.[18]

That is the essence of *esperpento*, a literary style for a Spain in crisis in the early twentieth century, resonant in the twenty-first as well. Made of sarcasm, caricature and the grotesque deformation of reality, *esperpento* exists because sometimes one needs to deform nature in order to understand it.

So, I end with a message to the arrogant xenophobes of our time. If you are going to love your country, love it for what it is, including its imperfections, because for its virtues it will be loved by everyone else. Love it for what you dare to see, not for the nostalgic remembrance of a time that never quite was the way you imagine it. Love the reflection in front of the concave mirror, because when you hold up a concave mirror to idols, the deformed image you receive is their true nature.

---

[18] Ramón María del Valle-Inclán, *Luces de Bohemia* (Arganda del Rey: Verbum, 2019), 65–6: "*El sentido trágico de la vida española sólo puede darse con una estética sistemáticamente deformada. . . . España es una deformación grotesca de la civilización europea. . . . Las imágenes más bellas en un espejo cóncavo son absurdas. . . . La deformación deja de serlo cuando está sujeta a una matemática perfecta. Mi estética actual es transformar con matemática de espejo cóncavo las normas clásicas.*"

Time Line

- 1808–1814: Napoleonic or Independence War.
- 1833–1840: First Carlista war.
- 1846–1849: War of the *matiners* ('early risers'), a Carlista confrontation essentially confined to Catalonia.
- 1873–1874: First republic.
- 1872–1876: Second Carlista War, at the end of which Basque Medieval powers of self-government (*fueros*) are taken away for good.
- 1878: A new scheme is set in place by which the Basque provinces levy their own taxes (*concierto económico*). Navarra has it since 1841 (*convenio económico*).
- 1874–1923: Restoration of monarchy with a parliamentary system where two parties take turns in power thanks to rigged elections.
- 1898: Spain loses its colonial territories in Cuba, Puerto Rico and the Philippines.
- 1923–1931: Dictatorship, led until 1930 by Miguel Primo de Rivera.
- 1931–1936: First democratic experiment, the second republic.
- 1936–1939: Civil War.
- 1939–1975: Franco's dictatorship.
- 1953: Concordat with the Vatican.
- 1955: Spain joins the UN.
- 1959: Emergence of ETA.
- 1973: ETA kills the prime minister, Luis Carrero Blanco.
- 1975: Franco dies. He is buried in the Valley of the Fallen.
- 1977 (June): First free elections, won by Conservative UCD. Adolfo Suárez remains prime minister.
- 1977 (October): Amnesty Act.
- 1978: A new constitution is adopted.

- 1979: Signature of four agreements between Spain and the Holy See to reform the concordat.
- 1982: Felipe González, new prime minister (PSOE).
- 1986: Spain joins the European Communities.
- 1996: Conservatives (PP) are back in power, with José María Aznar as prime minister.
- 2004: PSOE wins the general election, led by José Luis Rodríguez Zapatero.
- 2007: Historical Memory Act.
- 2008–2016: Financial and socio-economic crisis.
- 2010: The constitutional court declares some articles of the new Catalan statute of self-government unconstitutional. Independence starts to gain significant social and political support in Catalonia.
- 2011 (October): ETA announces the permanent end of violence.
- 2011 (December): New prime minister, Mariano Rajoy (PP).
- 2017: Independence wins clearly in a referendum with low turnout that is declared illegal by the judiciary. Catalonia's autonomy is intervened for two months by the central government.
- 2018: After a motion of non-confidence in Mariano Rajoy, Pedro Sánchez (PSOE) is elected prime minister by a majority in parliament.
- 2019 (October): The supreme court sentences nine pro-independence politicians to between 9 and 13 years of prison for sedition and other crimes. Franco's remains are exhumed from the Valley of the Fallen.
- 2020: First coalition government since the 1930s, with PSOE and United Podemos. United Podemos includes Podemos, United Left and sister parties of the two in Galicia and Catalonia. Pedro Sánchez remains prime minister.
- 2021 (June): The Spanish government pardons the nine pro-independence politicians.

Bibliography

ABC. No. 11385, 22 August 1942. https://www.abc.es/archivo/periodicos/abc-madrid-19420822-6.html

———. "Rouco apela al olvido basado en 'reconciliación y perdón'." 24 November 2008. https://www.abc.es/sociedad/abci-rouco-apela-olvido-basado-reconciliacion-y-perdon-200811240300-911474347777_noticia.html

Academy Awards Acceptance Speech Database. http://aaspeechesdb.oscars.org/link/072-12/

Act on the Succession to the Head of State, of 26 July 1947 (BOE no. 208, 27 July).

Act 44/1967, of 28 June, about the exercise of the civil right of freedom of religion in education centres (BOE no. 156, 1 July).

Act 62/1969, of 22 July, whereby it is decided on the succession to the Head of State (BOE no. 175, 23 July).

Act 1/1977, of 4 January, of Political Reform (BOE no. 4, 5 January).

Act 46/1977, of 15 October, of Amnesty (BOE no. 248, 17 October).

Act 24/1992, of 10 November, approving the cooperation agreement between the State and the Federation of Evangelical Religious Entities of Spain (BOE no. 272, 12 November).

Act 25/1992, of 10 November, approving the cooperation agreement between the State and the Federation of Jewish Communities of Spain (BOE no. 272, 12 November).

Act 26/1992, of 10 November, approving the cooperation agreement between the State and the Islamic Commission of Spain (BOE no. 272, 12 November).

Act 57/2007, that recognises and broadens the rights and establishes measures in favour of those who suffered persecution or violence during the Civil War and the Dictatorship, of 26 December (BOE no. 310, 27 December).

Act 27/2011, of 1 August, to update, adapt and modernize the social security system (BOE no. 184, 2 August).

Act 29/2011, of 22 September, on the Recognition and Comprehensive Protection of Victims of Terrorism (BOE no. 229, 23 September).

Act 3/2012, of 6 July, of urgent measures for the reform of the labour market (BOE no. 162, 7 July).
Act (Basque Country) 4/2008, of 19 June, on the Recognition and Reparation of Victims of Terrorism (BOPV no. 124, 1 July 2008).
Act (Basque Country) 12/2016, of 28 July, of declaration and reparation of victims of unjust suffering as a consequence of the abuse of their human rights, produced between 1978 and 1999 in the context of politically motivated violence in the Basque Country (BOPV no. 151, 10 August).
Act (Catalonia) 24/2015, of 29 July, of urgent measures to tackle the emergency on housing and energy poverty (DOGC no. 6928, 5 August).
Act (Navarra) 16/2019, of 25 March, of recognition and reparation of victims of politically motivated acts caused by far-right groups or by civil servants (BON no. 62, 1 April).
Adams, John. *A Defence of the Constitutions of the United States*. London: C. Dilly, 1787.
Aduriz, Iñigo, and Olías, Laura. "Iglesias dice que la derogación de la reforma laboral debe ser total como se firmó con Bildu después de que el PSOE limitase su alcance." *eldiario.es*, 20 May 2020. https://www.eldiario.es/politica/psoe-unidas-podemos-eh-pp_1_5971827.html
Agencia Tributaria. "Statistics of Income Tax Statements since 2003." http://www.agenciatributaria.es/AEAT.internet/datosabiertos/catalogo/hacienda/Estadistica_de_los_declarantes_del_IRPF.shtml
Agirreazkuenaga, Joseba. "Las oportunidades de construcción del Estado liberal español: La 'España Foral'." *Ayer* 35 (1999): 121–46.
Águeda, Pedro. "Muere por coronavirus el expolicía acusado de torturas 'Billy el Niño'." *eldiario.es*, 7 May 2020. https://www.eldiario.es/politica/fallece-expolicia-billy-nino-covid-19_1_5957352.html
Aguilar, Paloma. "Judiciary Involvement in Authoritarian Repression and Transitional Justice: The Spanish Case in Comparative Perspective." *International Journal of Transitional Justice* 7, no. 2 (2013): 245–66.
———. *Memory and Amnesia: The Role of the Spanish Civil War in the Transition to Democracy*. New York & Oxford: Berghahn Books, 2002.
———. "The Memory of the Civil War in the Transition to Democracy: The Peculiarity of the Basque Case." *West European Politics* 21, no. 4 (1998): 5–25.
Aguilar, Paloma, and Payne, Leigh A. *Revealing New Truths about Spain's Violent Past: Perpetrators' Confessions and Victim Exhumations*. Oxford: Palgrave Macmillan, 2016.
Aguilar Hendrickson, Manuel, and Arriba González de Durana, Ana. "Crisis económica y transformaciones de la política de garantía de ingresos mínimos para la población activa." *Panorama Social* 29 (2019): 91–103.
AIREF. *Los programas de rentas mínimas en España*. Madrid: AIREF, 2019.
Alguacil, Aitana, et al. *La vivienda en España en el siglo XXI: Diagnóstico del modelo residencial y propuestas para otra política de vivienda*. Madrid: Foessa, 2013.

Alvaredo, Facundo, and Sáez, Emmanuel. "Income and Wealth Concentration in Spain from a Historical and Fiscal Perspective." *Journal of European Economic Association* 7, no. 5 (2010): 1140–67.
Álvarez Junco, José. *Spanish Identity in the Age of Nations*. Manchester: Manchester University Press, 2011.
Álvarez Junco, José, and De La Fuente, Gregorio. *El relato nacional: Historia de la historia de España*. Madrid: Taurus, 2017.
Amnesty International. *Acabar con la doble injusticia: Víctimas de tortura y malos tratos sin reparación*. Madrid: Amnesty International, 2004.
———. *Wrong Prescription: The Impact of Austerity Measures on the Right to Health in Spain*. London: Amnesty International, 2018.
Anderson, Benedict. *Imagined Communities: Reflections on the Origin and Spread of Nationalism*. London: Verso, 1983.
Archivo online sobre la violencia terrorista en Euskadi: Fondo Euskobarometro. https://www.arovite.com/es/fondo-euskobarometro/
Arrese, José Luis. "No queremos una España de proletarios, sino de propietarios." *ABC*, 2 May 1959. https://linz.march.es/Ficha.asp?Reg=r-73814
Artola Blanco, Miguel, et al. "Wealth in Spain, 1900–2014: A Country of Two Lands." *WID.world Working Paper Series*, no. 5 (2018).
Ayala, Luis, and Cantó, Olga. "Los efectos redistributivos de las prestaciones sociales y los impuestos: un estado de la cuestión." *Observatorio Social de la Caixa*. Palma: Fundación La Caixa, 2020.
Badcock, James. "Spain is Flirting with Another Civil War." *Foreign Policy*, 27 September 2017. https://foreignpolicy.com/2017/09/27/spain-is-flirting-with-another-civil-war/
———. "Spanish Province Passes Historic Motion to Split from 'Fictitious Region'." *The Telegraph*, 29 December 2019. https://www.telegraph.co.uk/news/2019/12/29/spanish-province-passes-historic-motion-split-fictitious-region/
Banco de España. *Encuesta Financiera de las Familias: Descripción, Métodos y Resultados Preliminares*. Madrid: BDE, 2004.
———. *Encuesta Financiera de las Familias 2008: Métodos, Resultados y Cambios desde 2005*. Madrid: BDE, 2010.
———. *Encuesta Financiera de las Familias 2014: Métodos, Resultados y Cambios desde 2011*. Madrid: BDE, 2017.
———. *Encuesta Financiera de las Familias 2017: Métodos, Resultados y Cambios desde 2014*. Madrid: BDE, 2020.
Bar, Antonio. "A Nation of Nations? A Reply to Joseph H.H. Weiler." *International Journal of Constitutional Law* 17, no. 4 (2019): 1307–14.
Barrero, Abraham. "Sobre la Libertad Religiosa en la Historia Constitucional Española." *Revista Española de Derecho Constitucional* 21, no. 61 (2001): 131–85.
Barrio, Astrid and Rodríguez-Teruel, Juan. "Reducing the Gap between Leaders and Voters? Elite Polarization, Outbidding Competition, and the Rise of Secessionism in Catalonia." *Ethnic and Racial Studies* 40, no. 10 (2017): 1776–194.
BBC. "Spanish Civil War 'Martyrs' Beatified." 13 October 2013. https://www.bbc.com/news/world-europe-24515567

———. "Vatican Condemns Spain Gay Bill." 22 April 2005. http://news.bbc.co.uk/2/hi/europe/4473001.stm

———. "Vatican Honours Spanish War Dead." 28 October 2007. http://news.bbc.co.uk/2/hi/europe/7066094.stm

Beatley, Meghan. "The Shocking Rape Trial that Galvanised Spain's Feminists—and the Far Right." *The Guardian*, 23 April 2019. https://www.theguardian.com/world/2019/apr/23/wolf-pack-case-spain-feminism-far-right-vox

Bergantiños, Noemi, Font, Raquel, and Bacigalupe, Amaia. "Las rentas mínimas de inserción en época de crisis. ¿Existen diferencias en la respuesta de las comunidades autónomas?." *Papers: Revista de Sociología* 102, no. 3 (2017): 399–420.

Billig, Michael. *Banal Nationalism*. London: Sage, 1995.

Bombey, Daniel. "Spain's Tight Budget Puts Squeeze on Coronavirus Response." *Financial Times*, 24 June 2020. https://www.ft.com/content/65f22d03-fca2-4ac9-a4e4-65789e19cf9f

Boyd, Carolyn P. *Historia Patria: Politics, History, and National Identity in Spain, 1875–1975*. Princeton: Princeton University Press, 1997.

———. "The Politics of History and Memory in Democratic Spain." *The ANNALS of the American Academy of Political and Social Science* 617, no. 1 (2008): 133–48.

Brenan, Gerald. *The Spanish Labyrinth*. Cambridge: Cambridge University Press, 1943.

Buck, Tobias. *After the Fall: Crisis, Recovery and the Making of a New Spain*. London: Weidenfeld & Nicolson, 2019.

Butler, Judith. *Precarious Life: The Powers of Mourning and Violence*. London: Verso, 2004.

Cadena Ser. "Manuel Sánchez: 'Fuimos aprendiendo a base de muertos'," 30 November 2017. https://play.cadenaser.com/audio/001RD010000004818359/

Cañizares, Antonio. "Oremos por España." *La Razón*, 13 June 2018. https://www.religionenlibertad.com/opinion/816507801/Oremos-por-Espana.html

Carr, E. H. *What is History?* 2nd edition. London: Penguin, 1990.

Carreras, Albert, and Tafunel, Xavier. "National Enterprise: Spanish Big Manufacturing Firms (1917–1990), between State and Market." *Economics Working Paper 93*. Barcelona: Universitat Pompeu Fabra, 1994.

Casla, Koldo. "La hermana del Estado de derecho." *El Periódico*, 29 September 2017. https://www.elperiodico.com/es/opinion/20170929/la-hermana-del-estado-de-derecho-koldo-casla-referendum-articulo-6320534

———. "The Rights We Live In: Protecting the Right to Housing in Spain through Fair Trial, Private and Family Life and Non-Retrogressive Measures." *International Journal of Human Rights* 20, no. 3 (2016): 285–97.

Casqueiro, Javier. "¿Hay una forma de vivir a la madrileña como dice Ayuso? Los candidatos opinan." *El País*, 29 April 2021. https://elpais.com/espana/elecciones-madrid/2021-04-29/la-singularidad-de-ser-o-vivir-a-la-madrilena.html

Causa, Orsetta, and Hermansen, Mikkel. "Income Redistribution through Taxes and Transfers across OECD Countries." *Economics Department Working Papers no. 1453*. Paris: OECD, 2017.

Central Intelligence Agency (United States). "Terrorism Review." 19 January 1984. https://www.cia.gov/readingroom/document/cia-rdp84-00893r000100340001-3

Centro de Investigaciones Sociológicas. *Barómetro de diciembre 1980, Estudio 1258*. Madrid: CIS, 1980. http://www.cis.es/cis/opencm/ES/1_encuestas/estudios/ver.jsp?estudio=250
———. *Barómetro de enero 2020, Estudio 3271*. Madrid: CIS, 2020. http://www.cis.es/cis/export/sites/default/-Archivos/Marginales/3260_3279/3271/es3271mar.pdf
———. *Barómetro de enero 2021, Estudio 3307*. Madrid: CIS, 2021. http://datos.cis.es/pdf/Es3307marMT_A.pdf
———. *Barómetro de junio 2004, Estudio 2568*. Madrid: CIS, 2004. http://www.cis.es/cis/export/sites/default/-Archivos/Marginales/2560_2579/2568/es2568mar.pdf
———. *Barómetro de noviembre 2008, Estudio 2778*. Madrid: CIS, 2008. http://www.cis.es/cis/opencm/ES/2_bancodatos/estudios/ver.jsp?estudio=8920
———. *Barómetro de noviembre 2018, Estudio 3231*. Madrid: CIS, 2018. http://datos.cis.es/pdf/Es3231mar_A.pdf
———. *Barómetro de septiembre 2018, Estudio 3223*. Madrid: CIS, 2018. http://datos.cis.es/pdf/Es3223mar_A.pdf
———. *Memorias de las Guerra Civil y el Franquismo, Estudio 2760*. Madrid: CIS, 2008. http://www.cis.es/cis/export/sites/default/-Archivos/Marginales/2760_2779/2760/ES2760Cat.pdf
Cercas, Javier. *Anatomía de un instante*. Madrid: Random House Mondadori, 2009.
Cinco Días. "Los incentivos fiscales inflaron más de un 30% el precio de las casas." 16 March 2016. https://cincodias.elpais.com/cincodias/2016/03/15/economia/1458052566_248112.html
———. "Los 460.000 beneficiarios del ingreso mínimo estarán obligados a presentar declaración del IRPF." 24 March 2021. https://cincodias.elpais.com/cincodias/2021/03/24/economia/1616586386_793539.html
Code of Canon Law. http://www.vatican.va/archive/cod-iuris-canonici/eng/documents/cic_lib3-cann793-821_en.html
Cohen, Mark R. *Under Crescent and Cross: The Jews in the Middle Ages*. Princeton: Princeton University Press, 2008.
Colino, César. "Decentralization in Spain: Federal Evolution and Performance of the Estado Autonómico." In *The Oxford Handbook of Spanish Politics*, edited by Diego Muro and Ignacio Lago, 62–81. Oxford: Oxford University Press, 2020.
Collier, Andrew. *Critical Realism: An Introduction to Roy Bhaskar's Philosophy*. London: Verso, 1994.
Colomer, Josep M. "Political Institutions in a Comparative Perspective." In *The Oxford Handbook of Spanish Politics*, edited by Diego Muro and Ignacio Lago, 153–70. Oxford: Oxford University Press, 2020.
———. *The Spanish Frustration: How a Ruinous Empire Thwarted the Nation State*. London: Anthem Press, 2019.
Committee on Economic, Social and Cultural Rights. *Ben Djazia v. Spain (Communication 5/2015)*. UN doc: E/C.12/61/D/5/2015, Views of 20 June 2017.
———. *Concluding Observations: Spain*. UN doc: E/C.12/ESP/CO/6 (2018).
Concordat between Spain and the Holy See, 27 August 1953. https://www.vatican.va/roman_curia/secretariat_state/archivio/documents/rc_seg-st_19530827_concordato-spagna_sp.html

Conferencia Episcopal Española. "Ante la crisis, solidaridad." statement, 3 October 2012 (Boletín Oficial de la Conferencia Episcopal Española no. 90, 31 December): 189–94. https://conferenciaepiscopal.es/wp-content/uploads/boletin/BOCEE090.pdf

———. "El secretario general de la CEE apela a trabajar por el bien común." press release, 20 April 2020. https://conferenciaepiscopal.es/el-secretario-general-de-la-cee-apela-a-trabajar-por-el-bien-comun/

———. "El 63% de los alumnos eligen religión católica." press release, 24 May 2020. https://conferenciaepiscopal.es/el-63-de-los-alumnos-eligen-religion-catolica/

———. "Sobre nación y nacionalismos." press release, 7 January 2005 (Boletín Oficial de la Conferencia Episcopal Española no. 74, 30 June): 33–4. https://conferenciaepiscopal.es/wp-content/uploads/boletin/BOCEE074.pdf

Consejo Económico y Social. *La emancipación de los jóvenes y la situación de la vivienda en España*. Madrid: CES, 2002.

Consejo General del Poder Judicial. "Datos sobre el efecto de la crisis en los órganos judiciales: Desde 2007 hasta 2016." 12 December 2016. http://www.poderjudicial.es/portal/site/cgpj/menuitem.65d2c4456b6ddb628e635fc1dc432ea0/?vgnextoid=311600fe2aa03410VgnVCM1000006f48ac0aRCRD&vgnextchannel=a64e3da6cbe0a210VgnVCM100000cb34e20aRCRD&vgnextfmt=default

Constitución de la República Española (Gaceta de Madrid no. 344, 10 December 1931).

Constitución Española (BOE no. 311, 29 December 1978).

Constitutional Court of Spain (*"Tribunal Constitutional"*). Judgment 76/1983 (5 August).

———. Judgment 52/2008 (14 April).

———. Judgment 69/2008 (23 June).

———. 107/2008 (22 September).

———. Judgment 31/2010 (28 June).

———. Judgment 63/2010 (18 October).

———. Judgment 131/2012 (18 June).

———. Judgment 198/2012 (6 November).

———. Judgment 153/2013 (9 September).

———. Judgment 130/2016 (18 July).

———. Judgment 144/2016 (19 September).

———. Judgment 97/2018 (19 September).

———. Judgment 91/2021 (22 April).

Dalli, María. "The Content and Potential of the Right to Social Assistance in Light of Article 13 of the European Social Charter." *European Journal of Social Security* 22, no. 1 (2020): 3–23.

De Blas Guerrero, Andrés. "El problema nacional-regional español en los programas del PSOE y PCE." *Revista de Estudios Políticos* 4 (1978): 155–70.

De Fuenmayor Fernández, Amadeo, and Granell Pérez, Rafael. "Evaluación de la desgravación fiscal a la adquisición de vivienda." *Presupuesto y Gasto Público* 59 (2010): 157–75.

Decree of 14 February 1947, Mortgage Regulation (BOE no. 106, 16 April).

Decree (Basque Country) 107/2012, of 12 June, of declaration and reparation of victims of unjust suffering as a consequence of the abuse of their human rights, produced between 1960 and 1978 in the context of politically motivated violence in the Basque Country (BOPV no. 119, 19 June).
Del Pino, Eloísa. "Welfare State." In *The Oxford Handbook of Spanish Politics*, edited by Diego Muro and Ignacio Lago, 526–41. Oxford: Oxford University Press, 2020.
Delegación del Gobierno contra la violencia de género. "Fichas de víctimas mortales." https://violenciagenero.igualdad.gob.es/violenciaEnCifras/victimasMortales/fichaMujeres/home.htm
Della Porta, Donatella and Portos, Martín. "A Burgeois Story? The Class Basis of Catalan Independentism." *Territory, Politics, Governance* 9, no. 3 (2021): 391–411.
Dellepiane, Sebastian, Hardiman, Niamh, and Las Heras, Jon. "Building on Easy Money: The Political Economy of Housing Bubbles in Ireland and Spain." *Paper presented at the 7th ECPR General Conference*, 2013.
Diario de Sesiones de las Cortes. No. 105 (10 December 1918).
Diario de Sesiones de las Cortes Constituyentes. No. 55 (13 October 1931).
———. No. 165 (13 May 1932).
Diario de Sesiones del Congreso de los Diputados. No. 24 (14 October 1977).
———. No. 116 (21 July 1978).
Diario de Sesiones del Congreso de los Diputados. Pleno y Diputación Permanente. No. 178 (14 July 2010).
———. No. 2 (4 January 2020).
———. No. 106 (26 May 2021).
Dirección General de Arquitectura, Vivienda y Suelo. *Agenda Urbana Española 2019*. Madrid: Ministerio de Fomento, 2018.
Duva, Jesús, Intxausti, Aurora. "El Gobierno indulta por segunda vez a un guardia condenado por torturas y a otro compañero." *El País*, 6 May 1995. http://www.cat.elpais.com/diario/1995/05/06/espana/799711228_850215.html
Edgerton, David. *The Rise and Fall of the British Nation: A Twentieth-Century History*. London: Allan Lane, 2018.
El Diario. "Adolfo Suárez no sometió a referéndum la monarquía porque las encuestas le dijeron que perdería." 18 November 2016. https://www.eldiario.es/politica/adolfo-suarez-referendum-monarquia-encuestas_1_1158112.html
El Mundo. "Rouco: 'El matrimonio gay es la rebeldía del hombre contra sus límites biológicos'." 24 May 2008. https://www.elmundo.es/elmundo/2008/05/24/espana/1211622271.html
———. "Zapatero afirma que España juega en la 'Champions League' económica." 11 September 2007. https://www.elmundo.es/mundodinero/2007/09/11/economia/1189506158.html
El País. "Acebes: 'Mi mayor desprecio político y personal'." 27 February 2003. https://elpais.com/diario/2003/02/27/espana/1046300408_850215.html
———. "El Rey defiende en Guernica la democracia y las instituciones tradicionales vascas." 4 February 1981. https://elpais.com/diario/1981/02/05/espana/350175602_850215.html

———. "Interior anuncia 'acciones legales' contra quienes acusan de tortura a la Guardia Civil." 27 February 2003. https://elpais.com/diario/2003/02/27/espana/1046300409_850215.html

———. "Rubalcaba: 'Los miembros de ETA aducen siempre que son torturados'." 9 January 2018. https://elpais.com/elpais/2008/01/09/actualidad/1199870225_850215.html

———. "'Una guerra civil no es un acontecimiento conmemorable', afirma el Gobierno." 19 July 1986. https://elpais.com/diario/1986/07/19/espana/522108013_850215.html

El Periódico. "Casado apela a la Reconquista después de Vox: primero Andalucía, luego Asturias." 11 January 2019. https://www.elperiodico.com/es/politica/20190111/casado-reconquista-vox-7241163

Encarnación, Omar. "Democracy and Dirty Wars in Spain." *Human Rights Quarterly* 29, no. 4 (2007): 950–72.

———. *Democracy without Justice in Spain: The Politics of Forgetting*. Philadelphia: University of Pennsylvania Press, 2014.

———. "Memory and Politics in Democratic Spain." In *The Oxford Handbook of Spanish Politics*, edited by Diego Muro and Ignacio Lago, 47–61. Oxford: Oxford University Press, 2020.

———. "Spain after Franco: Lessons in Democratization." *World Policy Journal* 18, no. 4 (2001/02): 35–44.

Encyclopédie méthodique ou par ordre des matières, Géographie moderne, Vol. I. Paris: 1782.

Euronews. "Spanish MPs Vote Down Far-Right Vox Party's No-Confidence Motion in PM Sanchez." 22 October 2020. https://www.euronews.com/2020/10/21/spanish-government-faces-no-confidence-vote-accused-of-pandemic-mismanagement

European Commission. *Country Report Spain 2019*. Brussels: European Commission, 2019.

———. *Spain: Memorandum of Understanding on Financial-Sector Policy Conditionality*, 20 July 2012.

European Committee of Social Rights. *Conclusions XX-2: Spain*, 2014.

———. *Conclusions XXI-2: Czech Republic, Denmark, Germany, Poland, Spain, UK*, 2018.

———. *Digest of Case Law*. Strasbourg: Council of Europe, 2018.

European Court of Human Rights. *Argimiro Isasa v. Spain* (Judgment of 28 September 2010).

———. *Arratibel Garciandia v. Spain* (Judgment of 5 May 2015).

———. *Ataun Rojo v. Spain* (Judgment of 7 October 2014).

———. *Beortegui Martínez v. Spain* (Judgment of 31 May 2016).

———. *Beristain Ukar v. Spain* (Judgment of 8 March 2011).

———. *Etxebarria Caballero v. Spain* (Judgment of 7 October 2014).

———. *Otamendi Egiguren v. Spain* (Judgment of 16 October 2012).

———. *Portu and Sarasola v. Spain* (Judgment of 13 February 2018).

Eurostat. "Children at Risk of Poverty or Social Exclusion." https://ec.europa.eu /eurostat/statistics-explained/index.php/Children_at_risk_of_poverty_or_social _exclusion#General_overview

———. *Government Finance Statistics—Summary Tables. Data 1995–2019. 1/2020*. Luxembourg: Publications Office of the European Union, 2020.

———. "Immigration by Age Group, Sex and Citizenship." https://ec.europa.eu/ eurostat/databrowser/view/migr_imm1ctz/default/table?lang=en

———. "Social Scoreboard of Indicators." https://ec.europa.eu/eurostat/web/european-pillar-of-social-rights/indicators/social-scoreboard-indicators

———. "Taxation in 2018: Tax-to-GDP ratio up to 40.3% in EU." press release, 30 October 2019. https://ec.europa.eu/eurostat/documents/2995521/10190755/2 -30102019-AP-EN.pdf/68739572-f06a-51e4-3a5b-86e660a23376

Euskal Herriko Unibertsitatea—Universidad del País Vasco, *Eusko Barometro: Estudio periódico de la opinión pública vasca* (June 2019). https://www.ehu .eus/documents/1457190/1525260/EB_int_Junio19.pdf/25ff5c39-0988-d46e-a028 -d5b688693cf1?t=1563537212000

Fernández-Morera, Darío. *The Myth of the Andalusian Paradise: Muslims, Christians, and Jews under Islamic Rule in Medieval Spain*. Wilmington: Intercollegiate Studies Institute, 2016.

Fernández-Soldevilla, Gaizka. "Mitos que matan: La narrativa del 'conflicto vasco'." *Ayer* 98 (2015): 213–40.

Ferrer, Álvaro, and Gortazar, Lucas. "Diversidad y libertad: Reducir la segregación escolar respetando la capacidad de elección de centro." *EsadeEcPol Insight* 29 (April 2021). https://www.esade.edu/ecpol/en/publications/segregacion-escolar-esadeecpol/

Ferrera, Maurizio. "The 'Southern Model' of Welfare in Social Europe." *Journal of European Social Policy* 6, no. 1 (1996): 17–37.

Field, Bonnie N. "Legislative Politics in Spain." In *The Oxford Handbook of Spanish Politics*, edited by Diego Muro and Ignacio Lago, 210–23. Oxford: Oxford University Press, 2020.

———. "The Evolution of Substate Nationalist Parties as Statewide Parliamentary Actors: CiU and PNV in Spain." *Nationalism and Ethnic Politics* 21, no. 1 (2015): 121–41.

Fishman, Robert M. *Democratic Practice: Origins of the Iberian Divide in Political Inclusion*. Oxford: Oxford University Press, 2019.

———. "Spain in Comparative Perspective: Contributions of the Spanish Case to Comparative Political Analysis." In *The Oxford Handbook of Spanish Politics*, edited by Diego Muro and Ignacio Lago, 15–31. Oxford: Oxford University Press, 2020.

Fominaya, Cristina Flesher. "The Madrid Bombings and Popular Protest: Misinformation, Counter-Information, Mobilisation and Elections After '11–M'." *Contemporary Social Science* 6, no. 3 (2011): 289–307.

Font, Juan. "The Quality of Democracy." In *The Oxford Handbook of Spanish Politics*, edited by Diego Muro and Ignacio Lago, 297–312. Oxford: Oxford University Press, 2020.

Ford, Richard. *Gatherings from Spain*. London: John Murray, 1846.
Fraser, Ronald. *Napoleon's Cursed War: Popular Resistance in the Spanish Peninsular War*. London: Verso, 2008.
———. "Spain on the Brink." *New Left Review* I-96 (1976): 3–33.
Frazer, Hugh, and Marlier, Eric. *Minimum Income Schemes in Europe: A Study of National Policies 2015*. Brussels: European Commission, 2016.
Gellner, Ernest. *Nations and Nationalism*. Oxford: Blackwell, 1983.
Gillespie, Richard. "Between Accommodation and Contestation: The Political Evolution of Basque and Catalan Nationalism," *Nationalism and Ethnic Politics* 21, no. 1 (2015): 3–23.
———. "The Contrasting Fortunes of Pro-sovereignty Currents in Basque and Catalan Nationalist Parties: PNV and CDC Compared." *Territory, Politics, Governance* 5, no. 4 (2017): 406–24.
Gilson, Erinn. "Vulnerability, Ignorance and Oppression." *Hypatia* 26, no. 2 (2011): 308–32.
Giménez Barriocanal, Fernando. *Principales cifras de la economía de la Iglesia Católica en España: Año 2018*. Madrid: Edice, 2020.
González-Enríquez, Carmen, and Sebastian Rinken. "Spanish Public Opinion on Immigration and the Effect of VOX." *Real Instituto Elcano* ARI 46/2021 (April 2021).
Government of Spain. "España revalida en España revalida en 2019 su liderazgo mundial en donación de órganos y aporta el 20% de los donantes de la UE y el 6% del mundo." press release, 7 September 2020. https://www.lamoncloa.gob.es/serviciosdeprensa/notasprensa/sanidad14/Paginas/2020/070920-trasplantes.aspx?gfe=1
———. *Response to the Special Rapporteur on Torture*. UN doc: E/CN.4/2004/G/19, 4 March 2004.
———. *Sixth Periodic Report to the UN Human Rights Committee Submitted under Article 40 ICCPR*. UN doc: CCPR/C/ESP/6, 10 May 2013.
Gray, Caroline. "A Fiscal Path to Sovereignty? The Basque Economic Agreement and Nationalist Politics." *Nationalism and Ethnic Politics* 21, no. 1 (2015): 63–82.
———. *Territorial Politics and the Party System in Spain: Continuity and Change since the Financial Crisis*. Abingdon: Routledge, 2020.
Guillén, Ana M. "The Politics of Universalisation: Establishing National Health Services in Southern Europe." *West European Politics* 25, no. 4 (2002): 49–68.
Hannah-Jones, Nikole. "What is Owed." *New York Times*, 30 June 2020. https://www.nytimes.com/interactive/2020/06/24/magazine/reparations-slavery.html
Hernández, Adrián, Picos, Fidel, and Riscado, Sara. "Moving Towards Fairer Regional Minimum Income Schemes in Spain." *JRC Working Papers on Taxation and Structural Reforms*. Brussels: European Commission, 2020.
Hierro, María José. "Regional and National Identities in Spain." In *The Oxford Handbook of Spanish Politics*, edited by Diego Muro and Ignacio Lago, 494–508. Oxford: Oxford University Press, 2020.
His Majesty the King of Spain. Message of 3 October 2017. https://www.casareal.es/sitios/listasaux/Documents/Mensaje20171003/5_20171003_mensaje_en_rey_felipe_5.pdf
Hobsbawm, E. J. *Nations and Nationalism since 1780: Programme, Myth, Reality*, 2nd edition. Cambridge: Cambridge University Press, 1992.

Hoekstra, Joris, Heras Saizarbitoria, Iñaki, and Etxezarreta Etxarri, Aitziber. "Recent Changes in Spanish Housing Policies: Subsidized Owner-Occupancy Dwellings as a New Tenure Sector?." *Journal of Housing and the Built Environment* 25, no. 1 (2010): 125–38.

Housing Europe. *The State of Housing in Europe 2021*. Brussels: Housing Europe.

Human Rights Committee. *General Comment no. 20: Prohibition of Torture*. UN doc: HRI/GEN/1/Rev.7 (1992).

Human Rights Watch. "Spain: Police Used Excessive Force in Catalonia." 12 October 2017. https://www.hrw.org/news/2017/10/12/spain-police-used-excessive-force-catalonia

Hussey, Andrew. "The New Spanish Civil Wars." *New Statesman* 148, no. 5492 (11 October 2019): 30–3. https://www.newstatesman.com/world/europe/2019/10/new-spanish-civil-wars

Iglesias, Pablo. "Understanding Podemos." *New Left Review* 93 (2015): 7–22.

Instituto Nacional de Estadística. *Censo de población y viviendas 2011. Nota de prensa*, 18 April 2013. https://www.ine.es/prensa/np775.pdf

———. "Economically Active Population Survey," online scoreboard: https://www.ine.es/dyngs/INEbase/en/operacion.htm?c=Estadistica_C&cid=1254736176918&menu=ultiDatos&idp=1254735976595

———. *Encuesta Continua de Hogares 2019. Nota de prensa*, 2 April 2020. https://www.ine.es/prensa/ech_2019.pdf

Instituto Vasco de Criminología. *Proyecto de investigación de la tortura en el País Vasco (1960–2013) Memoria-Resumen de la actividad realizada*. Vitoria-Gasteiz: University of the Basque Country and Basque Government, 2016.

Instrument of Ratification of the Agreement between the Holy See and the Spanish State, held in the Holy See on 28 July 1976 (BOE no. 230, 24 September).

Instrument of Ratification of the Agreements between the Holy See and the Spanish State, held in the Holy See on 3 January 1979 (BOE no. 300, 15 December).

Inter-American Court of Human Rights, *Velásquez Rodríguez v. Honduras*, Judgment of 29 July 1988.

Jessoula, Matteo, and Natili, Marcello. "Explaining Italian 'Exceptionalism' and Its End: Minimum Income from Neglect to Hyper-Politicization." *Social Policy Administration* 54, no. 4 (2020): 599–613.

Jones, Sam. "Spain Plans to Turn Franco's Former Burial Site into Civil Cemetery." *The Guardian*, 15 September 2020. https://www.theguardian.com/world/2020/sep/15/spain-plans-to-turn-francos-grave-site-into-civil-cemetery

Juliá, Santos. "Apenas quedan ya regiones en España." *El País*, 6 November 2017. https://elpais.com/elpais/2017/11/03/opinion/1509724272_541783.html

Kabeer, Naila, and Waddington, Hugh. "Economic Impacts of Conditional Cash Transfer Programmes: A Systematic Review and Meta-Analysis." *Journal of Development Effectiveness* 7, no. 3 (2015): 290–303.

L.A. Times. "Pope Beatifies 233 Martyrs of 1936–39 Spanish Civil War." 12 March 2001. https://www.latimes.com/archives/la-xpm-2001-mar-12-mn-36630-story.html

La Sexta. "Salvados" Program, Season 6, Episode 29, 12 May 2013. https://www.atresplayer.com/lasexta/programas/salvados/temporada-6/capitulo-29-sed-justicia_5ad0958c7ed1a88d4ef812b9/

La Vanguardia. "Rivera proclama a C's heredero de los liberales de la Constitución de 1812." 19 March 2017. https://www.lavanguardia.com/local/sevilla/20170319/421014133070/rivera-proclama-a-cs-herederos-de-los-liberales-de-la-constitucion-de-1812.html

———. "Zapatero asegura que España superará a Alemania en renta per cápita en 2010." 15 January 2007. https://www.lavanguardia.com/economia/20070115/51301092633/zapatero-asegura-que-espana-superara-a-alemania-en-renta-per-capita-en-2010.html

Laborda, Julio López, Marín González, Carmen, and Onrubia, Jorge. *Observatorio sobre el reparto de los impuestos y las prestaciones monetarias entre los hogares españoles. Cuarto informe—2016 y 2017*. Madrid: FEDEA, 2019.

Landman, Todd. *Issues and Methods of Comparative Politics*, 3rd edition. London: Routledge, 2008.

Lannon, Frances. "Modern Spain: The Project of a National Catholicism." *Studies in Church History* 18 (1982): 567–90.

Le Monde. "Le régime espagnol se dit chrétien mais n'obéit pas aux principes de base du christianisme." 14 November 1963. https://www.lemonde.fr/archives/article/1963/11/14/le-regime-espagnol-se-dit-chretien-mais-n-obeit-pas-aux-principes-de-base-du-christianisme-declare-au-monde-l-abbe-de-montserrat_2218960_1819218.html

León, Sandra, and Jurado, Ignacio. "Multilevel Governance in Spain." In *The Oxford Handbook of Spanish Politics*, edited by Diego Muro and Ignacio Lago, 224–40. Oxford: Oxford University Press, 2020.

Lijphart, Arend. "Comparative Politics and the Comparative Method." *The American Political Science Review* 65, no. 3 (1971): 682–93.

Linz, Juan J. "Church and State in Spain from the Civil War to the Return of Democracy." *Daedalus* 120, no. 3 (1991): 159–78.

———. "Los nacionalismos en España: Una perspectiva comparada." *Historia, antropología y fuentes orales* 7 (1992): 127–35.

———. "Religion and Politics in Spain: From Conflict to Consensus and Cleavage." *Social Compass* 27, no. 2–3 (1980): 255–77.

López, Isidro and Rodríguez, Emmanuel. "The Spanish Model." *New Left Review* 69 (2011): 5–28.

Machado, Antonio. *Campos de Castilla*. Madrid: Alianza, 2013.

Maestre, Antonio. *Franquismo S.A.* Madrid: Akal, 2019.

Martín Jessica. "Santiago Cantera, de candidato de la Falange a prior del Valle de los Caídos." *RTVE*, 9 October 2019. https://www.rtve.es/noticias/20191009/santiago-cantera-candidato-falange-prior-del-valle-caidos/1981181.shtml

Martín, Unai, et al. "Migraciones internas en España durante el siglo XX: un nuevo eje para el estudio de las desigualdades sociales en salud." *Gaceta Sanitaria* 26, no. 1 (2012): 9–15.

Martínez, Isabel C. *ETA en la prensa internacional: Una aproximación al tratamiento del terrorismo en los diarios franceses, británicos y estadounidenses de referencia*. Vitoria-Gasteiz: Centro Memorial de las Víctimas del Terrorismo 2019.

Martínez, Manuel. "Algunos aspectos de la coyuntura económica española." *Ruedo Ibérico* 1 (1965): 17–32.

Martínez Pagés, Jorge, and Maza, Luis Ángel. *Análisis del precio de la vivienda en España, Documento de Trabajo no. 0307*. Madrid: Banco de España, 2003.

Mathers, Nicholas, and Slater, Rachel. *Social Protection and Growth: Research Synthesis*. Canberra: Department of Foreign Affairs and Trade Australian Government, 2014.

Matsaganis, Manos. "Safety Nets in (the) crisis: The Case of Greece in the 2010s." *Social Policy Administration* 54, no. 4 (2020): 587–98.

Mazur, Amy G., and McBride, Dorothy E. "State Feminism since the 1980s: From Loose Notion to Operationalized Concept." *Politics & Gender* 3, no. 4 (2007): 501–13.

Mees, Ludger. "Nationalist Politics at the Crossroads: The Basque Nationalist Party and the Challenge of Sovereignty (1998–2014)." *Nationalism and Ethnic Politics* 21, no. 1 (2015): 44–62.

Michielse, H.C.M., and van Krieken, Robert. "Policing the Poor: J. L. Vives and the Sixteenth-Century Origins of Modern Social Administration," *Social Service Review* 64, no. 1 (1990): 1–21.

Millás, Juan José. "Tuve que decidir si se volaba a la cúpula de ETA. Dije no. Y no sé si hice lo correcto." *El País*, 7 November 2010. https://elpais.com/diario/2010/11/07/domingo/1289105554_850215.html

Minder, Raphael. *The Struggle for Catalonia: Rebel Politics in Spain*. London: Hurst & Co, 2017.

Ministerio de Educación y Formación Profesional. *Sistema estatal de indicadores de la educación*. Madrid: Ministerio de Educación, 2019.

Ministerio de Fomento. *El ajuste del sector inmobiliario español*. Madrid: Ministerio de Fomento, 2012.

Ministerio de Justicia. "Map of Graves Online." https://mapadefosas.mjusticia.es/exovi_externo/CargarInformacion.htm

Ministerio de la Presidencia, Relaciones con las Cortes y Memoria Democrática. "Estudio sobre la inmatriculación de bienes inmuebles de la Iglesia Católica en el Registro de la Propiedad desde el año 1998 en virtud de certificación del diocesano respectivo." February 2021.

Ministerio de Sanidad, Servicios Sociales e Igualdad. *El Sistema Público de Servicios Sociales: Informe de Rentas Mínimas de Inserción—Año 2012*. Madrid: Ministerio de Sanidad, 2013.

———. *Estadística de Gasto Sanitario Público 2014: Principales Resultados*. Madrid: Ministerio de Sanidad, 2016.

Ministerio de Transportes, Movilidad y Agenda Urbana. *Observatorio de Vivienda y Suelo. Boletín especial vivienda social 2020*. Madrid: Ministerio de Transporte, Movilidad y Agenda Urbana, 2020.

Moore, Margaret. "On National Self-Determination" *Political Studies* 45, no. 5 (1997): 900–13.

Moradielos, Enrique. "Ni gesta heroica ni locura trágica: nuevas perspectivas históricas sobre la guerra civil." *Ayer* 50 (2003): 11–40.

Mujal-León, Eusebio. "The Left and the Catholic Question in Spain." *West European Politics* 5, no. 2 (1982): 32–54.
Muro, Diego. "Nationalism and Nostalgia: The Case of Radical Basque Nationalism." *Nations and Nationalism* 11, no. 4 (2005): 571–89.
———. "Territorial Accommodation, Party Politics and Statute Reform in Spain." *Southern European Society and Politics* 14, no. 4 (2009): 453–68.
———. "When Do Countries Recentralize? Ideology and Party Politics in the Age of Austerity." *Nationalism and Ethnic Politics* 21, no. 1 (2015): 24–43.
Natali, David, and Stamati, Furio. "Reassessing South European Pensions after the Crisis: Evidence from Two Decades of Reforms." *South European Society and Politics* 19, no. 3 (2014): 309–30.
Navarro, Vicenç. *El subdesarrollo social de España: Causas y consecuencias.* Madrid: Diario Público, 2009.
Neiman, Susan. *Learning from the Germans: Confronting Race and the Memory of Evil.* London: Allen Lane, 2019.
North, Douglass C. "Economic Performance through Time." *The American Economic Review* 84, no. 3 (1994): 359–68.
Núñez, Xosé-Manoel. "Spanish Nationalism since 1975." In *The Oxford Handbook of Spanish Politics*, edited by Diego Muro and Ignacio Lago, 479–93. Oxford: Oxford University Press, 2020.
———. "The Region as Essence of the Fatherland: Regionalist Variants of Spanish Nationalism (1840–1936)." *European History Quarterly* 31, no. 4 (2001): 483–518.
Observatorio de Vivienda y Suelo. *Boletín Especial: Alquiler Residencial.* Madrid: Ministerio de Fomento, 2017.
Observatorio Estatal de la Sostenibilidad. *Cambios de ocupación del suelo en España: Implicaciones para la sostenibilidad.* Alcalá de Henares: Universidad de Alcalá de Henares, 2006.
Oliveira, Ivo. "Portugal's Costa questions Dutch commitment to EU." *Politico*, 10 April 2020. https://www.politico.eu/article/portugal-antonio-costa-questions-dutch-commitment-to-eu-coronavirus-covid19/
Oliver Araujo, Joan. "La cuestión religiosa en la Constitución de 1931: Una reflexión sobre un tema clásico." *Revista de Estudios Políticos (Nueva Época)* 81 (1993): 175–83.
Orriols, Lluis and Cordero, Guillermo. "The Breakdown of the Spanish Two-Party System: The Upsurge of Podemos and Ciudadanos in the 2015 General Election." *South European Society and Politics* 21, no. 4 (2016): 469–92.
Ortega y Gasset, José. *Obras Completas.* Vol. I. Madrid: Occidente, 1946.
Orwell, George. "Notes on Nationalism." 1945. Reproduced at: https://www.orwellfoundation.com/the-orwell-foundation/orwell/essays-and-other-works/notes-on-nationalism/
Oxfam Intermón. *Armando el Puzle: Avanzando hacia el sistema de garantía de rentas que deberíamos tener.* June 2021.
Payne, Stanley G. *Spain: A Unique History.* Madison: University of Wisconsin Press, 2011.

———. *Spanish Catholicism: An Historical Overview*. Madison: University of Wisconsin Press, 1984.

———. "Spanish Conservatism 1834–1923." *Journal of Contemporary History* 13 (1978): 765–89.

———. "Spanish Nationalism in the Twentieth Century." *Review of Politics* 26, no. 3 (1964): 403–22.

Pew Research. *Global Views on Morality* (April 2014). https://www.pewresearch.org/global/interactives/global-morality/

———. *The Global God Divide* (July 2020). https://www.pewresearch.org/global/2020/07/20/the-global-god-divide/

Philips, Adam, and Taylor, Barbara. *On Kindness*. London: Penguin, 2009.

Pi i Margall, Francesc. *Las Nacionalidades*, 2nd edition. Madrid: Imprenta de Eduardo Martínez, 1877.

Pierson, Paul. "Increasing Returns, Path Dependence, and the Study of Politics." *The American Political Science Review* 94, no. 2 (2000): 251–67.

Piketty, Thomas. *Capital and Ideology*. Cambridge, MA: Harvard University Press, 2020.

Politico. "Brussels Playbook." 15 June 2020. https://www.politico.eu/newsletter/brussels-playbook/politico-brussels-playbook-corona-kills-trust-britains-dangerous-menage-catching-up-with-oettinger/

Pope John XXIII. *Mater et Magistra: Encyclical on Christianity and Social Progress*. 1961. http://www.vatican.va/content/john-xxiii/en/encyclicals/documents/hf_j-xxiii_enc_15051961_mater.html

———. *Pacem in Terris: Encyclical on Establishing Universal Peace in Truth, Justice, Charity and Liberty*. 1963. http://www.vatican.va/content/john-xxiii/en/encyclicals/documents/hf_j-xxiii_enc_11041963_pacem.html

Pope Pius XI. *Divini Redemptoris: Encyclical on Atheistic Communism*. 1937. http://www.vatican.va/content/pius-xi/en/encyclicals/documents/hf_p-xi_enc_19370319_divini-redemptoris.html

Prados de la Escosura, Leandro. "Inequality, Poverty and the Kuznets Curve in Spain, 1850–2000." *European Review of Economic History* 12, no. 3 (2008): 287–324.

Preston, Paul. *A People Betrayed: A History of Corruption, Political Incompetence and Social Division in Modern Spain 1874–2018*. London: William Collins, 2020.

———. *The Spanish Holocaust: Inquisition and Extermination in Twentieth-Century Spain*. London: Harper Collins, 2012.

Público. "El Gobierno resta importancia a las condenas de Europa por no investigar torturas: 'Son solo nueve'." 28 March 2018. https://www.publico.es/sociedad/gobierno-resta-importancia-condenas-europa-no-investigar-torturas-trato-degradante-son-nueve.html

———. "España, tierra de impunidad para torturadores." 24 April 2017. https://www.publico.es/sociedad/espana-tierra-impunidad-torturadores.html

———. "Urkullu admite que el Gobierno vasco debió haber actuado 'antes y mejor'." 5 June 2015. https://www.publico.es/politica/urkullu-pide-perdon-victimas.html

Quiroga, Alejandro. *Making Spaniards: Primo de Rivera and the Nationalization of the Masses, 1923–30*. London: Palgrave, 2007.

Raguer, Hilari. *Gunpowder and Incense: The Catholic Church and the Spanish Civil War* London: Routledge, 2006.

Real Academia Española. "Nuevo Tesoro Lexicográfico de la Lengua Española." https://www.rae.es/recursos/diccionarios/diccionarios-anteriores-1726-1992/nuevo-tesoro-lexicografico

Religión Digital. "Osoro se desmarca de la cúpula de la CEE y anima al nuevo Gobierno a 'alcanzar acuerdos' por un 'proyecto común'." 7 January 2020. https://www.religiondigital.org/espana/Osoro-desmarca-CEE-Gobierno-alcanzar-polarizacion-psoe-podemos-sanchez-cee-blazquez-canizares_0_2193080692.html

———. "Santiago Cantera: 'Lo que realmente molesta no es Franco, es la Cruz, es la comunidad benedictina'." 5 March 2020. https://www.religiondigital.org/espana/Santiago-Cantera-franco-exhumacion-valle-caidos-cruz-odio_0_2210178963.html

Renan, Ernest. *What Is a Nation? And Other Political Writings*. New York: Columbia University Press, 2018.

Rhodes, Martin. "Southern European Welfare States: Identity, Problems and Prospects for Reform." *South European Society and Politics* 1, no. 3 (1996): 1–22.

Riveiro, Aitor. "Las negociaciones por la ley de vivienda revelan profundas diferencias entre el PSOE y Unidas Podemos." *eldiario.es*, 2 February 2021. https://www.eldiario.es/economia/negociaciones-ley-vivienda-revelan-profundas-diferencias-psoe-unidas_1_7187986.html

Roberts, Yvonne. "'If I'm Not in on Friday, I Might be Dead': Chilling Facts About UK Femicide." *The Guardian*, 22 November 2020. https://www.theguardian.com/society/2020/nov/22/if-im-not-in-on-friday-i-might-be-dead-chilling-facts-about-uk-femicide

Rodríguez Coma, Magdalena. "Incidencia distributiva de la política de gasto en vivienda en el IRPF 2006." *Papeles de Trabajo del Instituto de Estudios Fiscales* 59 (2010).

Rorty, Richard M. *Achieving Our Country: Leftist Thought in Twentieth-Century America*. Cambridge, MA: Harvard University Press, 1998.

Royal Decree 1867/1998, of 4 September, which modifies the Mortgage Regulation (BOE no. 233, 29 September).

Royal Decree 233/2013, of 5 April, on the Housing Strategy 2013–2016 (BOE no. 86, 10 April).

Royal Decrees 456/2021 to 464/2021, of 22 June, pardoning Dolors Bassa, Jordi Cuixart, Carme Forcadell, Joaquim Forn, Oriol Junqueras, Raül Romeva, Josep Rull, Jordi Sánchez and Jordi Turull (BOE no. 149, 23 June).

Royal Decree-law 8/2010, of 20 May, to adopt extraordinary measures to reduce public deficit (BOE no. 126, 24 May).

Royal Decree-law 3/2012, of 10 February, of urgent measures for the reform of the labour market (BOE no. 36, 11 February).

Royal Decree-law 16/2012, of 20 April, of urgent measures to guarantee the sustainability of the National Health System and to improve the quality and safety of its benefits (BOE no. 98, 24 April).

Royal Decree-law 7/2018, of 27 July, on the universal access to the National Health System (BOE no. 183, 30 July).

Royal Decree-law 10/2018, of 24 August, that modifies the Historical Memory Act of 2007 (BOE no. 206, 25 August).

Royal Decree-law 7/2019, of 1 March, of urgent measures on housing and renting (BOE no. 55, 5 March).

Royal Decree-law 20/2020, of 29 May, to establish the minimum vital income (BOE no. 154, 1 June).

RTVE. "Los obispos vascos piden perdón por la ejecución de 14 religiosos a manos del bando franquista." 11 July 2009. https://www.rtve.es/noticias/20090711/obispos-vascos-piden-perdon-ejecucion-14-religiosos-manos-del-bando-franquista/284555.shtml

Sánchez-Cuenca, Ignacio. "Spanish Democratization: Transition, Consolidation, and Its Meaning in Contemporary Spain." In *The Oxford Handbook of Spanish Politics*, edited by Diego Muro and Ignacio Lago, 32–46. Oxford: Oxford University Press, 2020.

Santos, Antonio. "El Gobierno vasco estima que 3.300 personas vivieron a diario con escolta entre 1990 y 2011." *El Correo*, 8 April 2016. https://www.elcorreo.com/bizkaia/politica/201604/08/gobierno-vasco-estima-personas-20160408124700.html?ref=https:%2F%2Fwww.google.com%2F

Savio, Alfonso de. "Voltaire and Spain." *Hispania* 7, no. 3 (1924): 157–64.

Scheidel, Walter. *The Great Leveler: Violence and the History of Inequality from the Stone Age to the Twenty-first Century*. New Jersey: Princeton University Press, 2017.

Secondat, Charles de, Baron de Montesquieu. *The Spirit of Laws: Book XXV. Of Laws in Relation to the Establishment of Religion and Its External Polity*. Translated by Thomas Nugent. Revised by J. V. Prichard, 1748, 1752. http://classicliberal.tripod.com/montesquieu/sol25.html

Security Council (United Nations). Resolution 1530. UN doc: S/RES/1530, 11 March 2004.

Smith, Anthony D. *The Ethnic Origins of Nations*. Oxford: Blackwell Publishing, 1986.

Soler, Ricard. "The New Spain." *New Left Review* I-58 (1969): 3–27.

Special rapporteur on adequate housing as a component of the right to an adequate standard of living, Miloon Kothari. *Mission to Spain*. UN doc: A/HRC/7/16/Add.2 (2008).

Special rapporteur on the promotion of truth, justice, reparation and guarantees of non-recurrence, Pablo de Greiff, *Mission to Spain*. UN doc: A/HRC/27/56/Add.1 (2014).

Streeck, Wolfgang. "How Will Capitalism End?." *New Left Review* 84 (2014): 35–64.

Stora, Benjamin. "Les questions mémorielles portant sur la colonisation et la guerre d'Algérie" (January 2021). https://www.vie-publique.fr/rapport/278186-rapport-stora-memoire-sur-la-colonisation-et-la-guerre-dalgerie

Supreme Court of Spain (*"Tribunal Supremo"*). Judgment 101/2012 (27 February 2012).

———. Judgment 459/2019 (14 October).

Tilly, Charles. "Collective Violence in European Perspective." In *Violence in America: Historical and Comparative Perspectives: A Report to the National Commission on the Causes and Prevention of Violence*, Vol. 1, edited by Hugh Davies Graham and Ted Robert Gurr, 5–34. Washington, DC: US Government Printing Office, 1969.

Tremlett, Giles. "Bishops to Lead Gay Law Protest." *The Guardian*, 17 June 2005. https://www.theguardian.com/world/2005/jun/17/gayrights.religion

———. "How did Spain Get Its Coronavirus Response So Wrong?." *The Guardian*, 26 March 2020. https://www.theguardian.com/world/2020/mar/26/spain-coronavirus-response-analysis

———. *The International Brigades: Fascism, Freedom and the Spanish Civil War*. London: Bloomsbury, 2020.

Tribunal de Cuentas. *Informe no. 1382 de fiscalización sobre las actuaciones desarrolladas por la administración general del estado en materia de cooperación económica con las confesiones religiosas a través de los programas de ingresos y gastos contenidos en los presupuestos generales del estado, ejercicio 2017*. Madrid: Tribunal de Cuentas, 2020.

Trilla, Carme. *La política de vivienda en una perspectiva europea comparada*, Barcelona: Fundación La Caixa, 2001.

Tusell, Javier. *Spain: From Dictatorship to Democracy: 1939 to the Present*. Malden: Blackwell Publishing, 2007.

Valle-Inclán, Ramón (del). *Luces de Bohemia*. Arganda del Rey: Verbum, 2019.

Valles, Josep M. "The 1978 Spanish Constitutional Design: Assessing Its Outcome." In *The Oxford Handbook of Spanish Politics*, edited by Diego Muro and Ignacio Lago, 171–89. Oxford: Oxford University Press, 2020.

Valls-Montés, Rafael. *Historia y memoria escolar: Segunda República, Guerra Civil y dictadura franquista en las aulas (1938–2008)*. Valencia: Publicaciones de la Universitat de València, 2009.

Verge, Tània. "Gender Policy." In *The Oxford Handbook of Spanish Politics*, edited by Diego Muro and Ignacio Lago, 614–30. Oxford: Oxford University Press, 2020.

Vidal, José Manuel. "El IBI y la Iglesia católica." *El Mundo*, 20 May 2012. https://www.elmundo.es/elmundo/2012/05/19/espana/1337427855.html

Vtyurina, Svetlana. "Effectiveness and Equity in Social Spending—The Case of Spain," *Working Paper 20/16*. IMF: Washington DC, 2020.

Webster, Jason. *Violencia: A New History of Spain: Past, Present and the Future of the West*. London: Constable, 2019.

Weiler, Joseph H.H. "A Nation of Nations?." *International Journal of Constitutional Law* 17, no. 4 (2019): 1301–6.

Welles, Orson. "The Land of the Basques" (1955). Video available with Basque subtitles at: https://www.youtube.com/watch?v=hJlKx3NPuts

Went, Alexander. *Social Theory of International Politics*. Cambridge: Cambridge University Press, 1999.

White, Hayden. *Metahistory: The Historical Imagination in Nineteenth-Century Europe*. Baltimore: Johns Hopkins University Press, 2014.

Whitehead, Christine, et al. *The Private Rented Sector in the New Century: A Comparative Approach*. Cambridge: University of Cambridge, 2012.
Whitfield, Teresa. *Endgame for ETA: Elusive Peace in the Basque Country*. London: Hurst & Company, 2014.
Wieviorka, Michel. "Militantes del PNV analizan la lucha armada." *Ayer* 13 (1994): 211–35.
Woodworth, Paddy. "Using Terror against Terrorists: The Spanish Experience." In *The Politics of Contemporary Spain*, edited by Sebastian Balfour, 61–79. Abingdon: Routledge, 2005.
World Inequality Lab. *World Inequality Report 2018*. Paris: Paris School of Economics, 2017.
Yardley, Jim. "Facing His Torturer as Spain Confronts Its Past." *New York Times*, 6 April 2014. https://www.nytimes.com/2014/04/07/world/europe/facing-his-torturer-as-spain-confronts-its-past.html
Ysàs, Pere. "Democracia y autonomía en la transición española." *Ayer* 15 (1994): 77–107.
Zafra, Ignacio. "Estos son todos los cambios en la escuela que trae la nueva ley educativa." *El País*, 19 November 2020. https://elpais.com/educacion/2020-11-18/estos-son-todos-los-cambios-en-la-escuela-que-trae-la-nueva-ley-educativa-que-se-vota-hoy.html
Zuil, María. "El IMV sigue sin llegar a los hogares: solo lo recibe un 6% del millón que lo ha pedido." *El Confidencial*, 21 October 2020. https://www.elconfidencial.com/espana/2020-10-21/imv-sin-llegar-hogares_2798112/

Index

Abascal, Santiago, 53, 100. *See also* Vox
Acebes, Ángel, 96. *See also* Popular Party (PP)
Achilles' heel, 3, 6, 9–11, 13–14, 16, 21, 64, 101, 166, 171
Adams, John, 51
Aguilar, Paloma, 72, 79, 84, 92
Aguirre, Esperanza, 160. *See also* Popular Party (PP)
Alcalá-Zamora, Niceto, 43
Almodóvar, Pedro, 2, 158
Álvarez Junco, José, 18, 27–28, 30, 34
Amnesty, 78–79, 101
Amnesty Act 1977, 77–79, 90, 170, 177
Andalusia, 23–24, 28, 31, 37–38, 41, 105, 113, 126
Anderson, Benedict, 26
Añoveros, Antonio, 142
Antiterrorist Liberation Groups. *See* Grupos Antiterroristas de Liberación (GAL)
Arana, Sabino, 54, 148. *See also* Basque Nationalist Party
Arias Navarro, Carlos, 149. *See also* Franco, Francisco
Arrese, José Luis de, 115. *See also* Franco, Francisco
Arzalluz, Xabier, 77–78. *See also* Basque Nationalist Party

Azaña, Manuel, 149
Aznar, José María, 45, 87, 89, 107, 152, 178. *See also* Popular Party (PP)

Barrionuevo, José, 93–94. *See also* González, Felipe; Grupos Antiterroristas de Liberación (GAL); Partido Socialista Obrero Español (PSOE)
Basque Country, 3, 6–8, 24–25, 28, 30, 33, 35–38, 51–64, 73, 77–78, 81, 91–99, 101, 105, 113–14, 126–27, 132, 142, 147–48, 167; Araba, 53–55, 91–92; Basque language, 51–52, 91, 135; Bilbao, 9, 105, 142; Bizkaia, 53, 55, 91, 106; Ertzaintza, 97; *Euskaldunon Egunkaria*, 96; *Euskal Etxea*, 52; Gernika, Guernica, 56, 91; Gipuzkoa, 53, 55, 91; *ikurriña*, 58; *Iparralde*, 52; San Sebastian, 25, 61, 93, 136; Vitoria-Gasteiz, 92. *See also* Basque Nationalist Party; Euskadiko Ezkerra; Euskadi Ta Askatasuna (ETA); Ezker Abertzalea; *foralismo*
Basque Nationalist Party, 53–62, 77, 92, 138, 148–49, 167–68
Belloch, Juan Alberto, 95. *See also* Partido Socialista Obrero Español (PSOE)

Benedict XVI, 156
Boyd, Carolyn P., 148, 156
Brenan, Gerald, 23–24, 41, 146

Calvo Sotelo, José, 147
Cambó, Francesc, 42–43, 45
Campoamor, Clara, 4
Cañizares, Antonio, 160
Carles Gordó, Ricard María, 155
Carlismo, 34, 42, 55, 83, 145–48, 166–67, 177. *See also* Basque Nationalist Party; Catholic Church; *foralismo*; Franco, Francisco
Carrero Blanco, Luis, 59, 143, 149, 177. *See also* Franco, Francisco
Castelao, Alfonso R., 37. *See also* Galicia
Catalonia, 1, 3, 6, 8, 23–25, 28, 33–35, 37–51, 53–55, 57–59, 62–65, 78, 81, 101, 103, 105–6, 113–15, 126, 128, 148–49, 159, 165, 167–68, 171, 177–78; Catalanophobia, 45; Diada, 46; referendum October 2017, 1, 40–41, 48–49, 101, 168; statute 2006, 41, 43, 45–47, 49–50, 159. *See also* Convergència i Unió (CIU); Esquerra Republicana de Catalunya (ERC)
Catholic Church, 7–8, 15, 24, 123, 133, 135–61, 166, 174–75; Episcopal Conference, 8, 133; Holy See, 140, 143, 144, 150–51, 174, 178; Opus Dei, 7, 142; Vatican, 140–42, 148, 150, 152, 154, 156, 174, 177
Catholicism. *See* Catholic Church
Cervantes, Miguel de, 2, 143
Cirauqui. *See* Zirauki
CIU. *See* Convergència i Unió
Ciudadanos, 47, 50, 54, 96, 99, 165
Civil War, 1–2, 6–7, 24, 31, 34, 37, 43, 67, 71–72, 79, 81–83, 85–88, 92, 99–101, 104, 135, 138–40, 145, 155–58, 167, 171, 174, 177; International Brigades, 86, 88. *See also* Franco, Francisco
Colau, Ada, 114
Colomer, Josep M., 4, 146

colonialism, 3–4, 6, 26, 32–33, 42, 143, 173, 177
Columbus, Christopher, 25, 33, 69, 87, 146
Communist Party, 35–36, 44, 77, 86, 128, 143
Companys, Lluís, 43, 169. *See also* Esquerra Republicana de Catalunya (ERC)
Constitution: 1812 constitution, 32, 144; 1837 constitution, 144; 1845 constitution, 144; 1869 constitution, 145; 1876 constitution, 145, 165; 1931 constitution, 4, 139, 144–45; 1978 constitution, 6–8, 35–39, 41, 45, 49–51, 55–56, 65, 74–76, 78, 84, 87, 109, 113–14, 122, 124, 131, 140, 149–50, 152–53, 167, 169–70, 173, 174, 177
Constitutional court, 38, 40, 45–46, 49–50, 95–96, 113–14, 155, 178
Convergència i Unió (CIU), 45, 47–48, 58
Costa, António, 175
Covid-19, 7, 19, 76, 100, 130, 132, 133, 163, 175
Cuba, 4, 33, 42, 147, 177
Cuéntame Cómo Pasó, 86
Cuixart, Jordi, 50

Díaz Ayuso, Isabel, 37. *See also* Popular Party (PP)

EAJ. *See* Basque Nationalist Party
Entesa, 45
ERC. *See* Esquerra Republicana de Catalunya
Escarré, Aureli, 44
Escrivá, José Luis, 133
Esquerra Republicana de Catalunya (ERC), 43–45, 48, 64, 88
ETA. *See* Euskadi Ta Askatasuna
EU. *See* European Union
European Committee of Social Rights, 123, 125–27

European Court of Human Rights, 51, 95–97
European Union (EU), 9, 13, 19, 43, 65, 106–7, 109–11, 113, 120, 125–26, 129–30, 133, 151, 165, 172–73, 175; European Commission, 111, 119, 133; European Communities, 81, 83, 172, 175, 178; European Stability Mechanism, 111; Memorandum of Understanding, Spain-European Commission, 111, 119, 126, 133
Euskadiko Ezkerra, 35, 77. *See also* Ezker Abertzalea
Euskadi Ta Askatasuna (ETA), 2, 7, 53, 59–61, 78, 87, 91–99, 101, 142, 148, 167, 177–78. *See also* Ezker Abertzalea
Euzko Alderdi Jeltzalea. *See* Basque Nationalist Party
Ezker Abertzalea, 93, 98, 101; Amaiur, 55; EH Bildu, 59, 62; Herri Batasuna, 56, 61

Falange, 7, 24, 68, 138, 147, 157
Felipe II, 28, 67
Felipe V, 46
Felipe VI, 49–50
feminism, 4–5
Fernando of Aragon, the Catholic, 25, 32, 55–56, 69
Fernando VII, 31–32
Foral. *See foralismo*
foralismo, 36, 51, 54, 56–59; economic concert (concierto económico), 55, 58–59, 147–48, 177
Ford, Richard, 23–24
Fraga, Manuel, 16–17. *See also* Franco, Francisco; Popular Party (PP)
Franco, Francisco, 1–3, 6–7, 16, 24, 28, 31, 35, 37, 41, 43–44, 55, 67–69, 71–92, 94, 98–99, 101, 104–5, 135–36, 138–40, 142, 144–45, 147–49, 152, 157–58, 167, 170–72, 174, 177–78
Francoism, 2, 20, 35, 59, 74–83, 86–87, 90, 92, 99–101, 105, 123, 143, 155–57, 165, 170
Fraser, Ronald, 31, 44
fueros, 54–56, 59, 147, 177. *See also* Basque Country; Carlismo; Navarra

GAL. *See* Grupos Antiterroristas de Liberación (GAL)
Galicia, 6, 24, 28, 32, 37–38, 128, 167
Garzón, Baltasar, 89, 91
Gellner, Ernest, 26–27
Gesto por la Paz, 92. *See also* Basque Country; Euskadi Ta Askatasuna (ETA)
Gil Robles, José María, 147
González, Felipe, 45, 53, 86–87, 94, 178. *See also* Partido Socialista Obrero Español (PSOE)
Goya, Francisco, 83–84
Granada, 25, 31, 69; Al-Andalus, 2, 144
Greiff, Pablo de, 171–72
Grupos Antiterroristas de Liberación (GAL), 91, 93–94, 98
Guardia Civil, 28, 94–97

Hispanidad, 33, 146
historical memory, 85–91, 98–99, 101, 131, 136, 156, 170–71, 174, 176
Hobsbawm, E. J., 26

Ibarretxe, Juan José, 57. *See also* Basque Nationalist Party
Iglesias, Pablo, 100, 133. *See also* Podemos
Independence War, 30, 83, 87, 146, 177
Infante, Blas, 37. *See also* Andalusia
Isabel of Castilla, the Catholic, 25, 69
Izquierda Abertzale. *See* Ezker Abertzalea

John Paul II, 156
John XXIII, 67, 69, 141–42
Juan Carlos, King, 13, 56–57, 74, 87, 140

Kent, Victoria, 4
Kothari, Miloon, 116

Letamendia, Francisco, 36, 77. *See also* Euskadiko Ezkerra
Linz, Juan J., 144

Maastricht: convergence criteria, 107, 132; treaty, 109n22
Machado, Antonio, 4, 83
Macià, Francesc, 43, 169
Madrid (region and city), 1, 11, 17, 26, 28, 30, 35, 37–40, 42–47, 53, 54, 56–58, 60–61, 64, 67, 68, 76, 81, 86–87, 99–100, 103–6, 109, 113, 114, 126–27, 142, 152, 154, 160, 164–65, 167–70, 174
Mas, Artur, 47–48. *See also* Convergència i Unió (CIU)
Mola, Emilio, 135–36. *See also* Franco, Francisco
Morocco, 4, 33

Napoleonic War. *See* Independence War
Navarra, 6, 25, 36–37, 52, 54–56, 91, 98, 113, 126–27, 132, 135–37, 167
Nelken, Margarita, 4
Núñez-Seixas, Xosé-Manoel, 42

Ortega y Gasset, José, 4, 43–44, 81, 169
Orwell, George, 9, 41, 86
Osoro Sierra, Carles, 160

Pact of Silence, 73–85, 91, 94, 101, 156, 170
PAH. *See* Plataforma de Afectados por las Hipotecas
Partido Nacionalista Vasco (PNV). *See* Basque Nationalist Party
Partido Socialista Obrero Español (PSOE), 35, 38, 44–45, 47, 53–54, 56, 68, 86–89, 93, 95–97, 100, 106–7, 109, 114, 118, 128–30, 132, 151, 153–55, 157, 160, 178
Payne, Stanley, 18, 32, 55, 145

PCE. *See* Communist Party
Pelayo, Don, 31
Pérez-Rubalcaba, Alfredo, 97. *See also* Partido Socialista Obrero Español (PSOE)
Pi i Margall, Francesc, 36
Pinochet, Augusto, 89–90
Pius XI, 138
Pius XII, 138
Plataforma de Afectados por las Hipotecas (PAH), 114
PNV. *See* Basque Nationalist Party
Podemos, 3, 54, 96, 100, 103, 114, 128, 130, 132–33, 153, 160, 178
Political Reform Act 1977, 74, 76–77
Pope Francis, 156
Popular Party (PP), 7, 11, 31, 37, 39, 45, 47, 54, 56, 68, 78, 88–89, 92, 95–96, 99, 103, 107, 109–10, 113, 115, 128, 132, 152–55, 159, 178
Preston, Paul, 73
Primo de Rivera, José Antonio, 68–69, 71, 99–100, 147. *See also* Franco, Francisco
Primo de Rivera, Miguel, 28, 147, 177
PSOE. *See* Partido Socialista Obrero Español
Puigdemont, Carles, 43, 48, 50, 101
Pujol, Jordi, 47. *See also* Convergència i Unió (CIU)

racism, 6, 20
RAE. *See* Royal Spanish Academy
Rajoy, Mariano, 47, 54, 68, 89, 110, 128, 178. *See also* Partido Popular (PP)
Recaredo, 32, 173
Reconquista, 31
Renan, Ernest, 26, 170
Rodríguez Zapatero, José Luis, 45, 87, 89, 107–9, 118, 151, 154–55, 178. *See also* Partido Socialista Obrero Español (PSOE)
Rouco Varela, Antonio María, 154, 157
Royal Spanish Academy (RAE), 29–30, 39

Saint James the Apostle, 32–33, 146
Sànchez, Jordi, 50
Sánchez, Pedro, 51, 53, 68, 128, 157, 178. *See also* Partido Socialista Obrero Español (PSOE)
Sánchez Corbí, Manuel, 97
Santiago. *See* Saint James the Apostle
Suárez, Adolfo, 74, 149, 177. *See also* Unión de Centro Democrático (UCD); Transition

Tarancón, Cardinal Vicente Enrique, 142, 148
Tejero, Antonio, 99
Transition, 7, 18, 35, 74–79, 81, 84–85, 87–88, 92, 94, 99–101, 156–57, 170–71, 174; Moncloa Pacts, 124
Turull, Jordi, 50

Unión de Centro Democrático (UCD), 38–39, 154, 177
United Podemos. *See* Podemos

Valle-Inclán, Ramón María del, 4, 176

Valley of the Fallen, 3, 7, 67–73, 82, 88–89, 99, 101, 157, 158, 177–78; Cantera, Santiago, 157–58. *See also* Catholic Church; Civil War; Franco, Francisco
Van Boven, Theo, 96–97
Vera, Rafael, 93–94. *See also* González, Felipe; Grupos Antiterroristas de Liberación (GAL); Partido Socialista Obrero Español (PSOE)
Vives, Juan Luis, 122–23
Vox, 2, 5–6, 11, 31, 39, 47, 53, 96, 99–100, 114–15, 128, 131, 147, 150, 155, 165, 168

War of Independence. *See* Independence War
welfare state, 7–8, 12, 104–8, 123, 132–33, 172–73
Welles, Orson, 51, 53
Western Sahara, 4

xenophobia, 6, 115, 175

Zirauki, 135–36

About the Author

Koldo Casla is a lecturer in Law and the Director of the Human Rights Centre Clinic of the University of Essex, UK. Between 2013 and 2019, he worked as a researcher on social rights in Spain and the UK. Between 2011 and 2013, he was the chief of staff of Ararteko, the Human Rights Commissioner of the Parliament of the Basque Country, Spain. Casla holds a PhD in European and International Studies from King's College London, and is the author of *Politics of International Human Rights Law Promotion in Western Europe: Order versus Justice* (Routledge, 2019).

www.ingramcontent.com/pod-product-compliance
Lightning Source LLC
Chambersburg PA
CBHW062228300426
44115CB00012BA/2257